This book is dedicated to my wife,

Dorothy Pritchard (nee Thomson).

Born Birmingham on 9th May 1933.

Died Crewe on 6th June 2021.

The loving and caring mother of

Jacqueline and Robert.

The devoted and loving wife of Geoff

whom she encouraged to fulfil his ambition

to run his own advertising agency

and to write this book.

May she rest in peace

An Introduction to
'The girl on the number 64 bus'

Can you imagine the feelings of a country boy who was brought up in a quiet Cheshire village with 30 cottages and 3 farms with a total population of 50 adults and 9 children spread over an area of about five square miles where there were around 300 cows 800 chickens, 4 horses, 30 dogs and 20 cats to find himself in Birmingham, England's second biggest city which was devoid of a single blade of grass and not a solitary person that he knew?

It was Sunday evening and Birmingham appeared quite a daunting place. However this country boy had ambition and drive and the salary that he had been delighted to accept was around £575 per annum as a District Housing Officer in the Housing Department of the Corporation of the City of Birmingham, and in 1974 this was regarded as a good salary. He was to start work the following day but first he had to find somewhere to stay the night. He carried his small suitcase into the YMCA hostel who found him a bed he could have for three nights. Well anywhere was better than nowhere and perhaps over the next few days he could find himself something a bit more homely. He found what he considered to be adequate lodgings at a Victorian House on Gravelly Hill, Erdington which was a few miles from the city centre. On enquiring the best way to get there he was advised to catch the number 64 bus from Steelhouse Lane to Erdington. This he did without realising that the 64 bus would be instrumental in changing his life for the better and forever.

But there's no better place to start than the very beginning ... so here goes:-

Chapter 1 –
The Early Years

"He's going to be a boxer so he'd better have a crew cut" replied Bill to the barbers question "How would you like the lads hair done sir?" as young Geoff scrambled on to the barber's chair. Geoff was six years old and dads response had not only decided the boys future but publicly announced it to the seven or eight men all waiting for their customary 'short back and sides' which in the 1930's was about the only hair style for we chaps: excepting that is for the tough lot who fancied their chances in the boxing ring or more likely a brawl outside the pub who favoured a crew cut that basically was short all over which, had it been on the chin, would have looked as though he needed a shave.

Normally boys like Geoff who were born in the township of Crewe were destined to become employees of the LMSR just like their dads. Most of them would dream of driving one of the big powerful steam engines that wended their way anywhere between the capital cities of London and Edinburgh or through the Welsh valleys to Cardiff, but best of all was the magical Irish Mail train that took all the mail destined for anywhere in Ireland and returned with hundreds of mail bags intended for distribution throughout England and Wales. However it sounded as though this was not to be the future for young Geoff. On returning to their home in the village of Crewe Green Nellie, Geoff's mum, took one look at her son and shrieked "What have they done to the lads hair.   Oh dear God, it's bad enough having a son but they've made him look like a thug" Geoff's only flirtation with the noble art of boxing was listening with his dad to the big fights that were broadcast on the radio. Those renowned heavyweights Joe Louis and Tommy Farr were their particular favourites. These big fights were described in splendid colourful detail by that marvellous commentator Raymond Glendenning with his aide Barrington Dolby who gave inter-round summaries. What a team they were: you could almost feel the uppercut landing on an opponent's jaw by the Brown Bomber and squirm when a gush of blood erupted as a fist connected with an already gnarled nose: or the struggle of an opponent hauling himself off the canvas into a more dignified position.

The thought of actually being a contender did not exactly fill Geoff with a great deal of enthusiasm. At this time of his young life he was more concerned whether to get a pennyworth of sticky toffee or a sherbet fountain whilst listening to uncle Mac in Children's Hour on the radio or reading the latest pursuits of Desperate Dan in the Dandy. These were sufficiently demanding and taxing problems for someone who had only just learnt that nine nine's are er, er eighty something or other. In the days of his youth dad, who must have been a useful footballer had gone to Liverpool for a trial. However his mother had discouraged him from signing any papers by telling him to get a proper job and not mess about playing a rather daft game with a bunch of yobbos. So he stuck to his apprenticeship as a fitter in the railway works in Crewe. Much better than being a footballer and he was entitled to free passes on the railway !

Geoffrey Pritchard was to become a soldier, a telegraphist, a rent collector, an Insurance agent and an advertising executive, all totally different careers to what Bill had dreamed of for his son when it became obvious that he was not cut out to be a pugilist.

Geoff came into this world in 1931. His mother, Nellie, had been a nurse at the Cottage hospital in Crewe which she left at the age of 23 in order to have what she longed for a baby girl. So it was a massive disappointment when she became the mother of a boy. "Never mind, Nellie" said family and friends "better luck next time" "Next time" she retorted "I wish now there hadn't been a first time. A boy and there's only one thing worse than having a boy and that's having two boys – Oh my God, the very thought of that would send me to an early grave".

Nellie's determination not to have any more children never weakened so Geoff grew up to be an only child. "Yes I was an only one" Geoff would say "but I was never a lonely one" For the first four years of his life Geoff had lived in two houses. He could never remember anything of the first but he had vivid memories of the second which was close to the Grand cinema on West Street, Crewe. Mum, Dad and Geoff visited the Grand every Friday night no matter what film was showing and Dad gave Geoff a 'piggy back' in both directions. The front room of the house was used by Bills sister, Eileen as a Ladies Hairdressing Salon. Each day Eileen joined Nellie and Bill in their living room and they enjoyed the lunch and cups of tea that followed. It was at one of these lunches when Bill jumped up from his chair, grabbed his son by the scruff of his neck and asked in a rather menacing manner "What did you just say" When he repeated what he had said Bill roared "I thought as much, I'll teach you my lad" at which point he began to take off his leather belt from the waist of his trousers. What's the matter thought Geoff he asked me to say it again so I did and now it looks like trouble. Nellie and Eileen rose to their feet "Don't Bill oh don't, not the strap, you can't do that he's only three" pleaded Nellie. "For goodness sake man it's something he's heard someone say, he really doesn't understand what he's said" added Auntie Eileen."Mmm maybe not" said Bill "but if I hear you say that ever again" he said still holding his sons neck with his left hand and wagging a finger of his right hand in Geoff's face "I'll, I'll .." he trailed off menacingly.

Throughout his life Geoffrey never knew what it was that offended his Dad so much and even when he was in his forties he was tempted to ask but never ventured to do so. There are times when you just leave well alone. Geoff was four years old when a removal wagon pulled up at the front door and all the possessions were loaded into the back. Nellie and her son sat by the driver and Bill rode his bicycle to their new home in Crewe Green which was about three miles away.

Geoffrey could not believe it: they had a massive garden which had a holly/ hawthorn hedge on one side and at the rear, with a privet hedge at the front. "This" said Bill "is our new home, a country cottage with plenty of room for you to play in. You're going to love it here."

My golly he was so right. Geoff loved every brick and blade of grass: he was in heaven. It was a semi-detached cottage which was built in 1877 so when they moved in it was fifty seven years old and on a royal estate. The cottage consisted of a kitchen which was entered via the back door and the sole mod-con was a large stone sink with the one and only tap in the house which provided cold water. This stood high above the sink and had the appearance of the gallows. Off the kitchen was a small but adequate pantry that had one window that looked across to the village green and the four cottages on a minor B road that led further out into pleasant farm land and other villages.

Next to the pantry was 'the glory hole' which consisted of some useful shelving that held boots and shoes and a number of hooks to hang coats, smocks, aprons, hats and umbrellas as well as galoshes and a miscellany of other items. The door from the kitchen led into the living room. This was dominated on the wall opposite to the kitchen door by a magnificent black-leaded Excelsior range that had brass adornments which were polished with Brasso and plenty of elbow grease every week. In the centre of the range was a deep firebox with sturdy bars across the front to contain the burning fuel. To the left of the fire was a tank which was filled with water in jugfuls from the kitchen tap and fed into the tank by removing the lid on top. To the right was an adequate oven where the Sunday joint was roasted and where Nellie baked her delicious homemade cakes.

Above the fire basket a large hook was suspended which held the kettle to make a cuppa as and when required. There was also a rack above the fireplace on which washing could be aired before putting away. There were two windows: one looked north over beautiful green pastureland home to several oak trees and where cattle from the nearby farm grazed happily and rewarded the farmer with their delicious unadulterated milk: the other window was much smaller and looked west towards the town of Crewe.

The lounge – which was always referred to as the front room overlooked their well maintained lawn bordered by well nurtured rose beds. The bus stop for Crewe was immediately opposite to the cottage whilst the buses to Sandbach and Hanley stopped right by the front gate. However the dominant features were the village green and the village church which was dedicated to St. Michael and All Angel's on the east side of the green. The stairs to the three bedrooms were off the front room. The main bedroom was at the front and was of course used by Bill and Nellie whilst the second bedroom was that of Geoff. Both these bedrooms had small but adequate fireplaces which were seldom used except possibly in the case of illness when the patient was advised to stay in bed for a couple of days. The third bedroom was small and faced west. This was used as a box room where anything not in use could be stored. In later years it was converted into a bathroom.

The cottage had no electricity or gas supply so was lit by oil lamps. The one in the living room was an Aladdin lamp suspended from a hook in the centre of the room above the dining room table. The lamp had a mantle positioned above a container into which methylated spirit was used to light the mantle which straddled a wick which in turn was fed by paraffin oil. It could be quite a fiddle to light especially if the family had been to the pictures and it was dark when they got home. The mantles were adequate for the job but could crumble with a little carelessness. All the other rooms had free standing oil lamps which could be moved around to where they were most efficient or needed. There was no shower and taking a bath was to say the least extremely difficult as the zinc bath hung from a nail on the outside wall at the rear of the cottage. On bath nights, which were fairly rare, the zinc bath was brought in and placed on the floor in front of the fire. It was then filled with water from the range and from a primus stove located in the kitchen: so on bath night kettles and pans would be put on and taken into the living room where the bath was topped up as required. There were three brick built out-buildings at the rear of the cottage and were back to back with those of the next door neighbour. The first of these was for general purposes – storing tins of paint and a couple of bikes used by Bill and Nellie. Next to that was the wash house which housed a copper boiler above which was a cold water tap. Below the boiler was a fire box to heat the water on wash day, which was every Monday. Come sunshine, rain, hail, snow, frost, fog, or gale force winds – Monday was always washday.

Nellie would light the fire below the copper at 7.30 on a Monday morning: all the dirty washing would be put in the boiler and given a scrubbing. Once the water was hot enough to do the wash she would stir the dirty items from time to time, sometimes removing a few at a time, wring them out by hand and then put them back in for a final boiling. When she was happy with the results she would transfer the laundry into the dolly tub filled with cold water and using a dolly peg which was a wooden structure with three legs at the base and a handle bar at the top: this would enable her to swish away all the soapy water from the laundered items. Once this was completed everything would be put through the mangle. That was a job which young Geoffrey rather enjoyed doing. When they had been mangled the washed items would be put on the clothes line that ran from the house to a post further down the garden. But this last task could not be done if the conditions were unsuitable. Then finally in the evening, provided all had gone well Nellie would do the ironing. She had a few irons, but normally would use any two; the first one would go on the fire to heat it up: when it was 'right' she would remove it and put the second one on the burning coal so that it would be ready to use when the first had cooled. At the end everything would be neatly folded up and put away for further use. From start of the wash to the finish took about 7 hours plus ironing time.

The last of the buildings was the lavatory. This had not changed since the house was first built. It consisted of a wooden bench which went from wall to wall and occupied the full width of the six feet. In the centre of the top of the bench was a hole about 15 inches in diameter where one could sit in relative comfort whilst doing what nature demanded. Beneath the hole was a metal pan for the human waste. This was emptied each week by what were known as the "midnight soil men" who hoisted the pan and contents on their shoulders and deposited them in the specially made vehicle which went round the village. On that particular day it was advisable to keep all windows and doors closed as the smell hung around for about a hour or so after their visit. One of Geoffrey's jobs that he did each Saturday was to take the previous weeks Radio Times, which was a tabloid publication, and cut it down the spine and then cut it into pieces measuring about six inches by four inches. Once done the sheets were placed neatly on top of one another and a hole would be pierced in one corner through which a piece of string would be inserted and knotted then placed in the lavatory on a nail in the wall and served as toilet paper. Nothing was wasted.

AND SO TO SCHOOL

Crewe Green was a delightful village which consisted of three farms, about thirty cottages spread over quite a wide area, a school which had three classrooms, three good sized playgrounds which contained two sets of toilets: one for the boys and one for girls. Again, like the cottages the toilets had pans which were emptied weekly. At the back was a gate which led on to a playing field area and was destined to have a change of use in due course.

It was September 1935 that Geoff started his education in what was called the babies class where the teacher was Miss Buchan. The classroom contained a blackboard and several little desks and chairs as well as a rocking horse which was used to pacify any upset child. Being a Church of England school each morning began with prayers and singing a hymn. Each pupil was given a small blackboard and a piece of chalk together with an abacus which consisted of rows of wires on which were coloured beads with which the children learned to add and subtract. Every Monday morning each child took sixpence which was collected by Miss Buchan as this was the education 'fee' for the week.

Every morning the class would chant out in unison the ABC. A B C D E F G and so through to Z . This was always done in a singsong manner and everyone seemed to enjoy that.   This was all in conjunction with a simple book that started with a capital 'A' and a small 'a' together with the picture of an apple and the B for bird and so on through to Z. Again all the class would sing in unison. It was fun. On the little blackboards each child then had to write the letters of the alphabet which Miss Buchan would examine and correct if anyone didn't get it right. This was known as the three R's: Reading, (w)riting and (a)rithmatic. the 'rithmatic was the hard part but again all the class would sing out the times tables, and this was done with gusto -- Two twos are four , three twos are six, and so on right through to twelve twelves are a hundred and forty four.   On going into the higher class Geoff and his classmates had mastered all the tables up to twelve 12's.   At the time no one had realised it but they were learning social skills: how to treat fellow pupils: recognising who they could trust: who they should avoid if they possibly could: who were found to be disagreeable such as Ken the lad who lived in the adjoining village who, irrespective of the time of year or weather conditions constantly had a runny nose but never a handkerchief. He did however have a very stained blazer sleeve and, rather disgustingly, a longer than normal and active tongue. Ugh !

Actually years later it transpired that he had been very successful in a large menswear chain actually achieving managerial level.   Geoffrey was rather fortunate for he soon made pals with a couple of lads who had started school at the same time as himself. Both were called Brian. Brian Swinnerton lived in one of only a handful of detached cottages on the estate. The pathway from the front gate to the front door was bordered by the most magnificent rhododendron bushes. The remaining part of the garden consisted of a well manicured lawn on which were a handful of small but attractive trees. His father always wore a dark suit and bowler hat which identified him as an office worker for the railway company where he was in the control room. His mother was a lovely lady who became rather good friends with Nellie. Brian Parkinson came from Sydney the adjoining village which was almost a mile from the school which made it difficult for him to go home at dinner time. In consequence Nellie agreed that Brian could bring his sandwiches to her house and she would make him a drink.

Brian was an avid reader so he always brought a book with him whilst he munched his way through his butties. He was lucky that he seemed to have a photographic memory as well as a strange habit of always reading the last chapter of a book before he read the first. Geoff and Brian frequently loaned each other a book. Brian would say "wait till you read the third paragraph on page 76 it's really funny. In fact when the time came for him to take the entrance exam for secondary school he did no swatting whatsoever as he would sooner play tennis with Geoff. He passed with ease.

In the main Geoff rather enjoyed his time at the elementary school where he was until the age of ten. It was when they reached the top class that the pupils were assessed by the headmaster, who was nicknamed Gaffer, for their suitability for secondary school (later known as Grammar school) Those he thought stood the best chance of furthering their education found themselves sitting in a semicircle in front of his desk. He would then check on previous work by going round the group pointing a finger at one of the selected pupils and asking a relevant question. It was a lad called Fred to whom his finger pointed and asked him what was the capital of France "Dunno, sir" came the reply. "Well let me help you then, boy" and with that he stood up and jabbed the wooden pen about half a dozen times on Fred's head saying "perhaps this will help it sink in" as he said "Paris is the capital of France . now then boy can you remember what the capital of France is" "Yes sir the capital of France is Paris" "Well done, boy, and don't ever forget that" Fred never did forget, nor did anyone else who was in the group Did any of the pupils pass to go on to the secondary school.? Thankfully yes they did. The results came through during the holiday period so Geoff went to Gaffers house to let him know he had passed. 'Gaffer' was delighted.

This meant that Geoff would be off to the Crewe County Secondary School at the end of the holidays. But first he had to be rigged out with his new school uniform which consisted of a black blazer edged in orange and a school cap. Oh gosh that awful cap which was basically black with a orange band encircling it as well as another ring the colour of which denoted which 'house' you were in. The lads from other schools used to rag them somewhat by calling out "Watch out here come the ringworms".

Geoff did not have a happy time at the secondary school. He made pretty well of pals there but they were by no means as good as his mates he'd made at home. He was introduced to trigonometry, algebra, French, physics and so on. Geoff quickly made his mind up none of these subjects were going to be any use to him whatsoever. What he did shine at was mental arithmetic. This was mainly due to not having to write down the answer but call it out. With this he was often first to divulge the correct answer. Throughout his life he was quite quick with figures and impressed several of his colleagues who years later stumbled even when they had calculators. In fact he would check to see if the calculator had got it right!

The other subject Geoff rather liked was English, not Shakespeare or Keats or even the grammar, but he loved using his vivid imagination to write stories and often reading them out to the class. His writing was to help enormously in his working life. It was a very happy day when he said 'Goodbye' to school which did not have an abundance of happy memories for him.

FAMILY AND FRIENDS

Geoff was lucky, for in spite of the fact that his mother had yearned for a daughter she loved him very dearly and always welcomed his pals into their home and made them feel welcome. However her greatest failing as Geoff saw it when he was a youngster was that she was profoundly house proud. During this period of time it was seldom to hear of a mother going to work. Bill was the bread winner and worked hard in the Crewe railway works as a fitter.

Quite what a fitter did was something of a mystery to Geoff but he loved the finished product and knew most of the steam locomotives that dad had helped to build. Likewise Nellie also worked hard, and as she rightly pointed out on several occasions her work hours were far longer than any man. The cottage was kept immaculately clean and never a day went by without a hot meal.

Bill would arrive home for his dinner at around 12.40: the table would be laid for the three of them and Nellie would serve Bill first with his beef, Yorkshire pudding, roast potatoes, carrots and lashings of homemade gravy. This would be followed by apple pie and custard and inevitably a cup of tea. It was then back to work until knocking off time. At around 6pm Bill would sit down to his tea of 4 thick slices of dripping on toast. If Geoff had been playing with any toys prior to a meal he had to clear them away by putting them into his toy box so that nothing was out of place for Bills time at home.

In those day three meals a day meant breakfast, dinner and tea. 'Lunch' was a word only used if someone was taking a sandwich to his place of employment to have at his morning tea break. When dinner became lunch and tea became dinner was something that Geoff had never really thought of, for as long as it was food he was quite happy to call it whatever people wanted to call it.

Grandma and Grandad Pritchard lived at a cottage about two hundred yards away. Geoff adored his grandma and likewise she adored him. There was always a bag of sweets and a bottle of lemonade ready at hand. They had two dogs, Ben an Alsatian and Tan who was a black wiry haired type of mixed breeding. Ben was an outstanding guard dog and nobody could approach the cottage without being aware of his presence. His mouth would curl up in anger as he growled at each and every visitor to their cottage. No one, but no one would dare even to pat his head. That is with the exception of Geoffrey who, when he was three years old, grabbed Ben around the neck, scrambled on to the dogs back and told him to gee up. Who knows what the dog thought, but Ben and Geoff became close friends. Grandma was the daughter of an Irish immigrant by the name of Martin Welsh. It was never really known how the surname should have been spelt as the Irish records show it with a 'c' and the English records with 's'. One theory was that Martin, like many other people, would not have been able to read or write in the 1870's, so on landing at Liverpool docks the immigration office would likely have queried " Is that with a 's' " and would have received the reply of 'Yes' without knowing and probably without caring too much as long as his feet were on English soil.   He got a job as a farm labourer in Barthomley and later was promoted to position of waggoner.

Grandma had been a cook up at 'a big house' in the Salford area. How she came to leave such a pretty rural area as Barthomley and go to a rough place like Salford was in those days mystified Geoff.

Grandad was a very serious person who was brought up in the Police Station at Silk Street, Salford where his father was the sergeant. He had attended the local school so consequently mastered the three R's to good effect for a particular local 'businessman' who was a horse racing tipster.   He paid the schoolboy to write out the names of all the horses from a particular race on a slip of paper popping each slip into different envelopes then addressing them. The tips were then sent to the 'clientele'. Whichever of the runners won at least one person would have received the winning tip and paid a percentage of the winnings to the tipster.

Grandad's first name was William but grandma always called him Dad. In Salford he was employed as a bleacher but when they moved to Crewe in the early part of the 20th century he became a fitter in the thriving railway works which was attracting many newcomers into the town from Wales and Ireland. The family which consisted of three daughters, Alice, Annie, Eileen and their son who like his dad was named William lived in a small terraced house before eventually opening a picture framing business in Mill Street, Crewe. Although business was reasonably good Grandma yearned for a place in the country, and managed to rent a smallholding on the royal estate. It was barely sufficient to give them anything like a decent living wage so they bought a few cows, a couple of dozen hens to give them life's bare essentials. It must have been really hard work for both Grandma and Grandad who had no outside assistance. Geoff loved to go with his mum and dad each week but especially when it was haymaking time. What wonderful fun they all had cutting the hay then having gorgeous homemade pies washed down by delightful homemade nettle beer. In later years Geoff often wondered however his grandparents had managed to pack so much energy into their everyday lives.

Although Grandad was a quiet unassuming person he was not afraid of work, led a Christian life, seldom missed going to his local church on Sunday morning. Their home was a wonderful, welcoming place especially on Christmas day when all the family gathered for dinner wished everyone a happy Christmas and exchanged gifts. Nellie always gave Geoff two parcels: one for grandma and one for Grandad. On unwrapping hers Grandma always gave Geoff a kiss on the forehead and said what a lovely gift it was and gave her profuse thanks. Grandad never showed any enthusiasm but would take the gift off the boy but never opened it. He always said "Thank ee, lad". This was so mystifying to Geoff who simply could not understand why Grandad resisted opening up the package. Nellie later explained that he had no need to open it up as he knew they were a pair of socks that she had knitted and always had done since the first Christmas she met him.

The old man was very straight laced and had regular routines which were always observed. "That lads eyes are bigger than his belly" he would say at every meal time referring to Geoffrey "he sits there without chewing his food properly and searches around for what he can get down him next". Looking fiercely at his grandson he would always add "you should chew every mouthful thirty two times before you swallow it". His favoured saying was NEITHER A LENDER OR A BORROWER BE. That was something that Geoff failed to do in later life and regretted it. He was a proud independent man. He walked wherever he went; it's doubtful if he ever took a bus throughout his whole life. Geoff was once very embarrassed by Grandads independence.

It was after church on a very wet Sunday morning when Stanley, the church organist, who was one of the few people to have a car and lived almost next door to Grandad invited him to jump in and keep out of the downpour to which Grandad replied "Thank you very much for the kind offer, but I would point out to you that the good Lord gave me two perfectly good legs and whilst I can use them I have no need for a car ride, so I will bid you a good day" With that he set off on his two mile walk in heavy rain. Bill had three sisters, Alice and Annie who were born in Salford and Eileen who was born shortly after they moved to Crewe. Alice had one son. Eileen had three daughters. These were Geoff's cousins. More of those later.

THE LEESE'S

Geoff's maternal Grandparents lived in a village called Thurlwood. This was about eight miles from Crewe Green and involved two bus journeys. This meant he had less contact with them than he did with dads family. However their name was Leese and Grandad Fred was a self employed builder who owned a flat-back lorry on which he carried all the materials and accessories he needed for the business.

He had started work as a bricklayer on the North Staffs Railway Company where his duties were the maintenance of the canals owned by the railway company. They had three sons, the eldest of whom was Tom, then George and Frank. They also had three daughters, Nellie, Mary and Ethel. Grandad ran a successful business and was joined by two of his sons, Tom and George in the family concern.

Sadly Grandad Leese died when Geoff was only 5 years old so he could barely remember him. The eldest son Tom took over the business. He was a lovely, generous man. In fact in later years his generosity was the down fall of the family business. George was a fun loving single man who loved Geoffrey to bits. But again life can be cruel, and so it was with George who went on a rather venturesome holiday, as it was in the '30's, going abroad with his pal Ted to the Isle of Man.

On returning home Nellie who was visiting her mother asked George how he'd found the Isle of Man. "Absolutely loved it" was the reply "we'll be going again next year. But never mind about that our Nell come on read my leaves for me" Nellie had built up a good reputation for her skilful reading of the tea leaves left in the cups. She instructed George to swirl his cup three times and then place it upside down in his saucer. This he did. On looking in the cup she said "Oh George it's very clear to me that you will not be going to the Isle of Man next year as something is going to happen that will prevent you from going anywhere" "Well our Nell you are wrong this time because nothing will stop me".

A few months later George was taken ill and rushed into hospital where he was diagnosed to have meningitis. Days later he died at the age of 26: Nellie had read this in the leaves. Many years elapsed before she 'read' any more cups. Frank never went into the family business working instead for a local printer before taking on an insurance agency.

Mary was a nurse and remained single until marrying Harold, her childhood sweetheart and next door neighbour when they were both in their forties. Born in 1929 Ethel was more like a cousin than an aunt to Geoff and they remained close throughout their lives.   They managed to get into rather serious trouble in their younger days when they were taken by Nellie and Grandma Leese for a brief stay in the beautiful county of Herefordshire where Uncle Aaron and Aunt Ethel (Grandmas sister) had a small but pleasant cottage with the River Wye running close to the rear of their home.

This was the first time that Geoff had met Uncle Aaron who had been a farm worker all his life. He was quite intrigued by an old metal pan that propped open the back door where Uncle Aaron sat most of the day smoking his pipe. The pan was there not just to keep the door open but was used by Aaron to deposit his spent matches, to knock out the used 'baccy, but most intriguing of all it was used by what Geoff later found out was a spittoon.   Aaron would clear his throat and deposit the mucus into that pan from wherever he was sitting or standing.

Wow !! Geoff thought one day I'll be able to do that!   It was a rather lovely warm summers day and the adults decided to go for a short walk into the village. Some little time after they'd gone Geoff said to Ethel "Gosh something smells good, let's go into the kitchen and see what it is".   It was a freshly roasted chicken with beautifully brown crispy skin.   "Just look at this Ethel this must be what we are having for dinner. Smells good let's just try a little bit"   "We can't do that said Ethel they'll see it straight away and they'll know it's us"   "Don't be silly" came the reply "Look I'll show you what we can do"   With that he gently and very neatly lifted a piece of the crispy skin and tore off a small piece of the white meat and popped it into his mouth   "Oh Ethel that is gorgeous and look all I have to do is drop the skin back over and nobody will ever know"   Taking his advice Ethel did the same, but her piece seemed a little bigger than his so not wanting to be out done Geoff had some more and so it went on until there was barely any white meat left on the bird. However the brown crispy skin was now a poor disguise. Aunt Ethel was absolutely fuming when she saw that all that was left were wings, thighs and legs, and, of course the brown crinkly skin. Aunt Ethel had no children of her own and she exploded. "God, in heaven above" she exclaimed "what have these two horrible children done? All our dinners are ruined, they both want a darn good thrashing. Never again will I have them back here. Never - horrible, horrible children" She kept to her word they never went back, and Geoff so admired Aarons ability to hit that pot every time, but sadly he never witnessed it again. However it was on this occasion that he had a weird experience of déjà vu but he didn't realise what it was called at that time. For a brief spell he had the feeling that his mind was not in his body and that he had been here before.

As he stood on platform 3 of Crewe station waiting for the train from Manchester to Hereford he was aware that the engine would be coloured green, not the normal maroon or black. He also had a vision of the engines number. About five minutes later he heard the train entering the platform.

Nellie said "Geoff step back the trains coming and you're too near the edge of the platform" He felt bewildered he shook his head as around the curve came a green engine, with the letters GWR and the number he'd seen in his mind's eye. This was not the only such occasion on which something similar occurred so this might be the time to explain it. There was a crowd of about a dozen of the local lads larking about on the village green. "Look" said Fred somewhat mischievously. Every one looked in the direction he was pointing. "What are we supposed to looking at" asked Mick" "That fire is it at a cottage or is it a haystack" All the lads looked but could see absolutely nothing, no cottage, no smoke and certainly no fire. "There's nowt there" said Geoff "Aw come off it Fred" said Spider Webb "If there is a fire you'd best phone for the fire engine" "Good idea" said Fred "I'll ring them right away" With that he picked up a fallen twig which had a few leaves on it and spoke quite clearly. "Quick there's a fire at Crewe Green – don't know from here whether it's a house a haystack or whatever" As he threw the stick to the ground Fred said "Well that's it" In two minutes the lads could hear the bell clanging on a fire engine which swooped round the bend and pulled up. "Hey lads is there a fire round here" asked the driver "Dunno" said Geoff "I ain't seen one. have you Fred?" Fred was white and trembling "No, no, I anna seen one either" he managed to say.

"Funny that" said the driver "we had a call saying there's a fire at Crewe Green" Was that twig the first mobile phone.? Somehow Geoff doesn't think it was as they hadn't even been thought of in the 1940's.

Nellie was very close to her father throughout her life. On a Sunday she was the one who was given the top off Grandads egg as a special treat. All six children had to attend Sunday School at the same church where their father was the organist for many years. On Sunday's none of the children were allowed to read anything other than their Sunday school prizes. Sunday papers were banned from the home and if they wanted any music played on the family organ it must be something religious with hymns being greatly favoured. Frank was an extremely good organist and played it regularly. One particular Sunday he asked his father if he may be excused going to church as he felt unwell. This did not go down at all well with the stern Fred who stroked his auburn coloured moustache before submitting to Franks request on the proviso that he would play a few hymns. Frank agreed to this as he watched all the other family members set off on the three mile trek to church. The service started and the second hymn was being played when Nellie said to her brother "Tom there's something wrong at home I'm sure our Franks in some sort of trouble. Is it alright if I go and see?   "Don't be so stupid girl, he was OK when we left so however can you think that there's any trouble."?   "Tom I don't know what it is I simply cannot explain but I implore you let me go"   "If I let you go dad will kill me, so just sit down, shut up and follow the service"   "If you can't stand up to him I can. I'm going home"   With that she pushed her way past her brother, out through the door and went as fast as her legs would carry her back home. On reaching home she opened the door "Frank, Frank are you alright"   she called out as she took off her shoes and topcoat. There was no reply, no music, just complete silence. She opened the front room door Frank was sprawled on the floor unable to move. She glanced at the music sheet he'd been playing at the organ. It was the latest popular song. Retribution she thought. She shut the music away and went to fetch the doctor. Somehow Frank had fallen off the organ stool and had been knocked unconscious. He soon recovered but next Sunday decided he'd best go to church.

Grandad Leese died in 1936 at the age of 60. Nellie went to the funeral and took Geoff with her but left him in Grandads house with Ethel and Grandma who was busy preparing sandwiches for the wake. Generally in those days women were not encouraged to attend funerals. Ethel and Geoff were ushered out of the house as mourners came to pay their last respects. Geoff wasn't quite sure what being dead meant and Ethel was not much the wiser. The best, in fact the only thing they could get out of anyone was that Grandad was going to heaven. Minutes later all the mourners left the house and stood on either side of the wide driveway. The undertakers brought the coffin down from the bedroom and carefully placed it in the back of the hearse. Geoff was more confused than ever "Ethel that will never get as far as heaven. Heaven is right up there"   he said as he pointed up to the bright blue sky.

Grandma Leese lived into her early 90's but sadly pre-deceased four of her children including Nellie who died at the age of 60.

As Geoffrey got older he was able to cycle to see Grandma Leese who lived by the Thurlwood locks in a cottage which adjoined a farmhouse occupied by Mr and Mrs Smith. There he loved to see the horse drawn barges as they slowly but surely made their way to their respective destinations carrying all manner of things. He was fascinated by the wonderful sight of gaily painted metal pots and pans that were displayed on most of the barges. However there was one thing at Grandmas that he was rather scared of. At home he went down the yard to the lavatory, but here when he asked where the lavatory was he was shown into a tiny little room off the hallway where there was a small white porcelain washbasin and matching lavatory pan. "But grandma I can't do it in THAT inside the house and in a white shiny pan. Where do I really go"   She convinced him that this really was the place and that when he'd finished all he had to do was to pull this chain and everything will disappear. So he had no options, he was desperate to go, but even so he found it nothing less than revolting to do THAT in the house.   So 'go' he did and then wondered what would happen when he pulled that chain that seemed to look at him mockingly as it dared him to pull it.   His arms raised he grasped the handle of the chain and pulled hard. There was a sudden rush of gurgling water.   "Oh gosh I'm in terrible trouble now" he thought as he dashed into the living room   "Oh Grandma, Grandma, something awful has happened, but you told me to pull that chain and I did but it's letting in all the water out of the canal "Dad will slaughter me when he finds out what I've done he thought to himself. "I'm so sorry but you told me to do it" Tears of laughter were running down Grandmas face   "there, there" she said   "you've not let the canal water in. Come on let me show you".   She then went on to explain that this was called a water closet and that the water came out of the tank and would refill it for the next time. Geoff said nothing but thought there won't be a next time. What a disgusting thing to do inside the house. At home in the winter he may well have to put on his wellingtons, balaclava and his warm overcoat to go the lavvie with a storm lamp. But that was far better than this. Disgusting doing that inside the house! Wait till I see Grandma Pritchard, she'll simply not believe it! However years later Geoff was overjoyed when the spare bedroom at home was converted into a bathroom with one of those white shiny pans called a WC.

Geoff was lucky to have a whole lot of pals who loved visiting his home. He was never quite sure that it was his company that they found so pleasing or was it the beautiful Victoria Plum Trees that bore so many delicious plums that the branches had to be propped up so they would not break off: or was it those delicious small, very sweet, blushing apples. Maybe it was his mothers freshly home baked buttered scones laden with raspberry jam made from scrumptious berries direct from the garden; or possibly the dozens of bird's nests that could be found in the hedges of the cottage. or maybe they enjoyed the red but rather hard to bite pears that littered the lawn. Whatever it was he enjoyed their company and they were almost daily visitors with whom Geoff and his mates would swap their comics. The Dandy would be exchanged for Radio Fun, the Rainbow for the Beano, The Wizard for the Hotspur and so on. There really seemed to be no end to it. Then there was football and cricket on the village green. As they grew older they would be away on their cycles most of which were second-hand and refurbished; one or two may have a bike with gears but the majority had no such luxury.

But life was fun, life was to be enjoyed and enjoy it they did and there were so many 'characters' about. The lady everyone knew as Mary who walked around smoking a white clay pipe with a cigarette in the bowl, puffing away to her heart's content. Then there was the local vicar who had poor vision but made capital out of it. When he was going into Crewe he waited at the bus stop situated on the village Green - as a vehicle approached he would step on to the road holding his stick out. Most times it would be a car or a lorry which when it stopped he would say "I'm most awful sorry but my eyesight is so terrible I thought you were the bus: do forgive me" "That's alright vicar, not to worry hop in and I'll take you into town".   In those far off days the village church was the hub of everything that went on in the area.   In the cottage nearest to the church lived a lady by the name of Mrs Hewitt. She was the widow of a retired farmer who lived for the church and did a major part of the fund raising for its upkeep. Every Tuesday evening she held a whist drive in her lounge which was due to start at 7pm prompt.

People came from up to about a mile away and paid the modest entry fee, enjoyed a cup of tea and biscuits. The prizes were possibly a bar of chocolate, a tablet of soap, or something useful but it was the social gathering that was so enjoyable. However Mrs Hewitt could not understand why suddenly so many people started arriving late. "Mrs Hewitt" said Nellie   "we all love coming here but we also like to listen to that new serial that's started on the radio called The Archers. So it was agreed that in future the start time would be 7.15.

At Christmas time the village school had to be used as so many people wanted to attend as the prizes were then described as a Fur and Feather whist drive. The first prize being a chicken donated by a local farmer and the fur was a rabbit donated by the local 'hotshot'. Every month there would be a jumble sale again organised by Mrs Hewitt and held in the schoolrooms. These would start at 2 o'clock. They were so popular that frequently they were over by 2.30. Many of the customers were from Crewe who would come by bus and charge to the door to snap up the bargains. Another favoured evening was the Beetle Drive which was by no means as popular as the whist drives but had more appeal to the younger element of which Geoff was one.

Two popular characters were the road sweepers Charlie and a elderly gentleman who lived in Crewe and everyone knew simply as Grandad. They were responsible for cleaning the gutters and pavements for a two mile stretch which included Crewe Green. Charlie lived in a small but cheerful black and white cottage on Narrow Lane. Cars in those days were few and far between and most passers by were on bicycles so the two road sweepers were very well known and` were always popular. They had a hand cart a couple of brushes and a large shovel to deposit their sweepings into the cart. They always had a smile and a cheery word for everyone. They would have their pack of sandwiches and a flask of tea in a bag which hung from the handle of the cart.

Charlie and his wife were regular church goers together with their son George. They may best be described as simple, cheerful, honest folk who would harm no one or nothing. Charlie wore dentures which were ill fitting for his mouth which resulted in him clanking every time he spoke.

Geoff was rather taken back on one occasion when he was chatting to Charlie and his fellow sweeper that they both liked a bet on the horses. This was in the days before betting shops came into existence so they placed their bets with a local cobbler. Charlie told Geoff that they'd had a good winner the day before.   What they had done was to time their routine so they would be outside the cobblers at 1.45pm. There they would stop, have their sandwiches and a drink of tea. Charlie went into the cobblers who obliged Charlie by boiling a kettle of water for his flask. Charlie and Grandad opened up their butties and ate them outside. They had pre-arranged for a local pal to listen on the wireless for the winner of the 2 o'clock race: the pal wrote the winners name on a piece of paper, cycled past the handcart throwing the note into the cart which Charlie promptly reads and goes into the cobblers. "D'you know" he said to the cobbler "I forgot to put my bet on the 2 o'clock when I came in. Am I too late to put it on now - what time is it"   "The race will be over now" said the cobbler   "but I'll take it, you've been outside all this time so you can't know what's won" Neither of course would the cobbler know the winner until he got the evening paper.   And 'yes' Charlie was paid out. Geoff couldn't believe it, but it goes to show, you really can't totally trust anyone.

AND SO TO WAR

The main topic of conversation amongst the adults during 1937 and 1938 was about somebody called Adolf Hitler and the Nazi party who had got into power in Germany.

Mention was made of the 1914-18 war and the likelihood of it happening yet again, some thought it possible whilst others said that we were best to keep our noses out of it "Nowt to do with us and in any case we've got the channel between us and them so they'd never be able to invade us"   "And we've the best equipped navy anywhere in the world. They'll be ready to blow those Germans right into kingdom come" Geoffrey found all this sort of talk somewhat bewildering, but was soon to find out what war was all about.

In 1938 everything seemed as though we were going to live in peace in spite of what many people thought because the British Prime Minister, was seen waving a piece of paper in his hand that was a formal undertaking from Adolf Hitler that he would not invade us. But that was not to be and in 1939 Chamberlain made a speech to the nation to the effect that he had given an ultimatum to the Germans to leave Poland but going on to say that "as no such undertaking has been given we are now at war with Germany".

However the next morning seemed very much as it was yesterday. In fact life in Crewe Green just went on as if nothing had happened. But behind the scenes a lot was going on – the railway works stopped building steam locomotives and turned their production plant into making tanks. Similarly the car production plant of Rolls Royce turned their efforts in to making aero engines.

In the village though the farmers were still ploughing, sowing, reaping and milking Those of military age began to disappear as they were called up for military service in His Majesty's armed forces.

All the road signs were taken up and presumably either went into storage or to make something for the war effort. Wherever they went they were not going to tell any invaders which way to go. Even the clanging of all church bells throughout the country was abandoned. Blackout curtains had to be put up at all windows so that in the long winter nights not a chink of light must be seen, and there were Air Raid Precaution Officers (ARP's) to make sure that as far as possible everything would be in darkness. In addition every household had to have a sticky gauze sheet to go on the inside of all the windows. This was to prevent flying glass in the event of the windows being broken by bomb blast if there should be an air raid. Then, due to the fear of a gas attack everyone was supplied with a gas mask which had to be carried everywhere in the accompanying cardboard box which had a sufficiently long cord for it to be hung around the neck, and woe betide you if you should be seen without it. If you were challenged to identify yourself you could simply show your newly introduced Identity Card. Geoffrey's number was LGJA93 and was later used to form the holders National Insurance number.

Those lovely school playing fields remained mostly as they were but had the addition of two quite large air raid shelters with wooden seating along both sides. There were two entrances to each shelter the main one was down some steps and the other was through a metal tower at the other end to the door. These could be exited by a metal ladder. All the children quickly recognised them to be very similar to submarines complete with a conning tower. There was another addition to the field as Gaffer thought it would be a splendid idea for the boys' to have a vegetable patch. This proved to be a very popular introduction that was far superior to the three R's. The road through Crewe Green was quite strategically placed for any invading Force: on the west side of the village was a rather important roundabout, close to the railway station so it was decided to slow any enemy forces down by building a barricade. This consisted of eight pre-cast concrete rollers roughly 5 feet deep 4 feet in diameter and filled with concrete . These were strategically placed on the roadway so traffic from either direction was slowed down to a mere crawl. They could quite easily have been converted into a machine gun post should the need have arisen. Fewer and fewer cars were seen on the highways as petrol was available only for the use of essential commercial traffic and military purposes.

Most days would see army convoys with some vehicles carrying troops whilst others would be towing anti-aircraft guns and heavy artillery or conveying newly built tanks – all on their way to the battlefields or defence locations to dampen the enthusiasm of those Luftwaffe pilots All this resulted in the vast majority of car owners deciding to make the best of a bad situation by retiring their vehicles for the duration. However some people saw this as a golden opportunity and bought up the obsolete cars at very attractive low prices. In later life Geoff was to meet one such person best described as a shrewd entrepreneur.

The most prolific form of private transport was the humble bicycle. Every household had at least one bike and these were very much in evidence as people made their way to work and clocked on. At lunch time and again at knocking off time there was an amazing sight, particularly on West Street where the majority of the entrances to the various works were located, when swarms of cyclists were spread-eagled across both lanes of the road eager to get home. Bus drivers on that route would frequently stop to have a cigarette allowing the cyclists a clear passage. There were pretty well of buses normally packed to capacity some passengers travelling on the platform clinging on to the safety rails.

Crewe Hall lost its days of grandeur by becoming a camp for a battalion of Grenadier Guards. When they moved out it became home to American troops, first came white Yanks followed a little later by black Yanks. In those days apartheid was very much in evidence in the States. After their departure the Hall became a prisoner of war camp first for German and then Italian troops.

One day when Geoff was getting gooseberries for his mother to make delicious jam a man came down the pathway to the back door . He was followed by a group of around ten boys and girls: none of whom Geoff knew. When Nellie got to the door the man asked "How many of you live here"   "My husband and son as well as myself" "How many bedrooms have you got?"   "Three" replied Nellie "but what's this all about?"   "You and your husband in one bedroom and the lad in another means you've got a spare room for an evacuee. What d'yer want boy or girl"?   "Don't want either" was the reply   "Got enough with him"   "Take a girl then misses, be able to help you around the house Here what about this one? Comes from Liverpool don't you Sweetie?"   "Yes mister"   "And you'll help the nice lady wont you my dear"   "Yes mister"   "There we are then Mrs tell the lady your name sweetheart"   "I'm Lizzie"   "But I don't want an evacuee"   "There is a war on my dear you've got to have one. Now come on Lizzie get yourself inside and the nice lady will show you to your room"   So that was it we were stuck with a girl   "ugh"   thought Geoffrey Lizzie came from Liverpool and she was visited on a few occasions by her mother who after a fairly short period of time was so upset at leaving her daughter in this God forsaken place decided to take her back home. That was the last they heard of her.

As part of the national line of defence barrage balloons were introduced to protect potential targets and Crewe soon witnessed their presence. In fact it was on a Sunday afternoon when Geoff who was washing his hands at the kitchen sink saw what he thought were German Zeppelins hovering around.   "Dad, dad ! ! there are two or three Zeppelins coming what shall we do"   Bill came to have a look at what his son had seen.   "They are nothing to be afraid of, they are what they call Barrage Balloons, and they are there to stop German bombers getting too low, for the higher they are the higher the planes have to be to avoid entanglement with the heavy duty wires that hold the balloons"   "I'd better go and tell Grandma she won't know what they are when she sees them."   With that Geoff ran as fast as he could to Grandmas cottage to explain what these monstrous things were for. The balloons were to be manned by the Royal Air Force, and in order to do that, the men had to be found local accommodation.

Grandma was delighted to do her bit for the war effort by accommodating a young airman from Belfast whose name was Jack Armstrong.   All the family got to know him well and enjoyed his company. He was treated like a family member.   Geoff's cousin Eileen who was two years his junior had the most beautiful natural curly hair and Jack always referred to her as   "My own little Shirley Temple" who was a popular American film star. She loved it!

Most of the other airman were billeted in the cottages and almost every week they, together with several village folk, including Geoff and his mum, would catch the bus into Crewe where they would visit one of the six cinemas. On the way back they frequently popped into the local Chippie for a fish and chip supper wrapped in newspaper. These were eaten on their walk back. The newspapers would be scrunched up into balls and used as a football or thrown good naturedly at one another.

In those days nearly every boy had two prize possessions a toy gun and a knife. Everyone had a penknife which folded up into its own protective casing and was kept in the pocket. Some had sheath knives which were about six-seven inches long and each one was lovingly sharpened - each boy tried to outdo the others for sharpness. Having such possession years later were seen as anti-social and dangerous. However it is not knives that are dangerous it's those who possess them that are the danger. The misuse was never or seldom heard of for mostly lads were aware of what could happen, and actually did happen to Geoff. In the school playground an evacuee from London by the name of Roger Umpleby had a particularly sharp knife. Roger was chasing a number of the girls around the playground whilst holding his sheath knife and waving it in the air. Geoff who wanted to show some heroics went to grab Rogers arm but missed his arm and got a slashing from the knife which left his right hand thumb hanging loose with blood pouring everywhere. He screamed his head off and Roger was horrified at what had happened. The teacher Miss Buchan came rushing out to see what the matter was, took Geoffrey to the washbasin and ran the cold water tap whilst somebody else got the first aid box, splashing on some iodine which made him yell even more, bandaged his thumb up and took him home to explain to Nellie what had happened. The wound healed up and nothing more was said. In fact in later years he became rather proud of his scar which is still in some slight evidence today. Many years later there was an interview on TV with a gentleman who was associated with the forestry commission, his name was Roger Umpleby. Could there really be another person of that rather unusual name. Geoff intended to contact the BBC to find out if it was the one he knew - but never got round to it.

After a few weeks of being at war there were significant changes, neighbours and passers by that we'd seen in civvies a few days ago were now in army or air force uniform. Thankfully they all came home safe and sound but one by the name of Fred Astbury was taken as a prisoner of war by the Germans.

Uncle Frank was called up right at the beginning of the war. As he had been in St John's Ambulance Brigade he went into the Royal Army Medical Corps. He was one of the survivors at Dunkirk but had the experience of being torpedoed on one of the rescue boats. It was at this time that Geoffrey had to go to the railway station and the sight that met his eyes was very upsetting as a train going north pulled into the platform where a dozen or so ladies were handing out cups of tea to the troops who filled the train. As they alighted he saw that they all had kitbags, and rifles but sadly some were on crutches, many were bandaged up and blood stained. A lump came into his throat as he now realised that this was what war was about. Thank goodness he thought that his dad was exempt from military service because he was involved in tank building.

Even so dad and many of his colleagues joined the Home Guard. This meant he had an army uniform which he wore when he was on duty. His working week was from7.30 am to 5.30pm from Monday to Friday, but at weekends he only worked until 12.30pm. So after a day's work there were nights when he had to go on guard duty which finished in the early hours of the morning.

In addition to all this he turned the lawns into a vegetable garden growing potatoes, carrots, cabbage, parsnips, broccoli, Jerusalem artichokes onions and Brussels sprouts. In addition to all this he turned the pigsty at the bottom of the garden into a hen-cote with perches and nesting boxes installed. He then invested in a dozen chickens and a duck who was christened Donald. A gap was then made in the hedge adjoining the hen run so that they could get on to the field where there was plenty of scope for free food. When it came to feeding time Donald would go into the field quacking until the hens came back for their feed. The hens provided more eggs than Nellie could use when they were fresh so some were preserved in big toffee jars containing waterglass to use when the poultry stopped laying, others would be used for a bit of bartering. If a neighbour wanted any eggs Nellie would swap it for possibly sugar or some other rationed commodity. Family came first with Nellie as it did with the majority of women and Geoff certainly had a role to play: preparing food for the hens which normally consisted of the crust off a loaf of bread, any leftover food all went into a bowl together with sufficient hot water to mash everything together with bran. Neighbours, particularly those who came for eggs would bring any leftovers for feeding the hens – not forgetting Donald. Geoff would then take the mash and put it into the trough. Nothing was wasted: broken crockery was ground down to a fine dust and given to the poultry as potash which was to make the egg shells stronger. Geoff loved it when there were strong winds as he knew there was a good chance of trees or their branches being blown off as he would go searching for those that would make good logs to supplement the coal ration. Another of Geoff's chores was to get any newspapers, thoroughly soak them from the rain water-butt squeeze them so they still had some moisture mixed the squashy paper with the coal slack so making them into coal bricks measuring about six inches by four inches. Nothing must go to waste. Rationing was introduced early in the war and everyone was given a ration book which you were required to register with a grocer of your choice. As we had no car it made no difference to us that petrol was the first thing to be rationed.

In January of 1940 everybody was entitled to 4 ounces of bacon a week, butter 2 ounces, and 8 ounces of sugar. All this was so very necessary as the Germans sank many of our merchant ships that were bringing much needed food to our shores. It also helped to control the price of foodstuffs so the richer people could not benefit. In March 1940 meat was rationed so that everyone had one shilling and two pence worth of meat a week. 2 ounces of tea and 4 ounces of margarine. In July Jam was rationed, but you were allowed 2 ounces of cheese per head. Clothing and coal were also rationed in July. In 1942 it was the turn of rice, dried fruits, soap, to be rationed but to Geoff the biggest blow of all was also in 1942 when chocolate and sweets were rationed quickly followed in August by the humble sausage. Bread was not rationed until after war. Rationing finally finished in 1954.

Things like oranges and bananas were hardly ever seen, but dried bananas were introduced by some enterprising company who processed them shrinking them by less than half their original size so made them easier to transport in bulk. On one visit into Crewe there was a queue all the way around the inside and outside of the Marks and Spencer's store. On enquiring what they were queuing for the people just ahead of her said "Dunno really dear but it must be something good for all these people to be waiting" Further enquiries along the queue thought that it was for unrationed sweets. "In that case we'll wait shall we son" "Oh yes. It'll be worth it" It was almost an hour's wait and when they got to the front the sweets turned out to be red jelly cubes with a thin covering of icing sugar. Ah well we live and learn. Nellie wasted nothing and tried to use all the resources to good use: even the gas masks were put to good use when it came time to pickle the onions from the garden. Nellie, Bill and Geoff would sit in the living room they would each have a knife to scrape the skin off the onions, a pretty thankless task as they normally brought tears to their eyes, but the gas masks made it a more tolerable job.

Nellie visited Mrs Hewitt who told her that she was forming a ARP group and persuaded Nellie to join as her services would be quite invaluable.

Geoff was both thrilled and amused when his mother came home with a tin helmet and a armband which read 'DISPATCH RIDER'. The reason she was selected was that she was the only one to possess and ride a bike. Her duties were to take any messages to nearby villages informing them of any enemy activity. Her services were never called upon which were very much to her relief.

Nellie was a regular church goer and made sure that Geoff followed suit by encouraging him to go every Sunday afternoon to Sunday school. Before long he was invited to join the church choir which he was happy to do. The choir consisted of about eight men, four ladies and about a dozen boys. One of the ladies had a remarkable voice and was asked to sing solo on many occasions. Her name was Marjorie Shires she joined the Sadler Wells Operatic Company where she met her husband to be who was an Australian. They married and went to live in Australia: she was greatly missed by the Crewe Green community. Mr Collins made regular visits to his parishioners who generally made him most welcome. He had a habit of knocking and opening the door at the same time calling out as he did "Morning Nellie have you got the kettle on" She would reply "Oh vicar how is it you always seem to catch me when the house is in such a mess. I've done practically no cleaning at all today, but at least I can put the kettle on" She always said this to visitors to her home which generally was impeccable. Even when she went to answer the door she would be dusting whatever there was on the way to it. She was house proud beyond belief. If Geoff had been reading a book and went for a drink of water Nellie would have put the book back in the book case and straightened the cushion on his chair.   "What have you done with my book"   he would ask "I've only been in the kitchen for a minute and it's gone"   "It's gone where you should have put it"   came the retort One particular day Bill was at home and Mr Collins as usual did his best to get him to attend church. Bill came up with what Geoff thought was a brilliant response.   "Vicar, some weeks I work seven days building tanks for the war effort I go on regular Home Guard duty each week.   You vicar are with God when you are in the pulpit but I feel Gods presence when I am in the garden growing vegetables to keep my family alive and I look at the fruits of my labour and I say "Thank you Lord for your help".

Grandma Pritchard made jams and pickles which were sold for church funds, but her big occasion was the Harvest Festival. With terribly distorted hands due to arthritis such chores were extremely difficult, but every year she grew marrows from seed. When they got to about six inches long she would carefully write an inscription on the skin of two marrows with the point of a needle. As she nurtured and fed them the writing would increase as the marrows grew into maturity At the Harvest Festival they were carefully laid on the table at the entrance to the church. Everyone admired them as they walked into church and read the inscriptions: one was   "THE LORD WILL PROVIDE"   and the other THE LORD'S MY SHEPHERD, I'LL NOT WANT"   Geoffrey was so proud of his Grandmas handiwork that he stood by the door   "Grandma did that"   he told everyone as they entered. Many years later he decided to try and emulate his Grandma's efforts and whilst it was legible it was not nearly as good as hers.

The vicarage at Crewe Green was a large well cared for house where the vicar and his wife brought up Elizabeth their only daughter. They had a full time live in maid who did everything from answering the door to cooking the family meals and ensuring the home was kept clean and tidy. They also had a gardener who worked part time keeping the lawns and flowerbeds in good order. However the family also had a number of volunteer workers including Bert Garner who was a railway passenger guard. Bert worked many different shifts. It wasn't uncommon for him to finish around 7am, go to the church and cut the grass, then go to the vicarage to do some outdoor decorating. He would arrive back home around 4pm, have a cup of tea, go to bed for three hours, then back to the church where he'd find some task to do before going on duty at 9.45pm and be in the guards van on a return trip to Glasgow. During his waking hours he would have smoked around eighty woodbines. He died at the age of 69 and is buried close to the vestry of the church he loved so much.

His passing was a great blow to the church in particular and to the youth of the area for Bert had encouraged them to form a youth club for boys and girls. The first was held in the attic of the vicarage stables where meetings were held every week. Although the venue was good it was decided to move into the outbuildings of a nearby house called the Oakland's. Bert explained to the owner who was a single lady that we could not afford to pay any rent, but it was a great location for local youth and that he would arrange for members to paint the outside of the house in exchange. This she was delighted to accept and work started the following weekend all under the supervision of Bert. It was through this that many new and long lasting friendships were formed.

Geoff became lifelong friends of two brothers Jeff and Stan Farmer. They and their parents became active members at the church. Meetings were held every Thursday evening where they occasionally had a guest speaker, but the main attraction was table tennis.

As the years rolled on and the members began going to work Jeff who was an apprentice pattern maker made a superb new table tennis table as well as all the bats that they needed. All very resourceful and run in a business-like manner. It was at the club where Geoff got his first insight into working on a committee where he took on the role of treasurer. Not a position he at all relished or enjoyed but it did teach him, how to look after simple records.

The club was a wonderful way for the members to learn how to socialise and how to recognise the good as well as the bad habits of their fellow members. Eventually they would go fishing, shooting together and to attend league football matches, eventually going on holiday together. Through the club they learned social skills and respect for the other persons point of view. One or two marriages came about from relationships formed at the club. If there were any misgivings about a member it was dealt with by the committee, but Bert was always there to guide them through any problematic matters.

Geoff was interested to discover how his parents had come to meet up in the first place and was intrigued to learn that Dad had been admitted to the local hospital to have his appendix removed.

He was attracted to one nurse by the name of Nellie and likewise she was attracted to him and promised him that when he was discharged from hospital she would gladly ride pillion on his new motorbike.

The next bed to Bill was occupied by a man with a broken leg by the name of Harold Beasley who had been involved in a most bizarre accident on his tandem for he had a lady friend by the name of Maggie who he'd invited to ride on the back of the tandem. She however had never ridden a bicycle and was very wary of actually going on the back of a bicycle made for two. As she claimed that she really could not pedal a bike Harold came up with a perfect solution. He tied a length of elastic around the top of Maggie's knees and the other end was tied to the handle bars so aiding her ability to pedal and as he was on lead she really had to go through the motions. All went well after a few short practice runs so they were now both confident that they could go on a visit to a local beauty spot.

All went well until they came to the top of a steep hill on which the road had several fairly severe bends. As it was downhill Harold said that they no longer needed to use the pedals. He hadn't taken into account the elastic and Maggie simply could not stop pedalling with the result they picked up speed so much that the tandem took control of the outing and plunged through a fence into a field at the bottom of which was a rather large lake. Before they reached the water they took a nasty tumble in which Harold suffered a broken leg. He was admitted to hospital and was in the next bed to Bill who he had never met previously. Bill was discharged from hospital and shortly afterwards he and Nellie were married, as were Harold and Maggie. They became great friends for the rest of their lives going on holidays together with their respective offspring Alan the son of the Beasley's and of course Geoff. Like their parents the two boys also became good close friends. They went fishing together as well as with their fathers. In fact during the war years seaside holidays were not too pleasant as many of the beaches were closed off with barbed wire entanglements to protect us from a possible German invasion. So it made good sound sense to go on a fishing holiday which were taken mainly in Wales at a delightful place called Berriew where there was a canal, large lake and a couple of rivers. Ideal for any fisherman. However war was still raging throughout Europe and in the Far East against the Japanese who had entered into the fray.

But life had to go on. On the home front rationing and shortages of foodstuffs that had been readily available pre-war were now at best difficult to find and if you found any you had to have sufficient coupons to buy them. This applied particularly to clothing, but if Nellie wanted a new dress and had used her coupons she could use Bills coupons who more often than not at that time was mainly wearing overalls at work.

Grandma Pritchard had always taken great pride and derived much pleasure for providing what may be described as a right royal feast at Christmas when she loved to have all the family around on the big day. The family had now grown somewhat. No longer was Geoff her sole grandchild for Auntie Eileen was now married and had three daughters the eldest being Eileen so was always referred to as little Eileen to differentiate her from her Mum. In fact some years later it would have been more appropriate to reverse the 'little' tag as the daughter grew to be much taller than her Mum. Next was Kathleen followed by Judith. Although Geoff was fond of the three girls he had much more to do with Eileen as she was much closer in age to him. Auntie Annie, who spoiled all her nephews and nieces, never had any of her own children mainly because she was so late in life getting married. Auntie Alice had one son called Clive and it was through him that Geoff felt the first pangs of jealousy. That came about one summers day when Clive was a baby and the family had all met up in Grandmas home. She thought it would be nice to have a picture of her sitting in the garden holding her latest grandchild while 'young' Eileen and Geoff stood on either side. Geoff felt his nose had been pushed out: fancy Grandma holding this baby in her arms. The picture was taken and Geoff was given a print of it. He's kept it all his life and even now can look at that picture and recall his feelings towards his new cousin.

Looking back over the years Geoff never could understand how Grandma had coped when she had everyone to Christmas dinner with all the trimmings as well as a Christmas pudding she had made. They had roast goose with all the accompaniments. At tea time they were served with cold roast turkey, sandwiches and cakes, all home-made. As if that wasn't sufficient they had cold, roast pheasant and potato crisps for supper together with a glass of wine.

However the last time such a spread was possible was 1939 after which the shortages became so acute that everything had to alter. With the growth in the family and Uncle Arthur, Auntie Eileen's husband, being called up for service in the Royal Navy it meant that the number to sit down to a meal at Christmas had risen to thirteen. There was no way Grandma would sit thirteen down for that occasion and she had to find somebody to make it up to fourteen as it was easier to do that than to reduce the number to twelve. She invited a friend of Auntie Annie who was glad to accept the invitation.

Every Boxing Day Grandma Leese was invited to Crewe Green together with her family, Aunt Mary, Uncle Harold. Ethel and Roy, her fiancée of that time. They always came for the afternoon and evening where Nellie would have put on a delicious cold spread as well as her speciality a beautiful rich sherry trifle.

As they finished Nellie would ask   "Anyone for anything more? what about you Harold you seem to have had practically nothing at all"   "Thank you Nellie but no you've done us proud and I've certainly had my fill"   he replied and that was the general concensus, except that is for Geoff" I'll have some more trifle please"   "No you won't" was the response   "you've already had too much"   Why ask then he thought. This was the one and only day in the year when Bill volunteered to do the washing up with Geoff drying the dishes. When the guests had settled themselves into the front room Nellie went to the kitchen to see everything was going alright. "Why did you ask everyone if they wanted more trifle and when I said   "Yes please you said I couldn't have any"   "Nor could you because it's all been eaten up" came the reply   "And suppose Harold had said yes please: what would you have done then" "Well I know my customers so well that I knew they would not ask for more" "But just suppose they had what would you have done then? persisted Geoff "I would have gone into the kitchen and returned with an empty trifle dish saying "I'm so sorry Harold our Geoff must have gone into the kitchen and finished off all the trifle. I'm so sorry".   We would sit down in the front room by a roaring log fire and play pontoon.

Home entertainment in those days for all families was the wireless. As there was no electric the family had to use a wireless that was run off a dry battery and a wet battery. The life of a dry battery was quite long but the wet battery had to be recharged each week and this was another job for Geoff who cycled the two miles to the Charlesworth's Shop which stocked a range of radios and electrical appliances and carried out the battery charging service. Bill had purchased two such batteries and one was changed for the other every Saturday morning. There was a charge of sixpence for this service. Occasionally the battery would go 'flat' on Friday evening which meant that the family were without the luxury of listening to the radio. This was particularly so when that great war time leader Winston Churchill was addressing the nation on the radio. Because nothing must interfere with those inspiring and rousing addresses, about fighting them on the beaches, in the fields etc which everyone in the country found exhilarating. So much so that Geoff insisted on using one of the shot guns that Willie possessed in the event of a German coming to the house.

The radio and cinemas played a tremendous role in keeping up the spirits of the people at home. In Crewe there were six cinemas, some would have a main feature film on from Monday to Wednesday and change the programme for Thursday to Saturday. Seldom could you visit any of the cinemas without having to queue. Each film had a suitability certificate a 'U' picture was alright for all age groups the 'A' pictures were for adult only viewing but if a child was with a parent then they too could watch the 'A' film. 'X' films were adult viewing only.

The British Broadcasting Company (BBC) was brilliant. Geoff loved 'Children's Hour' which was on daily from 4pm to 5pm with Uncle Mac. Everything was so uplifting, so interesting, so entertaining and by and large in Geoff's opinion was far superior than most things that the BBC later churned out. People like Arthur Askey, Charlie Chester, Richard Murdoch, Vera Lynn and the stories of Valentine Dyall 'The Man in Black' who came after the war with his stentorian voice and real scary tales. Henry Hall and Billy Cotton and his Dance Band. All wonderful performers that entertained through those now dark long lost days. Although she died in 1943 Geoffrey still has wonderful and treasured memories of Grandma Pritchard. One lasting memory was when he called in on a Saturday morning. "I'm so glad you've come I'd like you to run an errand : I want you to get me six pennyworth of pigeons milk please" "I've never heard of that Grandma where will I get any? "Try the farms they'll probably have some if not any grocery shop will" He went to the farm opposite. "I've never heard of it" said the farmer's wife what's it for? "Grandmas baking a special cake and she needs some for that" Geoff replied .But no there was no success at the next farm either. He walked over a mile to the next village and went into each of the shops, but the response was all the same 'never heard of it, have you got it right?' Of course I've got it right he thought. Geoffrey turned back then walked about three miles into Crewe where he passed many grocery shops none of whom knew what he was talking about. The Home and Colonial would know he thought, they've got branches all over the place. But sadly they'd never heard of it. He plodded his way back to grandmas, he could feel tears welling up in the back of his eyes . he was letting his Grandma down.

On arrival at her home he explained why he'd been so long "I'm so sorry Grandma I tried everywhere but none of them knew what I was on about, I'm so sorry." "You've tried real hard, but you'd better look at today's newspaper and see what date it is" she said.   He was stunned "Oh Grandma it's April 1st, and you got me good and proper there I thought I'd let you down" She let Geoff keep the sixpence piece she'd given him for the pigeons milk. It was probably the hardest money he'd ever earned. That year although the war was still raging the allies were making good steady progress and things were turning in their favour.

There was still heavy loss of lives on both sides and dreadful destruction across the whole of Europe but generally there was a feeling that we were going to win through, and win we did when on 8th May 1945 the war in Europe came to a conclusion. Fighting in the Far East was still going on against the Japanese. However in October of 1945 the first atomic bombs were dropped on Hiroshima and Nagasaki, destroying both cities and many of their inhabitants. Peace was to reign throughout the world. Maybe it was an uneasy peace but it was peace and things started very slowly to get back to normality.

Chapter 2
IT'S TIME TO EARN A LIVING

This uneasy peace was provoked by the Russian leader Joseph Stalin.

This was mainly due to the German invasion of Russia. Towards the end of hostilities the Russians overthrew the Germans and then carried on through eastern bloc countries and Poland and into Germany going on to Berlin. Stalin refused to leave those countries and all fell under the communist flag including Poland the country whose defence we had initiated against Hitler. Churchill was furious with the Russians who held firm. Thankfully another war did not materialise, but it did not alter the fact that it would not have taken much provocation for another outbreak to start so we had to be on the alert. and be prepared for such an eventuality. In order to do this every boy had to go into the services on reaching the age of 18. This could be deferred for those taking apprenticeships until they were 21. So the thought of doing military service was never far away from the thoughts of teenagers including, of course Geoff who was now 14 years of age and his school days would soon be over. Bearing all this in mind he thought that if there were to be another war he would like his service to be in the Royal Navy, and so it may be an idea to sign on as soon as he possibly could to give himself a good start. When he told dad what he was thinking dad came up with a sensible proposal, pointing out that service life does not suit everybody and the minimum term to sign up for was five years whereas national service was only for eighteen months, and that if Geoff were to find out that service life didn't suit him then he could get out and get on with his life in Civvy Street This Geoff thought did make a lot of common sense.

Yes dad was right he thought but he was adamant in spite of his dads wishes and pressure that he did not want to go into the railway works.

"I think I would rather like to go on the railways but not into the Works I am sure that I would much prefer to go on to the running side, probably into the Control Room or something similar.

Dad agreed that probably his son was not cut out for engineering so a career on the running side may be much better for the lad.   With that Geoff wrote to the Railway offices and was sent an application form which he completed on its day of arrival and posted back. He was granted an interview where he seemed to have conducted himself favourably. Much to his amusement part of the test was to write about any railway journey he had made. This was easy mainly because he loved writing and secondly every Saturday when Stoke City were playing at home he always went on the train that was packed to capacity to see the team and in particular the great Stanley Matthews. The train to Derby left platform 6 at 1.35pm and called at all stations to Stoke on Trent. En route nobody got off, a few managed to squeeze in, but when it reached Stoke there was a mass exodus which was followed by a brisk walk to the Victoria Ground.

Geoff received a letter a few days later telling him that his application had been successful. He started work just few days after leaving school. He had to report to Mr Woolley in the Telegraph office which was up a flight of stairs off platform 5. Here he had to do a variety of things. The most important was to answer the telephone where somebody from anywhere on the station network would dictate a message which Geoff had to write down on a pad that was provided for this purpose and then pass on to the appropriate person for onward transmission. These were all Internal railway telegrams. It may be that an incoming train had a driver who did not know the route from Crewe on to Glasgow and requested a local driver to accompany him at least part of the way. On an odd occasion it may be the police in Birmingham asking for the Railway police in Crewe to meet a train on which there was a dubious character they wanted to interview. Also in the Telegraph were the 'tubes' these had a series of pipes which were about 3 inches wide and held cartridges that were about 4 inches long. These went to various departments on the station, but the furthest went to the engine sheds on the north side of the station. The tubes were operated by a compressed air system. A message would be folded into a cartridge placed in the tube, a handle was pulled and away went the message. Their receipt was acknowledged by the recipient pressing a button which rang a bell in the Telegraph office.

But the morse telegraph instruments dominated the large office which was heated by a massive coal fire at each end. There were also a couple of rows of teleprinters which were used to send internal telegrams to the busier stations like Euston, Manchester London Road and these were usually operated by female staff. Their fingers were never still all the time they were on duty as there were so many telegraph messages being sent the length and breadth of the country. Because of the nature of the work the telegraph office was open every day of the year for 24 hours a day. In other words it never closed. There were two smaller telegraph offices on the station: one for the upside traffic and one for the downside.

Geoff was rather taken back when he was told that on the railway the upside is all trains going south in the direction of London. You go up to London and down to Glasgow, Manchester and Liverpool etc.

There was no recognised formal training as we think of it today: however they were lucky to have a senior member of the staff, who when he was on duty, would tutor the newcomers. This he did by making them learn the Morse code. His name was Frank Wilding, fortunately he was a person who was so easy to get on with and had masses of patience which he needed with trainees. In fact there were only four newcomers at this time but none of them knew anything of the Morse code excepting for S O S which was three dots three dashes and three dots. Although he was not recognised as a trainer he enjoyed the training, and if he were on an instrument sending or receiving a message he would allow them to join him and see the routine. One of the instruments could be taken off transmission and they could practice on that which was very useful indeed.

Unfortunately Frank had something of a stammer which sometimes he would purposefully exaggerate. One particular day while he was training Geoff he said he had to go out for a short while. On his return he asked Geoff if he would like a rather nice looking red apple which he had in a bag. Not being one to turn down anything edible Geoff gratefully accepted. When he was about half way through eating it Frank stammerted "issssssit allllright?

To which Geoff replied it was very nice thank you. Frank said "Ohhhhhh ttttttthhhats gooood I found it ddddown theeee lavalavalvaatooory on number 5ppppllatfform. Ugh! Ugh! Ugh! Goodbye apple.

In due course they were allowed on to the morse instruments. They now knew the Morse alphabet from A to Z and were raring to give it a go.

They started off slowly by sending in what was known as E.   This meant that the sender would know that he had a beginner at the receiving end and would slowly send out the first word. At the end of that the receiver would tap one dot for E which meant that it was received and he was ready for the next word. If he'd failed to read it he would signal with a dash for T in which case the sender would repeat it until he got an E. As time went by, and Geoff progressed, he moved on to Slow G. As G was to send it at a transmitters normal pace the SG was a request to send continuously at a slower speed. If the recipient missed out on something he would stop the sender and ask for WA (word after) the last one he could be certain of.

It was fun and fortunately the operators at the other end were mostly very patient when the trainees were receiving or sending messages. Then that glorious day arrived when Geoff was to get his first pay packet which he had to go and collect from an office on platform 3.   He received Two pounds, two shillings and sixpence.

He was over the moon as he handed over his hard earned money to Mum and received from her five shillings to spend as he liked !

Bill however was not at all pleased when he saw Geoff's pay slip. It contained the name Geoffrey Pritchard. grade. Junior Porter. wage £2.2.6. "What the devils this? Junior Porter . Junior Porter! No lad of mine is a Junior Porter, what the devil are you training to do? Carry passengers luggage all over the place?"

Geoff tried to explain that it was merely a grade for the wages people and nothing more. In the office he made considerable progress by telling the operators that if they wanted to take a break to call him and he would take over their position for a spell. Geoff hated sitting around doing nothing and this would give him the experience to be useful and at the same time speed up his skills at being a telegraphist. From time to time an operator would have a stack of messages to send that he had no time to make a cuppa or have a smoke or with some, more importantly, to pick out the horses for his daily bet. Then they would call out "Come on Geoff I've got the "can on" a frequently used term that seemed to be restricted to the telegraph office as Geoff never heard it at any other place which in some respects seemed to have a vocabulary all of its own. He had taken over the duties of a senior man by the name of Norman. He was a smashing sort of chap, good natured and always ready for a joke and bit of fun. When Norman returned after about twenty minutes he asked Geoff if he ever had a bet on the horses to which he said no and that in fact he wouldn't know how to go about it.

Norman said that if he did want to make a bit of extra pocket money that a horse called Lucky White Heather was a dead cert to win his race. By the time Geoff had decided to give it a go he had to ask one of the other operators how to put a bet on as Norman had now gone off duty. There were no such things as betting shops in those days so it was suggested that he went to the Post Office and get a postal order to the value of the stake and send it together with his name and address to Littlewoods, Liverpool. He did this and put a two shilling PO in the envelope and posted it. The horse won but the trouble with that was the winnings would come in the post, almost definitely in an envelope bearing the name Littlewoods. So he had to be up before the post arrived at around 6.30am in order to avoid his parents seeing the evidence of his evil ways. The horse was an odds on winner and he had a return of about three shillings. All this trouble he thought it just wasn't worth the mither.

A door at the far end of the office led down a corridor to the railway telephone exchange which was operated by women during the day and by a junior member of staff throughout the night between 11pm and 7am. Geoff enjoyed the work including his occasional stint on the switchboard, but the shift work was not kind to his social life, particularly at weekends when he would much preferred going to the football match with his mates or going to the cinema on a Saturday evening, but the biggest upset would be in the event of him having to work Christmas day and miss out on the festivities at a family gathering. However he struck lucky because he came across Wally a member of staff who had six children and desperately needed extra cash. As a single man Geoff could get by on his wages and so asked Wally if he wanted to take on his Christmas shift he could do so. Wally was over the moon he would take on any extra shift if he could get it so that he could do more for the family. So in that aspect it served both parties very well and Geoff didn't have to work during the Christmas festivities.

Geoff reached the required grade to go into what was called the link. This basically meant that he would go on to the rota and be allocated his own morse instrument to work on. Sometimes this would be in the main office, but as a junior it was more frequently on either the Upside office on platform 4 or the Downside situated between platforms 1 and 2. Like the main office both the other offices were heated by coal fires which meant cleaning out the grate and making sure there was a adequate supply of coal for the next shift. These offices seldom had a visit from any of the bosses who confined themselves to the main office, but the workload was much more urgent than the main office as this dealt with trains on the move and reporting the time they left Crewe to various signal boxes and stations on the route. Rather than reporting that the 12.35 to Euston had left on time each train had a reporting number those on the up side had an even number and those going north had a odd number. It was a senior porter who was designated to give the number of the departing train together with the time it left. This person was known as the Train Reporter. However he was still basically a porter and was always anxious to get a tip by carrying luggage for a passenger. In consequence most of the Train Reporters gave their information as briefly and quickly as possible. So the telegraphist had to be ready for them. Sometimes he would get something like "146 Euston at 35, 162 Brum 37 and the Welshman at 39. With that the door was shut and the informant gone, so you had to be just as quick in getting the information down and passed on to the designated places. It was a fairly common practice for a train going from Glasgow to have certain carriages destined for London and some for Birmingham. Announcements to the travellers to that affect would be made saying the first six carriages were destined for London the other six were for Birmingham. On arrival at Crewe the train would be broken up and a different reporting number would be given to each train. So what might have been 236 became 238 for London and 240 for Birmingham. The breakup would not take more than about fifteen minutes as an engine would be waiting ready to take on the Birmingham section. It was not unknown for there to be a bit of a mix up and the driver of the London train could find himself leaving Stafford on the road to Birmingham. Geoff was thankful that as far as he was aware no such eventuality happened on his shift. He loved it when he was on the night shift in the main office where he could go outside on to the platform and see what was going on for a few minutes. In those days nearly all the letter mail and parcels went by rail. This meant that there were frequently more postal workers on the platforms than railway staff. The platforms would be piled high with bags of mail and all would be strategically positioned right by where the mail vans would come to a halt.

During the 1940's and 1950's the station was not just active and alive for 24 hours a day it was frequently busier at 3 o clock in the morning than the town centre on a Friday or Saturday lunchtime. The one train that passed through in the night that attracted Geoff was the Irish Mail. He found it fascinating to see it draw up in the platform and the activity that went on was so well organised. As a schoolboy he'd enjoyed, like his contemporaries, collecting engine numbers. The station used to be thronged with train spotters some of who would travel miles to be in this railway wonderland of Crewe.

Geoff was intrigued to see the wheel tappers at work on most of the long distance trains. They would walk the full length of the train at ground level and tap each wheel along the full length. Normally he would hear a clear bell like sound and then move on, but if he got a dull sound it meant there was something amiss he would know that there was a fracture in the wheel which meant the coach had to be replaced by something that was fit for use. These occurred very infrequently but when they did they would often lead to a long delay.

Now that he was a railwayman he was entitled to a certain amount of free passes and as many privilege as he wanted. With the privilege tickets the fare was about a quarter of the normal rate. So not unsurprisingly they were issued at what was known as the quarter fare office and every railway man knew where that was situated.

It was in 1948 that Frank Wilding asked Geoff if he would like to have a holiday in Ireland with himself and his friend Dennis who also worked in the telegraph office. Geoff jumped at the chance. They all had a free pass for the holiday and this entitled them to travel up to Stranraer and then on the ship to Larne in Northern Ireland. There they got the train that followed the coast up to Londonderry where they had a chance to have a walk around that town before getting their train to a place called Buncrana which was situated on Lough Swilly. The station at Buncrana seemed to have a staff of precisely one. He was the ticket collector who prior to collecting the tickets had to set the signal to 'go' and changed the points so that there would be no delay. He then took up a position on the platform, waved a green flag to the driver and for good measure blew his whistle for the train to get under way.

They were not sure how they would get to Rathmullan which was on the opposite side of Lough Swilly so they asked him and he pointed down to the boats. "O'ill be with you in a couple of minutes" he said I'll see you down there and put you right.

Put them right he did for he took the small amount of hand luggage put it on the boat then showed us where to sit. He briefly went in to an office and on his return he got into the boat and rowed across the Lough before returning himself to see to the next train. What an experience.

They found the way to the YHA hostel and met other guests. Every day for the week they were out walking along the pathways and over the hills of the delightful county of Derry. Ireland, or Eire, as it then was, had not been in the war so many things which were difficult still to get back home were readily available there. So after a very pleasurable holiday it was time to go home. They'd had a very enjoyable break now it was back to the dah di dah di di dah di which is morse for CR the call signal for Crewe.

But not for much longer as Geoff would soon be getting his call up papers for National Service.

NATIONAL SERVICE

The shrill ringing of Geoff's alarm clock wakened him from a deep, deep sleep. It was 6am on Thursday 21st July 1949. He got out of his cosy bed realising that today was an out of the ordinary one. Although he felt refreshed he was also very nervous and felt as though he was alone and that the next few hours were going to be tough. This was his last day in Civvy Street for what he thought would be eighteen months. He would have loved to get out of the house there and then for he knew that once he'd said his goodbyes and got through the front gate he would well and truly have to fend for himself more than ever before without having family and friends to fall back on. He went to let his dog Bruce into the house, patted his head, and said "I'm going to miss you so much Bruce"

Nellie, Bill and Geoff all had boiled eggs for breakfast with buttered toast and a pot of tea.

Dad said "It's a big day for you son but we will always be here for you if you need us but if you need to talk to me on anything that may be troubling you just give me a call on this phone number in my office" He then set off on his two mile cycle ride to work. Mum had by this time turned on the radio which was rather bad timing as the popular song 'A you're adorable' was being sung. He could see that his mother was touched by this and appeared to be on the verge of tears. Thankfully for both of them she managed to hold them back.

It was just after 8 o'clock when Geoff said that he'd best be on his way Nellie gave him a few words of advice " You are going to meet lads of your own age from all walks of life, some will be good, some will be bad, select your mates well but remember try to avoid any Welshman – they just cannot be trusted.

Geoff caught the 8.30 train to Manchester, London Road Station, On arrival about an hour later he made his way to Manchester Victoria Station where he got the train to Darlington where there were about three hundred 18 year old youths galloping their way to the platform where the train to Richmond would soon be departing. On leaving Richmond station there were about half a dozen army trucks and a number of sergeants and corporals waiting around and snapping out at everyone in general. "Come on you Mummies boys – as from now you are all soldiers that's a rank above being a Civvy. Civvies that's about as low as you can get so as from now don't forget you are a soldier and that's a step up in life"

"Come on, jump to it and get in the back of these trucks – there ai'nt no fare to pay but there ain't any nice soft seats to put your arses on – in fact there ain't no hard seats either. So all of you that's on now move down to the bloody front and hang onto anything or anybody you can hang on to. If you don't hang on you'll go flying out through the back on the hard road. Now move your big fat arses and let's see your nice new home"

The canvas covered trucks moved away, the lads at the front were in semi-darkness whilst those at the back could only see the following trucks.

The journey took the best part of half an hour. They arrived at their new home 7th Selection Regiment – Royal Corps of Signals, Catterick Camp, Yorkshire. On alighting they saw there were row upon rows of H block barrack rooms which had around twenty iron beds on either side. In the centre was a large fireplace. Geoff dumped his sparse belongings on to a bed which was adjacent to an open window.

Then a corporal came into the room "Stand to attention" he barked out "and stand by your beds and NOW" he roared "Let's get to know one another" "I am Corporal Mawdsley and this is Corporal McLellan. When you speak to us you address us as Corporal. Do you understand that lad" he said to a fair haired lad who responded

"Yes sir"

"Yes sir! Yes sir - I'm not a bloody sir, I'm a corporal, hell fire I just said you call me corporal. Got it lad"

"Yes corporal, sir" said the new recruit who was now visibly shaking.

"God almighty – I'm a corporal not a corporal sir, just corporal. Now pull yourself together lad or you'll be the first on spud bashing"

They were ushered outside where they fell into three ranks, turned right and marched to the bedding store where they were handed a thin mattress a couple of sheets and three grey blankets. Next stop was the Quartermasters store where they all received their uniform – denims – boots – ties – socks – top coat - cape – mess tins, plates and cutlery. "This battledress is too big for me" said one of the intake "You'll soon grow into lad, now get out"

On returning to the barrack room the two corporals demonstrated how to make the beds up ready for inspection on the following morning. It was known as the biscuit method. Two of the blankets were neatly folded to the same size, then the two sheets were also folded to the same size as the blankets. They were then placed blanket – sheet – blanket sheet and the third blanket around the outer of the others and a pillow on top.

July 1949 was one of the hottest summers on record at that time so all the windows were wide open. It was approaching 8.30 pm and it had now clouded over. They all now had to make up their bedding in the prescribed manner. This was something totally alien to anything Geoff had ever done in his life. He just hadn't a clue – but there again he did not appear to be alone on this. Having been given about ten minutes to prepare the two corporals proceeded on their inspection. Geoff compared his with the lads on either side and wished he'd paid greater attention to the procedure, but it was too late now.

He could hear the comments as the two corporals carried out their inspection. "What a mess lad do it again" they said as they threw the bedding of various ones across the barrack room.

Only a few of the new recruits had done a satisfactory job. Geoff knew his was even worse than some he'd seen, he was fearing the worst.

When they reached Geoff's bed the two corporals looked at each other, said nothing and then passed to the next bed.

Wow thought Geoff I've got away with it. I don't believe it.

But no – they wanted to make somebody's day really memorable. They completed their inspection and then the two corporals went back to Geoff's bed.   "Corporal McLellan have you ever seen such a bloody awful mess in all the time you've made these inspections" snapped Corporal Mawdsley.

"Corporal Mawdsley I can swear on oath that this is the biggest heap of shit I've ever seen" replied Corporal McLellan "I don't think this soldier deserves such kind understanding that we like to give to our men: let's put this heap where it belongs" They each put their drill sticks below Geoff's bedding and heaved it through the window. It was now raining quite heavy. Geoff went to go outside but was bawled at not to move until he had asked permission.

He wondered whatever his mother might have said. He thought he knew but decided to dismiss that.

"Corporal" he said "have I got your permission to fetch my bedding in please" "Granted" said corporal Mclellan "but we expect to see better tomorrow morning at reveille"

And they did. Never again did he ever fail a bed inspection. Reveille was at 6am. There was no bugler to awaken the new intake: instead both of the squadron corporals took great delight in clashing together two metal dustbin lids "come on you shower get yourselves up, let's go to that big beautiful parade ground and learn how to be soldiers"

Geoff thought to himself that although it was an early start he wouldn't have to do any more shift work, and getting up at 6am was better than having to get up, have breakfast and then be at work over a mile away by 6am. No, that at least was a plus point.

There was no specific induction into this way of life. Ablutions were carried out in that part of the 'H' that joins the two horizontals. Here there were about a dozen washbasins a couple of water closets and half a dozen urinals. These were used by the 80 recruits who had to do what they needed to do in order to be on parade for breakfast at 6.30. No! there was no leisurely stroll across to the mess hall for breakfast. In fact for each meal the recruits had to parade in three ranks outside their billet in order to have roll call to make sure that nobody had deserted. Names were called out in alphabetical order so Geoff was low on the list "Pritchard" bellowed the corporal. Geoff stood to attention "Here corporal" he called in a clear voice and so it went on down to Wilkinson the last man.

When satisfied that everyone was present the corporal gave the order to march on the spot – so basically the legs went left, then right without moving forward: the order to double march on the spot was then given and the same procedure was used except now it was more like running on the spot. To the delight of both corporals the hand held plates began to be dropped on to the hard concrete and smashed.

"Squad halt" came the order from corporal Mawdsley "Well just look here at all these broken plates, Oh dear corporal Mclellan - tell me corporal how are those who broke their plates going to eat their breakfast?"

"Do you know Corporal Mawdsley I really don't think they will be able to eat anything at all without a plate, perhaps the QM stores will have some spares, but I believe they will have to pay barrack room damages for the broken ones, let me see now - I know it's sixpence for a new plate and sixpence for the broken ones. So corporal I do believe that's one whole shilling."

"Bloody hell corporal McLellan a whole shilling I could have had breakfast at the Savoy for that, this lot must have money to burn"

There was a queue for breakfast in the mess hall but as there was no refinement in the service it did not take long to serve. There was a tray of fried eggs, another for bacon and a third for sausages. A member of the mess hall staff stood by each of the trays and slapped whatever was in front of him on to the recruits empty plate. Finally there was a stack of toast to help themselves to and of course a couple of tea urns for the lads to help themselves. Having been served the recruits would find a spot to eat and satisfy their hunger.

But this was the army and we couldn't have it quite as simple as that. Oh dear, no! Then the bawling started up from the squadron NCOs waiting by the exit.

"3 Squad get yourselves outside NOW. Come on double quick. If you haven't finished your brekklie too bloody bad, Get yourselves outside on parade SHARP".

Geoff was in 7 Squad and had eaten his egg and bacon but he'd barely touched his tea when it came "Squad 7 outside right away. Some of the lads were still in the queue. "Hey Corporal" called out one of the lads "some of us are still in the queue we ."But his voice trailed away when corporal Mawdsley bellowed. "Now means NOW not when you've had your bleeding brekkie get yourselves out here now. The last man out doubles five times around the parade ground. Got it? If you're hungry get yourself an extra spud at dinnertime. Now MOOOOVE".

What was said reminded Geoff of the words of wisdom given to him by Mr Day a bank manager who had served as a major in the army during WWII and now lived in Crewe Green. "Geoff" he'd said "The army will be exactly what you make it. It can be a good experience which will help you throughout your life or it can be a nightmare for you if you don't do what you are told immediately you are given an order.

Never argue with the corporals or the officers, don't question them as to why you are doing it, just do it, straightaway. One thing you can be absolutely sure of is that you stand absolutely no chance of winning. So make life as easy as you can for yourself by doing it immediately.

Every day was the same three meals a day, marching on the spot, broken plates. All part of the corporals fun. But the lads began to realise that they should take greater care of their crockery and gradually they learnt how not to drop it. However there was one task that would never change: when a meal was over each man was responsible for washing his own plate and cutlery. The facility for this was outside the exit door on a brick built platform which held a six foot long trough about two feet deep and eighteen inches wide. It was doubtful if that 'hot' water was ever anything other than barely warm. After about 500 squaddies had finished a meal and cleaned their possessions in the water there would be pieces of bread and thick grease floating on top with a bit of cabbage and left over carrots etc. Hygiene was not a word that came readily to mind but Geoff didn't have to wonder too hard as to what his mother would have had to say. After the shower of rain on Thursday evening the days had gone back to being lovely and sunny and everyone had to wear shirt sleeve order. They had been ordered to wear their denims and shirts but with the sleeves rolled up well above their elbows, hence the name of the order. They were not aware of it in the early morning but this was to be a fairly easy sort of day, which was itself a rarity. Following breakfast they were marched to the office block where they were to meet the squadron officer. They were told what was expected of them over the next four weeks of training. They would be going on to the square where they would be instructed on how to march properly, how to salute on the march, who to salute as an individual when out in the street. They would be issued with a rifle and bayonet and trained on how to use them. They would be told how to make their beds ready for the adjutant's inspection. They would be assessed for their trade training and then receive instruction and where that would take place. Everyone was supplied with an identity disc which was worn on a cord around the neck. They received their pay book and probably most important of all their army number.

The camp padre put in an appearance and told the new recruits where the church was, how to get there and what time the services took place. They were then handed back to the gentle and loving care of the two corporals. Corporal Mawdsley smartly saluted the padre who after he was out of ear shot said "So you might be going to church on Sunday morning!! Well let me tell you if you do then ask the good Lord to be with you on Sunday afternoon to help you peel a ton of spuds. Spud bashing is what we call it and spud bashing is what you'll do if, need I say any more. Remember you are in the army you are no longer a mister you've all been promoted to Signalman: we don't much care for misters around here do we corporal Mclellan.

"We certainly don't corporal Mawdsley but we have our bibles with us everywhere we go, isn't that so corporal"

"Of course it is" and turning to face the squadron he produced his pay book. "This is our bible and our prayer book. Never ever go anywhere without yours It's far more precious than the church bible . If ever you lose it I can't begin to imagine what will befall you By morning we expect you to have learned your army number. You may well find yourself doubling around the square if you've forgotten it"

Geoff kept mumbling his number to himself 2 2 1 5 9 5 6 8, 22159568 got it he thought to himself 22159568.

The corporals went through the woven cotton webbing they'd been issued with and were instructed to get themselves some Blanco and a tin of Brasso from the NAAFI. These had to be paid for out of their meagre wages The Blanco was like a khaki coloured cake and served the purpose of both cleaning and colouring the webbing. The application was simple enough as the brush was dipped into a dish of water and then rubbed on the cake of blanco and applied to the webbing. Normally the belt had to be done each day whilst the ammunition pouches, the water bottle holder and other items were done weekly. Possibly it was more important to make sure that the brasses that were attached to the webbing were done daily as these caught the eye better particularly if they had a good sheen. One of the intake was a particularly tiresome sort of youth who made it perfectly clear to all and sundry that he had better things to do in life that playing at soldiers. Well none of the intake particularly wanted to be here, but at least realised that had they been born a few years earlier they may well have seen active service with the chance of being injured, killed or taken prisoner so personally Geoff thought it was far better to be doing this in peacetime and know more or less when you'd be going home. Apart from which so many had given their lives to give us peace it's a pity some seem so begrudging to be grateful to those who achieved it and for us to be able to honour them by keeping the peace.

The order had been to Blanco all our equipment, and all of us knew that this meant all the webbing so we looked on in horror and amazement when the tiresome one spread his newly acquired greatcoat on the ground and liberally Blancoed it inside and out. When the corporals came to see how the lads were progressing this stupid jerk held his greatcoat up with joy. "There you are corporal you said to do ALL your equipment so that's what I've done".

The air was blue as the two corporals each took an arm of this weirdo and he disappeared never to be seen or heard of again.

It was becoming obvious to Geoff whilst all this was going on that they were all getting subconsciously competitive and taking pride in what they were doing. Geoff had not known anybody that had actually completed their National Service stint so had nobody to give him a few tips on what to expect and what he could do which a few of the others had. This was noticeable when it came to cleaning the boots. The boots of the corporals shone so brightly that to get them to ever look remotely like theirs seem an impossible task. The answer to it all was 'spit and polish' The boots all had a standard 13 studs: if even one was missing it had to be replaced immediately by the cobbler. The toe caps and heels of the boots had to have sufficient shine that you could see your face in them. The trouble as Geoff saw it was that the toe caps were somewhat 'pimply' yet those of the corporals were perfectly smooth. Most of the lads, like him were baffled by how to rid the boots of the pimples, but yes, it was basically spit and polish, because it wasn't the leather of the boots that shone it was the shoe wax. So the blacking was put on fairly heavily with a cloth, then spread over an area of the toe cap, which was then spat upon and using the same cloth lightly rubbed in a circular movement. The boots were clean, very clean in fact but this was a slow process. A variety of thoughts were expressed some sounded fairly convincing but to his own surprise it was Geoff who struck on the idea of putting the blacking on quite thick and then melting the blacking with a lit match. It worked . it actually worked the blacking spread out fairly quickly. It was allowed to cool down and then the circular motion on the cloth began its magic. Of course the pimples were still there but were less obvious. After a few days they were hardly noticeable and then they'd disappeared altogether. Although there was a perfectly good NAAFI on the site it was not used much by the new intakes who generally were far too occupied, but some of the lads did go there when there was a morning break for a cuppa tea and a pie or pasty just in case they missed out on the dinner again.

Geoff didn't particularly enjoy the drill but of course he tolerated it because there was no option: occasionally he, like several others would sometimes get the right wheel and right turn mixed up, but thankfully he never got his right turn mixed with the left turn which surprisingly quite a few did.

They were introduced to route marches of various lengths the average being 5 miles with just one of seven miles. Then there was an obstacle course which Geoff never thought that he would master but surprised himself when he actually did it rather quickly. There were frequent visits to the gymnasium where the one thing he excelled at was climbing the ropes. But above all of these he enjoyed rifle drill. They were introduced to the standard military 303 rifle all of which would have been used through the war. Geoff enjoyed firing it on the range then cleaning it with boiling water and a piece of 4 by 2. But above all this he loved being on the parade ground with the rifle. And the routine of sloping arms to presenting arms, trailing arms he loved them all and one occasion was called out by the corporal to show the squad how to do it. However there was a piece of drill which he and all the others hoped they could do and that was at the order FOR INSPECTION- PORT ARMS. This order was usually given by a NCO and involved the officer of the parade who would go along the three ranks to look down the barrel of each rifle to see that it was clean and clear of any rust. It was standard practice for the NCO to say that when it was our turn as individuals to port arms there would be a reward for anyone on the pararde who could hit the officer in the face before he'd had chance to make his inspection.

In fact throughout his time in the army he heard this said on every parade when the order to Port Arms was given. He never heard of any officer being caught out by this.

Pride, or attention to detail all the lads were eager to demonstrate their appearance: this would include everything from their webbing and their brasses to the cleanliness of their cap badges on their blue berets. All sorts of dodges were tried and tested. Geoff was particularly anxious to get the best pressed battle dress trousers with the sharpest crease down the front and back on each leg. He was prepared to try anything and the one that he favoured above all others which he used everywhere he went in his service. This was to turn his trousers inside out and then get a damp tablet of soap to run down the length of the trouser creases. Turning back he would then iron them. "Just look at them lads" he would say don't touch or you might cut your bloody fingers off" When on parade everyone wore gaiters into which the bottom of the trousers were tucked; in order to make them look a bit more flashy some of the lads found a way to get the trouser leg to hang rather smartly over the top part of the gaiters by using a length of cord with lead weights attached. This made the trousers hang perfectly to good effect. Geoff was all for trying this out himself – the result was very effective even though some of the NCO's rather frowned on this practice.

He was pleasantly surprised to find out that there was no objection to any of the lads going home for the weekend providing that they were not on duty and that they let the duty officer know of their absence. They must be back for first parade at 6.30 on Monday morning. With the August Bank Holiday looming it meant that they would be finished by 5pm on Friday and need not report back until Tuesday morning. Although they had to pay their own travel fare or make their own arrangements for going home many of the lads lived far away but Geoff was fortunate that he could still use his privilege ticket for rail travel as he was employed by the Railway company. One of the lads said to him "You're lucky mate, you live fairly close to and have got your cheaper travel I live in Portsmouth and cannot really afford to visit my folk. I'm only a pound short for the return fare I don't suppose you could lend me a pound until we get back could you?"

Geoff thought, he's right I am lucky and he knew how he would have felt if the roles had been reversed. "Course I can let you borrow a pound, but make sure that I get it back on pay day.

"Oh you are a mate, thanks, have a good leave."

Sadly that was the last he ever saw of him his 'pal' had been transferred to the Pioneer Corps.

A pound may not sound much now but in those long gone days it was the bulk of his £1 8 shillings a week wage. You were right Grandad he thought – never a lender or a borrower be. For the rest of his life Geoff gave a cheer when he heard the football results and Portsmouth had lost!

The basic training was to last for only four weeks and each weekend was free to go home if you so wished. However there was always a full parade of all squads early each Saturday morning for an inspection: sometimes it was called the Commanding Officers parade, or the Adjutants parade. Whatever they called it there was an inspection by the officer in accompaniment with the NCO's. Rifles had to be taken on these parades. Geoff could feel and see that all the intake were getting considerably better each time they paraded, and he felt a sense of pride that everyone seemed to be making such good progress. Anyone who was 'checked' by the officer of the parade had his name taken and was refused weekend leave. The weather was still sunny and even in the morning it was quite hot and some of the lads were in fact overcome by the heat that they actually fainted on parade. They would then be taken off in order to recover.

One of the lads in Geoff's intake was named Sid who came from Runcorn. Sid was a smashing friendly lad but he was one of those few people that no matter how hard he tried or whatever he wore he always seemed to have a dishevelled appearance. He loved the idea of going home at the weekends, but he had been checked on one occasion so had to stay in camp. On this particular Saturday the lads had completed their arms drill and there had been a few fainted. Sid turned to Geoff who was next to him and said "I betcha I don't fail this time" and with that he gently laid his rifle on the ground then stretched himself out on the parade ground as if he had fainted. It was so obvious to Geoff that Sid was play acting. However nobody saw what had happened - the medics came on - took him off the parade ground gave him a drink and told him to go home.

Well done Sid.

One very important part of the recruitment into army service was to take an allegiance to His Majesty King George VI. This was conducted en mass on the parade ground on to which all the squads had been marched. They then had to repeat after the officer the words of the allegiance

"I Geoffrey Pritchard swear by Almighty God that I will be faithful and bear allegiance to His Majesty King George VI and his Heirs and Successors and that I will do as in duty bound honestly and faithfully defend His Majesty, His Heirs and Successor's. So help me God"

It was drilled into the recruits that they must show respect to the officers both within and outside the camp by saluting them whenever we passed by. Most of the young second lieutenants were recruited as national servicemen like themselves, and it was obvious that some of them like the other ranks were tolerating rather than enjoying their time in uniform. A crowd of Geoff's mates were out one particular evening when there were a number of these young officers going in the opposite direction who they had to salute, and out of courtesy the officer had to acknowledge their salute by saluting back. If Geoff's crowd had all been together the officer would just give one salute to them. However he came up with the idea that they each walk about five paces behind one another. The first one in line saluted and got the appropriate response by the time the next lad saluted the officer hadn't the time to drop his arm, so he marched along at the salute for almost fifty yards. It gave the lads something to tell the others about when they got back into barracks. Basic training in the Signals was shorter than it was for any of the infantry regiments mainly because they were not foot soldiers or fighting soldiers but what might be called a support group. So it became necessary to be sorted out into groups for future 'trade training'. It seemed obvious to Geoff that he was in the Royal Signals because of his background in telegraphy. On the day they each had to be interviewed individually with the selection officer he was right in his assumption that they would try and send him on the course for Wireless Operators. However he really did not want to do that: he wanted to learn new skills.

As predicted the selection officer said "Wireless Op course for you" To which Geoff replied "I see why you say that, sir, but really I would have preferred to broaden my skills and do something a little different". "OK then" said the officer "but I would advise you that with your telegraph skills you would stand a good chance of getting early promotion as a tutor and furthermore you would almost certainly be guaranteed to stay here in Catterick"

Good grief Geoff thought Catterick was the last place on earth he wanted to spend eighteen months.

"Sir I do appreciate your thinking but I really would prefer to learn something fresh"

He was pleasantly surprised and pleased by the response "Very well then I will put you down for clerical training, is that OK"

"Yes sir, thank you, sir" with that he was dismissed and a few days later was sent on to the appropriate course. There they were trained on touch typing on a typewriter keyboard that had caps on each of the keys so nobody could look down as all their fingers became skilful in finding the required keys. It was not quite what Geoff had originally pictured in his mind's eye about the army but, as he was to discover later, there were a great number of perks which at that time he could never have imagined.

The next thing all the lads had on their minds was where would they be posted to. It could be the Far East, the Middle East, Germany or horror of horrors a home posting. He wanted to see a bit of the world, he was a reluctant soldier so he wanted His Majesty's government to pay for his travels. The day arrived when the postings were made known "568 Signalman Pritchard B A O R". Wow he thought BAOR, Germany that will do me very nicely. Geoff went home and told mam and dad that he was now on embarkation leave and would be going to Germany on 17th December. Sadly he would not be home for the family Christmas get together, but there was nothing he could do about it, unless he decided to dessert, but that was something he would never do.

He had to return to Catterick to get all his equipment together in his kitbag and all the required documentation and rail passes. The train went from York down to London then he had to make his way to Harwich and join the ship to sail across the North Sea to the Hook of Holland. It was packed with squaddies who were either drunk or in the course of getting drunk: the sea was relatively calm but even so the smell of vomiting Tommies was something he found quite obnoxious. But it was a free ride and they should be landing early in the morning. The military trains were really comfortable and pleasant, one could move about with ease and they were really clean. Geoff was posted to the headquarters of the Royal Corps of Signals who were based in the German town of Herford. The buildings had been specially built for and used by German troops during the war. They were rather magnificent when compared to the wooden built barracks he'd left behind in Catterick. In fact he had a single room which contained a bed and steel wardrobe as well as a small bedside cabinet. His window looked along the main road in the direction of Herford town centre. Herford was in the Ruhr district and looked as though it had not seen too much bombing during the war. However this turned out to be a short term stay for him as he was destined to be posted to 20th Liaison in the city of Cologne.

He received his travel warrant and instruction for the journey. The train left late in the afternoon. There were not many on the train which again had plush upholstered seating in which he soon dropped off to sleep. The stopping of the train woke him from his slumbers. It seemed to be quite a big place called Koln which he'd never heard of. As the train left the station he became aware that there was rather a big river that they passed over. Geoff had an eerie feeling that he was alone so he got up and walked along the corridor. No one was about, but then he came to a compartment with blinds down which read RTO (railway train officer). He knocked on the door which was opened by an officer who said to Geoff

"What the devil are you doing on the train, where are you going?"

"I've been posted to Cologne, sir, but I seem to be the only passenger"

"Colognes a bloody great big place, we stopped there a few minutes ago why the devil didn't you get out?"

"The only place I saw, sir was Koln"

"Oh hell" came the reply "that was Cologne. These bloody Germans don't know how to spell"

"What I'll do lad is to stop at the next station. You then cross the bridge to number 1 platform and the train that stops there will take you to K O L N get off there. Geoff had a wait of less than five minutes for the local train which had hard wooden seats occupied by downtrodden looking Germans. Being in uniform he felt somewhat uncomfortable by the looks he was getting from the occupants. On arrival he expected there to be transport waiting for him to take him to his new posting, but there was no sign of any such thing in sight as he left the station. There were some telephone kiosks close by so he phoned the CCG (control commission in Germany). He explained who he was, where he was and where he was destined to go. He received instructions from a friendly sounding person.

"Are you in uniform"

"Yes I am"

"Stay in the kiosk. Do not move out and let nobody enter. A driver will pick you up within ten minutes"

It had not really entered his head that here he was a 18 year youth in the uniform of their enemy country that had recently defeated them in the bloodiest of wars and equally as bad he was in the first German city to have been on the wrong end of the first 1000 bomber raid that had annihilated one of their biggest cities. The CCG were as good as their word and he was whisked away on the two mile trip to his new posting in Aachener Strasse, Koln or as he preferred it Cologne. It was a pleasant enough looking building which went by the name of CONTIHAUS and was reputed to have been one of the main offices of the Continental Tyre Company.

He arrived shortly after midnight. The duty corporal showed him to his billet a pleasant room that accommodated six. He was glad to get into bed and enjoyed his sleep. Reveille was at 6am and he barely had time to see much of the others as they went to do their ablutions. Geoff made himself look presentable to report to the Company Sergeants Major and advise him of his arrival. The CSM was popularly known among the lads as Bootsie.

"How the hell did you get here ?" he asked "I sent the Humber to pick you up at the station so what happened to you"

He explained his folly "Oh God help us. If you get lost in this world there's not much hope for you in the next one. Anyway go down to the first floor and get yourself some breakfast and then be on parade outside at 8 o'clock, sharp"20th Liaison was a very small unit with no more than 40 British troops. Germany at that time was divided into zones. The American zone was in the south in probably the most picturesque and desirable part of the country including the Black Forest the Russians were in the east to the Oder river: the British were mainly in the North West area with the Rhine and Ruhr. The French zone was in the South west. Belgium did not have a zone but were given a small part of the British Zone around the Cologne area: hence the reason 20th Liaison existed.

Geoff had crossed the Rhine in the train the previous night.

What a mixed bunch they were. The only regiment to have a decent number of men was the R A S C which had about six men, the others were made up of a Gordon Highlander, someone from the Black Watch, the Kings Own. Interestingly the Army Catering Corps had the one and only cook who was from Norwich. Geoff decided that he was the one who was going to be his best mate .And he was – for after all he was the only cook !

Geoff could not have dreamt what he was going to witness in the next few days. There was no parade ground at the camp but there was a piece of wasteland adjacent to Conti Haus where everyone assembled at 6.30 am for roll call. It was a flat piece of ground which had a fair bit of rubble on it and it served its purpose reasonably well., Geoff however asked what was causing the whisps of smoke coming from the surface. He was told that they were from the cellars of the old properties that had once been on the land which were bombed during the war and was where several German families were now living.   One of RASC lads went around collecting the kitchen waste from the bins every evening and took it to a contact who lived below ground for the German families to use. This unit was so small that you soon got to know everybody: the majority were regular soldiers including Sergeant Penman who Geoff worked with. He was a Scot, a really likeable sort who had been in the Black Watch during the war and had seen action on the front line.

It seemed to be the policy of the military in BAOR to use a certain number of German personnel and this was certainly so in Cologne where the cleaners were all German nationals who started work around 6am to get the offices spick and span ready for the day's work. Gerda, however, worked in the offices and most of her duties were with the major. Geoff was delighted to find that Sergeant Penman was very easy to get on with and had a good but firm manner but didn't stand on too much ceremony. The sole officer in the Royal Signals was Major Patterson who was small in stature, kindly but firm and had no inhibitions about letting all and sundry know that he was a Christian and did his best to get all ranks to attend the church service on a Sunday morning. Geoff was among the few that did actually go along most weeks. There were certain things the major seemed to strongly disapprove, bad language and drink being at the top of his list. When Sergeant Penman's phone rang it was usually the major who was calling. "Need to see you straight away sergeant" would come the command. Turning to Geoff as he stood to go out he would say "Och, the little shit wants to see me ... just keep an eye on things while I'm with him"

There were times when this was said in the presence of Gerda. However the Sergeant and Geoff were both shocked one morning when Gerda walked in with armful of files saying "Sergeant Penman, the little shit wants to see you"

"What did you say" asked the sergeant

"The little shit wants to see you"

He looked at Geoff and burst out laughing, but he simply could not let her get away with that"

"Do you know what you are saying" he asked

"Of course I do "shit" it's something that little dogs do when they go for a walk"

He looked at Geoff who was now convulsed in laughter "Do you know sarge, it's what you call him, she just thinks it's acceptable" "Listen my dear" he said looking at Gerda "I may say it but I shouldn't do so, so in future just say the major wants to see you. You'd have us all in the glasshouse if he heard you say that".

A few months after Geoff's arrival in Cologne Sergeant Penman had been drinking fairly heavily in the sergeants mess. He decided to take out the unit's big Humber car that was in the compound. He drove through Cologne at what was described as a very high speed. He returned to the compound where he wrecked the vehicle. It was at reveille next morning when another of the sergeants came into the billet to say that Sergeant Penman was dead. Apparently after the crash he had gone to his room on the top floor of Conti Haus and fell over the banister and dropped the sixty feet or so on to the entrance floor. There was a inquest at which it was revealed that during his war service he had received an injury in a battle in no-mans land, where his pal went to fetch him back to the British lines. His pal hauled him on his back to within a few yards of their own lines but never reached safety as he was killed from a shot in the back. This had given Sergeant Penman a deep personal hatred of Germans and his reckless driving had been in the hope of avenging his pals death by taking a few Germans in vengeance. The enquiry stated that he should never have been given a peacetime posting to Germany. A sad end to a lovely man. Being such a small camp it did not really warrant having a NAAFI, but there was a good canteen which had a perfectly adequate bar, tables and chairs as well as a good snooker table and, inevitably, packs of playing cards. In fact a crowd of the lads became obsessed with cards. Geoff would have a pack or two in his bedside locker and would play with four or five of his mates before and after breakfast until it was time to go on parade.

Geoff had never played snooker until he went to Cologne, but one of the lads Mick Mather got him to have a go. Geoff had a decent eye and soon got into the game but to nothing like the standard of Mick who played an outstanding game. Geoff was convinced in later life when snooker became popular on TV that Mick would have been good enough to turn pro. In fact he did things that Geoff can never recall being seen on TV. As an example when he and Mick were playing singles Geoff said "I've a feeling Mick that you are going to snooker me here" Mick replied "No way. That would be too easy for you to get out of so I'm going to angle you" This meant that he would play the ball towards a pocket but would leave the cue ball end in such a position that Geoff would have no option but to play away from the object ball. It was amazing.

Geoff had made a point of getting the cook, Arthur Tate, as his best pal and they really did hit it off very well together. Arthur was a heavy smoker and hated all sports but would have a go at snooker from time to time but he really hadn't much idea . Geoff would say "You can't play snooker with a fag hanging out of your mouth. play now smoke after".

It was the best part of half an hour walk into the city centre so sometimes they would get on to one of the trams which stopped right outside Conti Haus: in fact they got a bit brash and would hop and off but always refused to pay the fare. A quick "nein" and a shake of the head and the conductors used to know what was meant. It gave Geoff a good feeling when he and his mates went by public transport for two reasons. First many of the Germans who were on the tram would look at their boots and make comments and point them out to their wives. This even applied to the Belgian troops who looked at their boots, webbing and brasses. They never seemed to bother with such things.

Company Sergeant Major Hayes was sports mad. On several mornings a week they would go with him on the camp bus to the outdoor swimming pool which was about three miles away. It didn't matter what the weather he would always be first to run to the pool. Some mornings the water was frozen over but that wasn't going to put him off. He dived on to the ice and into the freezing water below. "That's the best way to do it lads, now come on in.

Close by the pool was the football stadium of Koln FC and they were given the privilege of playing on that ground up to three afternoons a week. Geoff didn't know what the ground capacity was in those days but the general opinion it was around 30,000. Most weeks 2oth Liaison would play against one of the Belgian units. Geoff could never recall anytime that the Belgians won a game. Arthur Tate would always look for an excuse not to play football. He was useless as an outfield player so CSM Hayes told him he should go in goal where he could have a quiet time and have a smoke as well ! That satisfied him: after all he didn't really have to stop the ball but it would keep Bootsie quiet.

There was one occasion when the officers were to entertain a group of local dignitaries and Arthur had been given a menu to prepare for the evening meal. However this coincided with the day that a special football match had been arranged. This was to be two sides from the unit playing against each other. Arthur told Bootsie that he had a massive meal to prepare for that evening. Bootsie seemed to know nothing of this and ordered Arthur on to the camp bus. Reluctantly he did, but on the way to the ground he said "Sergeant Major I hope you will take full responsibility if I fail to get the meal ready for tonight. There's a lot of preparation to be done and right now I can't see how I can possibly do it, and I don't think the commanding officer is going to be too pleased if I say that I hadn't the time to prepare it as Sergeant Major Hayes thought it more important for me to play in goal" "Tate, I don't know if you are taking the piss, but if you are I'll make sure you spend a long time in Bielefeld," (a tough military detention centre) "but now we haven't a goalie" "I'll have a go" said Geoff "he is my mate, so I'll give it a try"

When everyone had alighted at the stadium Arthur was driven back as the sole passenger to get on with his work.

It turned out to be a great decision for Geoff as it happened as Sergeant Foulkes who seemed to have a grudge against Geoff was the centre forward for the opposing side. Geoff's side were two up by half time and he was rather grateful that he'd not had a shot to save. The second half was a little different, the opposition had attacked more with a few shots on target which Geoff was pleased with the way he'd handled them. After half an hour into the second half one of the lads called Terry put in a shot which was beyond Geoff's reach to pull one back. There were only a few minutes left when the opposition were awarded a corner. Sergeant Foulkes was in a dangerous position waiting for the corner which came across at head height for the sergeant. Geoff stood his ground then spied his chance to fist the ball away. He went up and connected with the sergeants head instead. He was obviously in pain holding his hand to his head.

"Oh sarge I'm so sorry" said Geoff" I tried to fist the ball away" he said as he saw the sergeants bloodied nose.

The game ended and cups of tea were served with a packet of digestive biscuits. "Are you OK" Geoff asked Sergeant Foulkes. "I'll live" came the reply.

There were some characters among the lads in the unit.

Geoff was particularly intrigued by a very smartly turned out corporal who was another of the regular soldiers. He'd been in the army prior to the war and had served for some time in India. His home town was in Cardiff where his wife still lived. He had a tremendous appetite and was constantly on the lookout for anything left over by any of the lads. If there was no food he would eat glass or even razor blades! Geoff watched closely when Taffy was eating any of these objects. Was this some sort of trick? Geoff could not really believe what he saw but Taffy would gladly put a chunk of glass into his mouth and chew.

"You can't eat glass" said Geoff in disbelief.

Taffy would open his mouth to reveal a mass of chewed glass. Then he'd shut his mouth too, then open to reveal there was nothing there. Unbelievable !!Another character was an old soldier who must have enlisted prior to the war. He had three stripes but he was a private not a sergeant. His stripes were inverted and worn on the lower part of the arm and were awarded for good conduct and the length of service. His name was Fitzgerald but everybody knew him as Pop. he was responsible for the units Motor Vehicles, making sure they were kept clean and serviced regularly. Geoff did not find him a particularly pleasing sort of person but he kept himself out of any sort of trouble. However Geoff found that he was a rather sneaky sort of person and not to be trusted one little bit which was out of character with the others. On more than one occasion he tried to get Geoff into hot water usually over some petty matter, so nothing serious. However he was advised that at the end of his current term he would not be invited to sign on for continuation in the army.

The day before his release Geoff saw a softer side to him.

"Do you know lad I envy you and the other national service lads. I wanted to stay on because I've absolutely no one to go home to, I will have no place to live, no mates to look forward to meeting up with for a couple of pints "

"Oh come on Pops, you must know somebody in London where you are from. An old neighbour maybe or a sister you've lost touch with"

"There's nothing and nobody waiting for me, this place is my home and all the lads here are the nearest I've got to family. But you, you've got loving parents who will be looking forward to seeing you back, a comfortable bed in a nice warm loving home and a decent future to look forward to. As for me all I've got to look forward to is a hostel of some sort full of buggars like me . That'll be my home"

There was nothing more to be said to try to comfort this poor old soldier, but Geoff wondered can there be many more like him – old soldiers that have served king and country and are now society's outcast. Sadly the answer was 'yes'. Nobody ever explained to Geoff why one morning on the Daily Orders it stated that he had been promoted to corporal . What he'd done or why he'd been promoted was a mystery to him. He knew he'd taken on more responsibility following Sergeant Penman's death. However a clue did come when the adjutant told him that he was to be transferred to Minden as their squadron office routine was something of a shambles and they wanted somebody to sort out the mess. Geoff was quite thrilled with this. This resulted in him going through file upon file of documents and paperwork and getting some in to decent order and destroying some which were of no relevance.

From there he went on to do a similar exercise at a place called Celle. Each time he moved he had to put new 'flashes' on his battledress. The 'flash' identified which division he was in. The first flash he had was the Cross swords of BAOR. His favourite was a black bull on a yellow background of the 11th Armoured Division. However the one that gave him a good feeling of pride and amusement was that of the 7th Armoured Division which during the war years got themselves the name of the Desert Rats, because of the jerboa on a sandy coloured background. In Celle, perhaps unsurprisingly, they were known as the Cellar Rats. Again he was there for a fairly short spell before going on to what turned out to be his last posting. That was in the lovely spa town of Bad Lippspringe.

The accommodation here was quite pleasant, but the office was like a battle ground. Absolutely no organisation whatsoever, bits of paper, some marked Confidential were scattered all over the place. There was absolutely no filing system at all. On the first day he met the guy who had been responsible for the mess Private White. He was a very likeable sort of person, affable but irresponsible. However he had got away with it was beyond Geoff. But it was no use moaning and going into the whys and why not's. Unsurprisingly White was nicknamed Chalky and he and Geoff got on rather well. New approved systems were brought in and everything was knocked into shape. There was a very good social arrangement at Bad Lippspringe.

The officers had the Officers Mess for their recreational purposes, the sergeants had their own mess and the corporals had their own. Geoff found this to be unusual as the corporal's normally were regarded as other ranks along with the privates. So Geoff's evenings were mostly spent in the Corporal's Mess. It was in the Mess when a corporal who was much older than Geoff said to him "You don't remember me do you?" Geoff admitted that he was sorry but no he didn't ever remember seeing him previously.

"I'm glad about that" said the corporal "because if you don't remember me I just hope that nobody else will".

This is rather mysterious thought Geoff – but who the hell is he? "Well come on then tell me where we met before and why you hope others don't recognise you"

"OK I'm sure I can trust you not to give me away, but there are plenty of guys in the Signals who would gladly take me apart if they had the chance"

"Why would they want to do that" asked Geoff

"Remember your days at Catterick and being on guard one night when you had to call out the guard?

"I do remember it - I don't really know who was the most scared the driver who turned up without his works order or me who had to challenge him, but that still doesn't tell me who you are"

"I was the corporal of the guard that night, and you did the right thing now you remember?"

"I remember the incident well but I still can't place you"

"If I told you that I did not wear uniform during the day but had a red and black top with horizontal stripes..."

"Oh my God ! You were that bloody horrible PTI.! No damn wonder you don't want to be recognised – plenty of those lads would willing do you in if they had the chance. But don't worry about me I won't let on at all, your secret is safe. so come on let's enjoy a pint together.

They became really good mates. His name was Ted and he had really put them through it in the gymnasium at Catterick, but that was now history, and the circumstances had changed.

Geoff had six or seven weeks left before he was due to be demobbed and he was also entitled to a spell of leave. As his release wasn't too far off he decided that it might be a good idea to take full advantage of his situation and take local leave so that all his accommodation and travel would be quite inexpensive compared to the cost it would have been from the UK. He selected an approved military rest centre in Ehrwald in Austria. It was a fairly long journey which passed through not only the British Zone but ended up in the American Zone, but not before going over the border of the Russian Zone which they reached quite late at night. He had nodded off but was startled when the train came to a halt and he found himself with three armed Russian soldiers each pointing their rifles at him. It was just a little scary to be looking down three rifle barrels but all they wanted were to see were his travel documents: so that was soon dealt with.

On arrival at the destination he found that he was in a very pleasant chalet with eight

Chapter 3
A CHANGE IN DIRECTION

It was 19th July 1951 when Geoff walked down the garden path. He was back home.

To his delight and surprise his beautiful black Labrador remembered him: jumped up with his paws on Geoff's shoulders and tail wagging licked him all over.

"Oh Bruce it's so good to see you"   Geoff now knew he was welcome home. How lovely it was to see his mam and dad again, it had been so long, but they were all together again. Nellie though had a surprise for him "We are going away on Saturday to the Norfolk Broads for a week with the Beasley's and the Webb's so I've arranged for Grandma Leese to come and stay the week and look after you. "Why put her to that trouble, after two years in the army I would be quite capable of caring for myself for a week"

"Never mind she wants to come and I will feel a lot better if I know you are being looked after properly"

"You do realise that when you get back I've arranged to go to Rome for a week with Alan Beasly don't you and then it's back to work"

Although Grandma Leese did all the cooking and the cleaning it was Geoff who found himself with the task of feeding the hens every day, collecting the eggs and making sure they were locked up safely every evening.

Back home! How lovely no more getting up at 6am parades, no more kit inspections. On the other hand no more going to the NAAFI or popping into the corporals mess for a few 'jars' and a game of pontoon with the lads. No more competitions with the other corporals as to which of them would put the most squaddies on a charge during the week. Looking back Geoff was a little ashamed of himself that he'd won the pot more times than anyone else. Yes like thousands of others he had been a reluctant soldier. However he had gone in and served King and Country for two years and really had no cause to complain. In fact as he sometimes reminisced he knew it had done him and the vast majority of the other national service men more good than harm as it had given them the understanding of discipline which led to most of them coming home much more confident to face life. However it was good to see all his old mates, but as he pointed out national service had made a bit of a mess of his social life in civvy street.

As an example Geoff was pally with the brothers Jeff and Stan. Geoff and Jeff were both 18 years of age but because Jeff was serving an apprenticeship he was deferred from national service until he was 21. This meant that the friendship was disrupted four years for as Geoff finished his national service Jeff was going in and as Stan was younger still it meant that he was to go in as his brother came out. But like any situation in life they had to adapt accordingly.

Geoff and Alan went to Rome by train because their privilege tickets allowed them free travel. They first made their way to London Euston and then to Waterloo, there they got the train to Dover where they joined the ship which took them on to Calais. Then they got a train to Paris where they joined the train to Rome. Through enquiries at a tourist centre they found a bed and breakfast place quite close to the station. They visited quite a few places of interest including, of course, the Colosseum, where their imagination took over as they pictured Lions and Gladiators in their minds eye. The week flew by and so it was back home and the prospect of going back to work.

Most of Geoff's old colleagues were still there together with some new faces. Geoff wondered how he was going to cope considering he had done no morse for over two years. He need not have worried as it seemed to be second nature as he heard the familiar sounds of Dah di Dah Dah and so on.

It was not long though until he felt that this was not really a long term job for him. But what could he do? What would he really like to do for the rest of his working life? He was not at all sure but he would scour the vacancy columns in the local paper. The work itself was OK but it was regulating his body and his whole system to getting used to working shifts once more. Shift work was playing havoc with his gastric system. If he was on 6am to 2pm he really didn't want to have breakfast at 5.30.But there was a 20 minute break for breakfast at 9am, but it was a five minute walk to the canteen and the same going back: this left 10 minutes to queue up. then gobble it down. When knocking off time came at 2 o'clock he'd gone off wanting his dinner. Every shift seemed to have a drawback so he really must find something else to earn a living. But what?

In November 1951 he spotted a vacancy advert in the Crewe Chronicle that sounded promising, it was for a Housing Assistant in the offices of the Urban District Council of Nantwich. Geoff made his application and a few days later was invited to attend for interview with the Housing Manager, Sam Barlow at 7.30pm the following Thursday. What a strange time to go for an interview was Geoff's first thought. But he found out why when he met Sam Barlow who invited him to take a seat in the corridor until he was called.

After a brief wait he was invited in to what turned out to be the Council Chamber. On entering he was horrified to see that there were about thirty people seated on two rows of benches facing a higher placed bench from which the Mayor sat in his glorious robes of office with two stern looking gentlemen on either side who turned out to be lesser mortals but were officers of the council.

Geoff felt petrified as the mayor introduced himself and his entourage. Then came the questions: some straight forward enough asking where he was currently employed and why did he want to leave.

Had he done his military service, what rank had he obtained, in what capacity did he serve in the forces.

To add to Geoff's horror the other councillors were invited to ask him any questions they thought appropriate. They had no hesitation . Why do you want to work here? How far away is your home? How will you get here on time each day? Will you miss the travel benefits of the railway. How much notice would you have to give?

Good grief thought Geoff they'll be asking me what I've had for breakfast before long. However they didn't so they bid him a good night and thanked him for coming.

A few days later he received a letter offering him the job with a wage of £6.15.0 a week and to report to the Civic Offices at 9am on Monday morning in three weeks time. Geoff was delighted to write two letters: one to accept the job the other to give his resignation from the Railway company.

The Civic House was a lovely old building that at some time in its past had been the residence of what must have been a well to do citizen. It stood in its own grounds with a public pathway running through it that linked two pleasant roadways.

On arriving for his first day he reported to Mr Barlow who gave very brief details as what was involved in his job. Basically it was to record all the applications that were made for the tenancy of a council house. Before going into fuller detail Mr Barlow introduced him to Eddie who turned out to be totally blind but operated the switchboard as well as typing. He was somewhat older than Geoff. The other person was Geoff Harding. They seemed to hit it off straight away and appeared to be more or less the same age.

Finally, and most important of all Geoff was shown to a small but adequate attic room to meet a person named Malcolm who was moving on to pastures new, still in local government but with a borough council. Malcolm was in his final few days and was charged to train Geoff in the way things worked and where the many records were kept. It seemed to be fairly straight forward. When anyone wanted a council house they had to complete the appropriate application form. This required the name of the applicant, marital status, how many children they had what sex and ages they were. How many bedrooms in their current home. How many other people lived there and what age group they were in. The size of the bedrooms were needed : what cooking facilities, was there a bathroom was it shared by all the occupants. When the form was completed the number of points were added and recorded on the applicants card. This card then went into a desk top filing box The applicants with the highest number of points were assumed to have the greater need. All local authorities had a massive project for building houses to meet the needs of their residents. When a property was vacated or a new batch of houses were built it would be Geoff's responsibility to advise Sam who the likely ones were to be in line to get the keys to a house. In turn Sam would advise the council at the next meeting of the lucky ones. Geoff thought that he would really enjoy this and felt that he was doing something worthwhile in the process for the local community.

The all important morning tea breaks took place in the general office where the switchboard was located. Normally there would be five or six members of staff who would go there for tea or coffee and a couple of biscuits and of course a natter among themselves. It soon became obvious that Eddie was somebody who was doing a decent job, but it was work, Geoff thought, that was below Eddies mental ability. It didn't take him long to find out that Eddie who had never enjoyed good vision had been in the 8th army and served a great deal of the war in North Africa.

He had been a draftsman prior to the war and his skills were to be put to a very good use during his time fighting against the enemy. His workplace was below ground in a specially constructed room where the strategy to beat the Germans was to be planned. The officer commanding this unit gave Eddie the strategy and what the intentions of the generals were. This entailed Eddie to draw up the plans which were then passed on to the necessary groups who would be leading the attack. As the room was below ground it meant that they had to generate their own light. This resulted in Eddie working in artificial light for most of his service.

As the war ended he was demobbed and went back to his civvy job. One of the first initiatives of the council was to build a civic hall where residents could gather for a variety of events. Eddie was to draw up plans for this project which he was delighted to do. The council accepted his ideas and worked commenced. Unfortunately his eyes were deteriorating rapidly and in spite of medical treatment he became totally blind. The man who planned it never saw his finished work. So sad. But whenever there was an evening event on at the Civic Hall that the two Geoff's fancied attending they always asked Eddie to go along with them. He loved it and really joined in whole heartedly. Often these events finished later than the time of the last bus back to Crewe so Eddie insisted on Geoff going back to his home and staying the night. Eddies wife approved of this as she could see that it was lifting her husband's spirits.

The two Geoff's were rather keen Stoke City supporters and went to see the team play whenever they were at home. On a particular Friday prior to a home game they were making arrangements to meet at the top of Crewe station. Eddie surprised them by Saying "Heh you two buggars go off to the match but what about me, you never ask me to go with you" Both Geoff's looked at one another rather surprisingly. It was Geoff Harding who said. "Sorry Eddie I never thought you would want to go to a match but of course you would be welcome. I'll call for you then we can get the bus to the station and meet Geoff. Is that OK for you?"

It certainly was and they all went to the ground and took up a spot behind one of the goals. When the game started Geoff Harding who had a very good clear voice gave Eddie a brilliant running commentary on every kick and managed to make a fairly dull game sound a great deal better than it was. In fact after the match one of the nearby spectators said to him "Sounded a much better game than the one I was watching, well done pal, you should be doing that on the radio" A complement indeed.

Geoff (Pritch) soon got into the routine of his new job. In fact the only drawback was the distance he had to go to work. If he went by bus it meant he had to catch two buses. This he did on a few occasions but mostly he cycled the six miles which was OK when it was dry but it seemed an awful long way when it was raining. They were a friendly pleasant crowd of people that he worked with, the hours suited him, but he was not overjoyed at having to work Saturday mornings from 9 'til 12.

Each morning on his way to the office he would stop to get what was then his favourite newspaper, the Mirror. Whether he bought it because it had the strip cartoon of Jane or the fact that it was a tabloid paper he was never sure, but he did enjoy it when he was having a break. It was during one of these breaks that Bert the deputy clerk to the council walked in. "Ah Geoff I didn't know you were interested in horse racing". This took Geoff by surprise but the paper was open at the sports page on which the day's race cards were and Bert assumed that was what he was studying, but far from it as he was not at all interested in the horses. But he did say "Oh yes I like to see if I can pick out the winners".

"Have you anything good for today" enquired Bert.

"Oh yes" came the reply

"Well what is it then. I've got one sorted out but I want one to go with it in a double"

Geoff hadn't a clue but ran his finger down the race card at Haydock and said "Here it is in the 3.30"

"Are you backing it yourself" asked Bert

"No I really can't afford it" came the reply

Geoff thought nothing more about it until the next day when Bert came to see him. "Hey, thanks for that yesterday, a nice winner and it was at 8-1 what have you got for today?

Geoff hadn't got anything. In fact he was staggered to think he'd picked a winner out of the blue. So not wanting to appear unhelpful he went through the routine of the previous day before making his selection. The horse duly obliged at somewhat less odds, but, he thought a winner is still a winner.   Although his success carried on he began to find a few losers as well but not sufficient to make him feel that he had 'something of a talent' for picking winners. As betting shops had now come into being he decided he ought to give it a go himself. He was none too sure what to do, but he went into Nantwich during his lunch break and found a betting shop. He went in somewhat apprehensively but saw the lady who was taking slips and the cash, so he went to her and placed his bet. No it did not win but he was undeterred, maybe next time. The caretakers of the civic offices were a man and wife team who had things organised very well between themselves. Jack would fill all the coal buckets and light the fires when it was necessary. His wife, Amy did the vast majority of the cleaning around the offices.

They had a pleasant but small cottage that adjoined the big house.

It turned out that Jack followed the horses and had a bet most days. Geoff told him that he was now taking Bert's bet into town at lunchtime and that if he ever wanted a bet that he would be happy to take his along. It saved Jack a trip so he was happy to do this. Word spread around and before too long anyone who fancied having a flutter would see Geoff . Most of the bets were very modest in size but what struck him was that each day he seemed to be taking more money in than he ever got back on the total stakes.

So he decided to stand the bets himself "why line the bookies pocket" he wondered when I can make a little bit on the side to supplement my wages.

In order to do the thing properly he purchased a simple note book and kept accurate records of how much each of his clients had put on, the odds and the returns if indeed there were any. He got a old OXO tin from home and kept any money he had made in that together with his records and secured them in a drawer of his desk. The Grand National and the Derby were the big races when everyone wanted a gamble and Geoff was only too ready to help them.

His takings were growing rather nicely with £8.10 shillings and 3pence in the tin On one particular day Jack came into the office "Geoff I'm going to have a rather stupid bet today. Rather unusually for me I'm having a win double and both are at good odds, can you take it in for me please?"

"Of course I can" he replied "how much do you want on"?

"Half a crown double on Slippery Sam and Dandoleen both are at Sandown"

"That's a lot of money Jack are you sure about this?

"Yes, if it goes down I won't have another bet this week, but if it comes up, I've told the Mrs it will be a week in Blackpool".

Fat chance of that thought Geoff and in due course entered the details in his book. On his way home he purchased the evening newspaper and looked in the stop press for the winners. Slippery Sam had obliged by winning at 8 to 1. His fingers ran down the other racing results - Dandoleen first at 20 to 1. Cold shivers went up and down his spine, his head had taken on a swimmy feeling It's a lot of money he thought and calculated in his head that he would have to find £23.12.6 The six mile journey home seemed more like sixty and tonight he and his pal Ian Banks had organised a Coronation celebration in the School Hall at Crewe Green. He had nothing like enough in his OXO tin. Should he tell Jack that he'd forgotten to put it on? No of course not. What will dad's reaction be if I told him he wondered. He didn't know the answer to that but he had a pretty shrewd idea that Dad would let him have the money on certain provisos, whatever they were Geoff knew he would have to earn it by doing some chores in the garden and dad would want more than his money's worth.

Tea was ready when he got in. He really couldn't face any more than just a few nibbles, a cup of tea and a cake. Oh dear what a mess I've made of things He even considered going to see a bookie who lived in a council house in Nantwich and explain what had happened and to offer his services if this person, Ellis, would pay off his debt. But that too he rejected for the present at any rate.

It was a lovely evening in the school hall and everyone paid tribute to Geoff and Ian on their efforts. It was home time and the best thing he could do was to be honest and open and tell dad and take the consequences.

"How did things go then" enquired dad

"Not bad at all, nearly everyone from the village was there and they all seemed to have enjoyed themselves"

"Oh" said Nellie "it was first class : the two lads did a brilliant job and everyone was full of praise for them"

As nice as it was to hear these compliments Geoff was more concerned about his losses. "I'll just have a quick look at the paper before I go to bed" he said.

There was no getting away from it. At 8-1 and 20-1 he was in serious trouble. He turned to the back page to read up some of the sporting items. He glanced down at the 'stop press' on the back page. He didn't quite understand what he'd read: He looked at dad and asked the question "What does this mean"? There was an objection to the winner in the 3 o'clock race which was sustained.

"Well" replied dad "if the objection is sustained then the horse that finished second would be declared the winner. Now don't tell you've started backing horses".

"No fear I think betting is a mugs game" said Geoff "but a chap at work backed a horse called Dandoleen and it won but in the stop press it said the objection was sustained. That was bad luck for him, he stood to win quite a bit" Geoff slept easier that night.

The number of houses being built by the council was increasing at a very steady pace which meant that the councils rent collector Geoff Harding had more houses to contend with. So Geoff P was asked to help him out in this task.

As most employees in the area paid their staffs wages out on either Thursday or

Friday afternoons it made sense that rent collecting would be done on Saturday, Monday and Tuesday each week.

Geoff P rather enjoyed this duty as it got him out of the office for a few hours each week and he loved meeting so many new people most of whom paid their rent promptly. However the town clerk was concerned with the mounting arrears and wanted to have all collections completed by Monday lunchtime. He called a meeting of staff and asked for volunteers to work Friday evenings and Saturday mornings in an attempt to eliminate this problem. There were several volunteers from different departments and each was allocated properties for which they would be responsible. David Tudor, the town clerk was aware that not only were the rent arrears a problem but also that the rents actually collected did not always balance with the amount banked. Something was amiss and that something had to be rectified. In order to do this Mr Tudor gave Geoff Pritchard the task of being in the office when everyone had finished their collection, and checking the sheets which recorded the payments made and the cash handed in and banked. Once satisfied that the two balanced Geoff made a note and deposited the takings into the strong room in the cellar of the office.

On very rare occasions there were small discrepancies which the person responsible would make up the shortfall but by and large it worked out well and the arrears situation improved greatly. However there was one little incident that Geoff couldn't believe. One of the collectors had a particular tenant who was badly in arrears. It was late Saturday morning when Frank called at this house. The tenant opened the door and said "You'll be glad to know that I can pay the full arrears off but the money is in the bedroom I'll go and get it"

Just then the clock struck 12 and Frank called out "Too late now, I finish at 12 o'clock" and with that returned to the office. So instead of the arrears going down they went up. Ah well it takes all sorts.

Most weeks would see that the council would have two or three new houses completed and ready for occupation by the next family in line to be granted the tenancy. So it came as a great surprise when Ted the building foreman announce done Friday that there would be twelve new houses ready to let the following day. Geoff had a standard letter to send out to the potential tenants asking them to call for the keys between 11am and 1pm on Saturday. This was something of a red letter day having 12 houses ready. Mr Tudor would be delighted to think of the extra revenue. Geoff addressed the letters, tucked them into the envelopes put on the stamps and got them ready to drop in the post-box on his way home. As he went upstairs to bed he had a horrible thought. All those letters were still in the office waiting to be posted. There would be trouble over this if he failed to get the new tenants into their homes as a week's rent would be lost.

He was up early on Saturday and was at the office by 7.30. He knew the caretaker would be around so he got access, grabbed the letters put them all into the best journey order and promptly went to the dozen homes delivering them all by hand. By 9.15 he was finished and back in the office much to his relief and feeling rather gratified by his efforts. He made himself a cup of tea, lit a cigarette and relaxed in front of the freshly lit fire.

At 9.30 the door opened and Ted walked in looking somewhat sheepish. "Good morning Geoff , I suppose it's too much to hope that you didn't send those letters out last night?"

"Of course they went out Ted we need the revenue on them many houses. There's no problem is there?

"Well actually there is. The electricians were not able to complete the installation so there's a week's delay – sorry about that"

"No trouble at all Ted - when they come in for the keys all I have to do is apologise and ask them to come in the same time next week."

Thankfully the people concerned were very understanding but disappointed. Most people who were in need of a council house would call into the office for an application form: some completing it there and then, others would take them home to do. A very attractive fair haired young woman came in to say that she wanted a council house but admitted that she was useless when it came to filling in forms. So Geoff volunteered to assist.

All the usual questions were asked including the date of marriage : " Saturday 15th March 1952" she replied. "Have you any family" asked Geoff

"Yes a little girl"

"What was her date of birth"

"Saturday 15th March 1952" came the reply

"No" said Geoff "what was the date of your daughter's birth" insisted Geoff

"Saturday 15th March 1952" was the response

Geoff was insistent "No you were married on 15th March 1952"

"Well yes that's right we were married in the morning and she was born in the evening. Just in time you might say"

Geoff felt quite embarrassed but went on to complete the form.

Geoff was ambitious and he hoped to make progress in his work, but he was not academic and never had the discipline to study to gain any recognised qualification. He was good at his work but frustrated when he realised that the only way up the ladder in local government was to qualify in your chosen sphere . He had to think of his future. Things were OK as a single man but one day he would find the love of his life and wanted to have the best that he was capable of. He did think that if he were to move to a different authority that he may climb that ladder. So he and his pal Geoff Harding started to apply for jobs advertised in local government journals. They were both successful and Geoff Pritchard was accepted to work for the Borough of Malden and Coombe in Surrey, and Geoff Harding took an appointment in Newhaven.

Neither of them really settled into their new jobs and it was not many months before they were on the move. Geoff Pritchard applied for a vacancy in the Housing Department of the City of Birmingham as a District Housing Officer which sounded rather splendid. He was called for interview "what were your duties there, what hobbies have you got, did you do national service" all these fairly basic sort of things. However he was given a list of pounds, shillings and pence and asked to add the figures up and put the total at the bottom. It was a lengthy list but by the time the interviewer had got back to his desk Geoff had put his pen down.

"You are supposed to add them up" said Mr D

"Well yes that's what I've done" said Geoff

"You can't possibly have done it in that time" said Mr D

"But I have said" Geoff   "And what's the total then? " he was asked

"fifteen pounds, three shillings and nine pence" was the response

"Blimey" said Mr D "Not only quick but accurate as well"

A few days later he received a letter saying that his application was successful and his starting salary shot up to £575 a year. Wow he thought that's 15quid a week. All he had to do now was find a place to live. He was not familiar with the city so he decided that for a week he may as well stay at the YMCA which was in a fairly central position, and all importantly it was close to the office of the Housing Department. In fact he walked the distance in barely five minutes, so that was a great start.

As he arrived on a Sunday the place was fairly quiet but he was rather shocked to find that there was a cinema open for business. Open on a Sunday surely not! Has he come to a city of heathens? He didn't really think so but nobody back at Crewe Green would believe this. A cinema open on the Sabbath! His mother would be disgusted.

Geoff looked to see what film was showing. It was ' The Cruel Sea' a picture he badly wanted to see. He was about seventy miles away from Crewe, nobody would see him if he were to venture in and if they did they wouldn't know who he was. Dare he risk it? Just suppose somebody he knew were to see him going in or coming out he would never hear the end of it. But he had no place to go other than a room in a hostel. So rather against the grain he went up the steps of the cinema, somewhat sheepishly paid his two bob entrance fee and went in and just hoped that he would be spared the wrath of the Almighty.

He was not long in finding decent lodgings in a private house owned by Mrs Jones on Gravelly Hill in Erdington. It was a rather dark stuffy Victorian house filled with bric-a-brac from that area and displayed in a similarly aged display unit.

Geoff paid her £3 a week for full board plus a bit extra if she did his laundry, plus sixpence each time he had a bath.

She did have another lodger by the name of Ken who was quite a lot older than Geoff. He was a security guard at a large manufacturing concern and worked around the clock shifts. Ken related a story about one of his colleagues who had been off work due to illness for some considerable time. He had paid a visit to this persons home to cheer him up and took a basket of fruit round. On arriving at the house the colleagues wife invited him in.

The patients wife suggested that Ken went up to see her husband. This he did and they had a pleasant chat. Ken told him that all his work colleagues sent their best wishes and they hoped he would soon be returning.

As he went downstairs he was asked if he would like a cup of tea before returning home. He gladly accepted and sat down whilst he drank it.

It was then that one of the three young children of the house said to Ken "If me dad dies we're going to have a telly with his insurance money"

Ken was rather shocked to hear this but this was in 1954 when there were not too many homes with a TV.

The bus which Geoff used mostly stopped outside a newsagents shop which displayed several advertising cards in the window. He had a brief glance at them and spotted one that was offering 'Comfortable Digs. Apply within'. Geoff did just that. The newsagent said "You seem just the sort of chap Mrs Wilcox is looking for, so pop around and see her she lives in Minstead Road which was almost opposite to the shop. Geoff went round. It was a pleasant detached house, clean, TV and a delightful Dachshund dog by the name of Sammy. He saw the room that was on offer and gladly accepted the terms which were similar to what he was already paying. What a good move it turned out to be.

CHAPTER 4
DOROTHY MEETS GEOFF

It was early on in his time at his new job that Geoff was instructed to go to the office of Mr Evans the chief clerk. Here he was required to complete a form which asked a host of questions from what religion you were to who is your next of kin.

If there was one thing in life that Geoff detested doing was filling in forms, but it had to be done and whilst he was doing this onerous task Mr Evans picked up the phone on his desk and said "Send Miss Thomson in please" Seconds later in walked Miss Thomson, Geoff glanced up, admired the vision he saw coming through the door and said to himself 'my dear Miss Thomson I came here to make a better career move, but you are the icing on the cake I'm going to get to know you better.

He left the office at 5.30pm to catch the 64 bus which would take him to within a couple of hundred yards to his new 'digs'. As he walked down Colmore Row to get to the bus terminus he spotted Miss Thomson a few yards in front, so he increased his pace slightly until he caught up with her.

"Oh hello Miss Thomson you were in Mr Evans' office when I was filling in that beastly form! I'm just going down to Steelhouse Lane to get the 64 bus to Gravelly Hill"

"Oh hello: I too am going to Steelhouse Lane to get the 64 bus to Hunton Hill" "That's amazing" Geoff said "you'll be getting off the stop after mine, by the way my name is Geoff"

"And I'm Dorothy. Where were you working at before coming to Birmingham"

"I was in New Malden in Surrey, but my home town is Crewe"

So the small talk continued until Geoff alighted.

"I do hope we meet up around the office" said Geoff as he went "perhaps I could get you a coffee in the morning break tomorrow around 10.30".

"We'll see" was the reply.

They saw one another around the office or in the canteen most days. Geoff though was not office bound as his main task was to collect the rents. The system of collecting was quite different than it had been at the previous local authorities he had worked for: so in order to get the correct procedures he was given a week's training with an experienced housing officer by the name of Bert who was responsible for an estate in the Kingstanding area.

Geoff was allocated two pre-war estates as the rents on these were fairly low so the rents were collected fortnightly. The first week he had an estate to collect from in Wylde Green which fortunately was just a short bus ride away. On the next week he had the Brookvale Park Road estate, which was convenient but a little further from his 'digs'. It was a pretty 'cushy' sort of job and by and large without too much pressure, particularly if your cash balanced at the end of the day. There were some tenants who seemed to be permanently in arrears but not too badly. However Geoff did stress to them that, although they owed this money and that he did not push them to clear it, it was in their own interest to make sure that the arrears were cleared by the quarter end when the powers that be wanted to know every household that owed rent money. It worked well. In fact Geoff would make a special journey to their homes in the evenings in order for them 'to keep out of trouble'

However there was one household where he seemed to make very little impression at all. Although they had moved in from what was known as the central areas which consisted mainly of back-to-back houses into a rather pleasant house they were from the start always in arrears. It was quarter end and these tenants owed more money than the combined arrears of all the other properties on the estate. In Geoff's mind there was only one course of action – an evening visit when he assumed the husband would be at home He didn't really like doing this but he could think of no other action that may bring the desired result.

He reached the house and tentatively knocked on the door which was opened by Mrs H.

"Mrs H it's the quarter end your arre . . ." he got no further.

Mrs H stepped outside pulling the door towards her "Oh not now please we've just been told that our eldest son has been killed in a motorcycle accident. I promise you that I'll clear every last penny when you next call, but we are so upset right now." "Oh dear, I am sorry, so in the circumstances I won't speak to Mr H, but once again I'm so sorry to hear your sad news. Good night".

Geoff felt genuinely sorry for her and her family. The next time he was due to call. He said to one of the close by neighbours "How tragic it was to hear of Mrs H's son"

"Why what's happened?" she asked.

"Her eldest son was killed a few days ago on his motorbike".

"Rubbish" she said "He's as healthy as you and I, or at least he was an hour ago"

When Mrs H answered his knock at the door he said "Mrs H you told me."

She cut him short. I'm so sorry about that she said, but let me show you something. She lifted her skirt to show him the state of her legs which were black and blue with bruising, she opened her mouth wide and pointed inside where there were big gaps instead of teeth.

"That's what my husband does to me , and if he knew that I owed all this rent the bastard would really kill me".

This, thought Geoff, was not in the training. "Look" he said "Your husband is the tenant, it's his name that's on the rent book. He's the one I should be speaking to but does he give you the money to pay the rent"

It ended up with her swearing on her son's life that she would clear up the arrears. It took a few months to do so but eventually she did.

Rents were collected Monday, Tuesday and Wednesday. After the daily round was completed the money had to be balanced and paid in to the cashiers. Most of the collectors finished their rounds by about 2 o'clock. They would then make their way to the office where each of several large tables were adequate to occupy about ten collectors who would empty their satchels and count up the days takings and with crossed fingers hoped they would balance.

Geoff was intrigued by one of the long serving collectors by the name of Reg who never seemed to have a pile of coins in his satchel like everybody else did. "Hey, Reg how is it you don't have a mass of loose change and always seem to balance up in a matter of a couple of minutes" Geoff asked "Simple. I train them in how to pay. As an example most of my rents are £5.5.0

"So I tell the first three to each give me five one pound notes and two half crowns. Then from the fourth house they have to give me six one pound notes and I give them half a dozen half crowns, so at the end of the round all I have is pound notes and possibly six half crowns"

"And they all go along with that" questioned Geoff

"Never fails" came the response.

It was when he was going into the office one day that Geoff saw the placards of the Birmingham Mail announcing that "Council Rent Collector on murder charge" Whoever could that be he wondered . He couldn't get the money out of his pocket quick enough to get the paper from the street seller.

It turned out to be one of the collectors who he and Dorothy had sat by just a few weeks earlier. Such a nice couple they had said at the time - whatever had happened he wondered. The story ran that his wife rather enjoyed dancing and went to her favoured venue every week, whereas her husband just liked social dancing but did not go with her on her weekly outings. One night she returned much later than usual and he was in bed when she returned.

"Where the devil have you been until now" he stormed at her

"You know very well where I've been"

It was obvious she'd had some drink as she was somewhat unsteady.

"You been with a man"? he asked

"Yes I have, and he's not the first. In fact our Franks not your son ..

He took her by the throat and strangled her.

Dorothy was shocked when Geoff told her the story. "They seemed such a lovely devoted couple" she said.

He got a lengthy imprisonment sentence. Hell thought Geoff it just goes to show.

Geoff was amazed that how in the second biggest city in the country he had got a job in the same office as this one girl in a city of millions and that he had selected to live in a house which was less than a quarter of a mile to her home. It was uncanny.

One thing that they did not have in common was her love of dancing which Geoff thought must be most boring way to spend an evening. BUT, BUT she was such a lovely girl that he realised that he must make some effort to do something to overcome his two left feet. So when they dated she wanted to go to the dance at the Palace in Erdington on the 64 bus. As patient as she was with him he made little or no progress with dancing skills. But they still went because they wanted to be with each other. Thankfully there were plenty of cinemas both in the suburbs as well as the city centre and several theatres where they could enjoy an evening out.

Dorothy had been very friendly with Janet since childhood and they had a good relationship. Janet helped to run a club that was held in a room off Slade Road and went by the name of 'The Young Britons' which was a junior form of the Young Conservatives. Geoff went with Dorothy where they met Janet at the meetings together with a gentleman by the name of Alan.

There were plenty of varied activities appropriate to all of them in the age group which ranged from between twelve and sixteen. Everyone seemed to thoroughly enjoy themselves and join in the various activities.

Some weekends Geoff went back home and normally met up with mates to go to the football match in the afternoon and probably a dance or the cinema in the evening.

Before long Geoff was invited round to Dorothy's for tea on a Sunday afternoon when he was to meet her family for the first time. Geoff was quite shocked when Dorothy addressed her dad as Bertie which was his Christian name. Apparently this had always been the way she and her brother Stuart addressed him.

Bertie greeted Geoff with the question "and which one are you the one in the R A F, the one from the club or the one from the office?" He was rather taken aback at this but managed to say "well I suppose I must be the one from the office"

The one thing Geoff never liked buying were shoes but as his old ones were looking the worse for wear he had treated himself to a new pair for this first visit. The Thomson family had a dog called Bruce which they had taken on from a rescue home and seemed to be especially attracted to Geoff's new shoes. He lay at his feet as Geoff patted the dogs head, but Bruce was not interested in being fussed: not when he could see his reflection in these lovely new shoe caps which he was intent on licking. Geoff tried flipping the dogs nose with his shoe which seemed to make the dog worse. Geoff didn't want to upset things on his first visit and he certainly didn't want this to be his only visit so he just accepted the dog and let him get on with it.

When the time came for him to leave he discovered that Bruce had gnawed away the sole so that when Geoff got up the sole of his shoe was hanging off.

It was a long time afterwards that Geoff even told Dorothy about it. Geoff told Mrs Wilcox about Dorothy and she very kindly suggested to him that if Dorothy would like to go around to her house on a Friday evening, they could watch TV together in the lounge and have a bit of supper. That was such a lovely offer that they gladly accepted. Mrs Wilcox seemed overjoyed at having their company and Geoff walked Dorothy back to her home accompanied by Mrs Wilcox's dog Sammy who always seemed ready for walkies.

Mrs Wilcox had been married for some years before her husband died but she told Geoff that when she went to the altar she knew nothing of the facts of life. Her mother had told her that she would find things out for herself once she got married. They went to Blackpool on honeymoon and she was somewhat surprised what happened to her on the first night.

Monday morning she paid a visit to a local doctor. "I don't think I've seen you before my dear how can I help you" asked the doctor

"Oh doctor I hope you can help me but I have reason to believe that I'm pregnant"
"I take it you are married?"

"Of course I am otherwise I couldn't be having a baby, but I've had awful face ache since our first night and when I asked my mother before I was married how would I know if I was pregnant she told me that I would suffer face ache when I was".

"If you've got face ache my dear you really need a dentist, but while you are here let me take a quick look in your mouth" He thought she may need a filling!!

Mrs Wilcox had two sons: the first son was given the very best education that they could afford even when it meant going short themselves. He had what she described as 'a top job in the British Embassy in the United States".

When the second son Trevor was born they simply could not afford to be so lavish on him and could not afford any special education. However he was promised that when they died Trevor would get the full inheritance. This would not help him until his mother passed away but he had no scruples about coming around quite frequently to 'borrow' a few quid. She was rather soft with him but told Geoff after one of Trevor's visits that she was getting fed up with his constant scrounging and he should be standing on his own feet. Trevor was no fool and on his next visit he changed his strategy. He really did not like dogs of any sort and Sammy in particular. However he knew his mother loved Sammy to bits and nothing was too good for him. He went into the living room "Hello mam are you OK? and how's my little friend Sammy". With that he picked Sammy up above his head saying "Sammy you are such a lovely little chap and such a great companion for mum" But Sammy was not to be taken in and promptly bit Trevor's nose which bled profusely. Trevor threw him to the floor saying "You are a horrible spoiled little brat" In consequence he went home with no loan.

In the early 1950's the idea of having a car was just a dream for most people. So the bus service offered an affordable and easy means of getting anywhere in Birmingham. Be that going to Erdington to see a film or to the weekly dance the 64 bus was their means of transport. Dorothy's dad, Bertie was a Scot who had strict rules about his daughters upbringing, one of which she must be in by 10.30pm. This meant than on occasions they went to see a film at the Odeon in the city centre. It didn't matter if the main film hadn't finished before it was time to get the 64 bus they had to leave before the end to ensure Dorothy beat the deadline.

It came as a bit of a shock to him when Mrs Wilcox announced one evening that she was very seriously thinking of trying to find a place in Newquay. She said that she had a love for Cornwall and it would be rather nice to spend the remaining years of her life in such a lovely place.

"That means I'll have to find somewhere else to live" exclaimed Geoff "and I so love being here"

"I've thought about that" she said "I'm in no rush to go and live there, but I can buy a place so that when you get married or move on I will be able to sell up and go soon after"

This seemed remarkably good of her. Days later she told Geoff that she'd got details of a place in Newquay and she would be going down to view the following weekend.

Geoff went to Crewe Green while she was in Newquay. He hoped she would find somewhere nice, she really deserved it.

On Monday evening he asked her how she had got on "Oh Geoff it was a complete disaster. When I got to Newquay I asked for directions to the address. Only to be told "Sorry, love I've never heard of it" Eventually she went into the council office to enquire. "Let's see what we can do to help" said the receptionist. "Oh dear madam you are certainly in Newquay but the house you are looking for is in Cornwall not Wales. I'm so sorry"

Things were going well with Dorothy and Geoff: they met for coffee in the canteen when he was in the office. Most Fridays they went for lunch at Lyons Corner House. At weekends they would go to the Palais for the dancing, at which Geoff never got any better, or they would go to a theatre or the cinema. So it was special for both of them when Geoff took Dorothy to meet his parents and stay for the weekend.

Nellie and Bill took to her straight away, but being born and bred in Birmingham Dorothy was not too sure about being stuck in the countryside. However she met a lot of Geoff's mates and several of the girls from the area including Eileen a former girlfriend of Geoff who was now going out with his pal Jeff Farmer. They all got on well together. On the Sunday afternoon around 4 o'clock Nellie asked if they would be attending the Harvest Festival Service in the church that evening. They hadn't really thought about it, but yes that would be rather nice they said and asked what time does the service start. When Nellie said it was 6.30 Geoff said well we're OK to go across about quarter past 6.

"You won't get a seat if you leave it that late: you need to be there for 5.30 the latest as the church will be packed" Geoff thought his mother was exaggerating, but they followed her advice. Of the 120 seats in church there were only about 10 seats left. As time went on chairs had to be brought in from the nearby schoolroom.

Geoff enjoyed trips out with Dorothy and her mum and dad to places of interest in the area. The place he liked the best was the delightful Sutton Park where in the autumn they gathered chestnuts for roasting by the fire. By now Geoff knew this was the girl he wanted to spend the rest of his life with, so 'popped the question' on a visit to Sutton Park. He was kept waiting for the answer for a few days but appropriately Dorothy chose the top deck of the 64 bus to say "Yes I do want to marry you"

In due course they made arrangements to get married on the 27th April 1957 at the Parish church in Erdington.

Mrs Wilcox was delighted when Geoff told her the news and she very kindly suggested that his family could go to her home prior to the service, but there was one proviso: Geoff was to paint all the woodwork in the hall and stairway prior to the wedding. This he readily agreed to, so he set about the task as Mrs Wilcox had been so very good to himself and Dorothy. The night before the wedding Mrs Wilcox discovered a small patch of woodwork on the stair that had been missed. He did it on the Saturday morning dressed in his wedding suit!

Nellie and Bill arrived mid morning and Nellie unbeknown to Mrs Wilcox ran her white gloved finger along the coat stand in the hall; glanced at it, turning to Bill saying "Just look at this .. needs dusting"

The wedding reception was held in the Acorn Hotel which was adjacent to the Church. Dorothy had not many relatives who lived close to as most of them were in New Zealand. It was decided that it would be a wedding for immediate family, aunts and uncles, but no cousins. So as far as numbers go it was not a big wedding. About 32 guests attended including best man and bridesmaids. The reception was very pleasant. However Bertie said to Geoff "Good God! I hope you are going to be worth it. Just look here 10shillings and 6pence (about 52p) a head. You'll have me ruined!"

Geoff had been faced with something of a dilemma over who he would have as his best man: it could have been Alan Beasley, Jeff or Stan Farmer. Over the past few years he had not been so involved with Jeff because of national service commitments so he chose to have Stan. Janet Parkes and Dorothy had been friends since their school days as well as into their teenage years so really she could not have had a better choice for being bridesmaid.

Geoff had not been looking forward to giving a speech, but in the office they had kindly presented him with a very welcome cash gift so that he could get whatever he wanted. So when he was presented with that he was required to say a few words of thanks. The colleague who actually made the presentation said a few words which included "Geoff it would have been much cheaper for you to have bought a motorbike. This gave Geoff a wonderful opening for his acceptance speech. "Well thank you all for this handsome gift which will give us the chance to buy something to remember you all by, but I do not fancy going to bed with a BSA500 !!

They had some wonderful gifts from family friends, neighbours and all were displayed at Dorothy's home until they moved into their newly found flat. For the honeymoon they went from Birmingham's Snow Hill Station to Bournemouth where they were to stop for the week in the Meyrick Cliffs Hotel which stood a few yards back from the lovely beach.

They had absolutely no complaints about the hotel which was owned and run by a gentleman who had an apartment there and was waited on hand and foot. He had purchased the place for cash shortly after the war ended by money he had earned by buying cars off people who could not get petrol during the war and had been glad to get rid of them at a fraction of the original cost. He had stored them on land he owned and sold them when hostilities were over at a somewhat inflated price. They had a marvellous week and were sorry to be leaving but the stay was rounded off by all the staff lining up to wish them well for the future. A lovely gesture.

They returned to the flat that they had agreed to rent in Powick Road, a small but pleasant cul-de-sac off Gravelly Hill and almost opposite to Minstead Road. Little did they know then that this area one day would become part of the motorway network adjacent to the notorious Spaghetti Junction. The house was owned by Mr Oliver who it turned out was an alcoholic which they had not realised at the time they moved in. He was quite a charming man when sober and he had a lady who was his housekeeper. She had her own house but came frequently to carry out the domestic chores and to keep an eye on Mr Oliver when he had a bout of drinking.   As he recovered from his drinking sessions which could last a few days or even a few weeks she would accompany him on the Midland Red bus to his place of employment.

Frequently though as soon as she got the return bus he would leave work and get the next bus home and start drinking again. Not only was he a heavy drinker but he was a heavy smoker as well buying his Players cigarettes in tins of fifty. He would sit in his easy chair with a tumbler full of whisky in one hand and a cigarette in the other. Geoff was concerned that when he was in one of these sessions that he would be chain smoking and lighting one cigarette from another. As ashtrays filled up lighted cigarettes could roll off and possibly cause a fire.

Thankfully during these spells his housekeeper would take him to her home where she could keep better control of him. She told Geoff that in his absence they must feel free to go into the living room and watch the television whenever they wanted. This they did on a few occasions. The TV had a 10 inch screen with a magnifier over the top to enlarge the picture.

How anyone could let their life get into such a state was beyond the comprehension of the newly-weds who were so delighted with the flat with their bedroom at the back which overlooked a small garden beyond which ran a local railway line which ran from New Street station to Sutton Coldfield.

When sober Mr Oliver was a perfectly charming man who was full of remorse for his drinking habit. He explained to Geoff and Dorothy that as a younger man he had gone into the army and was posted to India. It was there that he was quite horrified and disgusted by several of his fellow officers who drank so much that he vowed that he would never touch any booze at all. Well intentioned as he was he found the heat of the day almost intolerable so decided to have just one drink. One went to two then on to a full bottle and before long he was as bad as the others and worse than most.

His absences from Powick Road became longer and longer so the couple enjoyed the privacy and the run of the house. It was there that they adopted 'Fred'. Fred was a lovely black and white cat who they found miaowing at the door and so gave him a saucer of milk and some little titbits. Where he came from or who owned him they didn't know so they adopted him and he contentedly 'lodged' with them.

Days after moving in Dorothy went to the butcher's shop which was at the bottom of the road on Gravelly Hill. The two assistants must have been suspicious that Dorothy was newly married for they confirmed this when she asked for a chop. One of them asked, "Certainly dear what sort would you like, beef OK"

"Oh yes that will be fine, thank you".

They roared with laughter at their little quip. "Newly married are you my dear, there's no such thing as a beef chop, you'd better take him lamb" Slightly embarrassed but somewhat wiser she went home to tell Geoff who counted himself lucky not to be tied to strict office hours so one day he decided to get a meal ready for when Dorothy got home from the office. He got a decent sized potato and cut in to chips that were hardly thicker than matchsticks. He fried an egg to go with them when he saw her nearing home. Dorothy came in and Geoff said "Surprise, surprise I've got your tea ready for you" and placed her plate in front of her at the table.

The chips failed to impress her: she didn't try them, she took one look at them "Chips these are nothing like chips they are more like those crispy things you get in a bag I don't want them"

Geoff was so disappointed: so they had words which led to Dorothy packing a bag and stormed off down the road.

Geoff suspected she'd gone back to mum, but decided not to go after her as she hopefully would see sense and come back. She was away about two hours Geoff was relieved to see her walking back, apparently she had only gone round the corner and to Gravelly Hill. "You never came to look for me" she said. She didn't realise how much he really wanted to dash out to find her, but did not admit as much to her.

Dorothy's dad seemed to have a rather good job he was Sales Manager for the Birmingham Chamber of Trade and Commerce. His duties were to sell membership subscriptions and advertising into the Chambers journals. He had quite a nice company car that was supplied and Geoff suspected an above average salary to go with it. His wife accompanied him most days acting in the unofficial capacity of route finder. She would have a list of the different prospects together with address details and phone numbers. She did not drive herself but sat next to Bertie with a map selecting the best and quickest route. Geoff wondered how do people get jobs with a car provided – and decided to look into it.

From his observations it seemed that many companies who employed sales staff provided them with a vehicle, but Geoff had no experience in sales and the majority of such adverts always seemed to ask for applicants with experience. But he thought how can you get experience in anything without being taken on for a trial.

Undaunted he decided he try to place himself in the position of the advertiser and came up with the thought that such a person may be looking for someone with initiative and enthusiasm rather than the normal Dear Sir, I was interested to see your advert etc etc. Instead he thought they may take more kindly to someone starting off by saying "Dear Sir, This I believe is a lucky day for both you and I. I find the challenge and opportunity to show potential customers the benefits that they could derive from using your product and so on.

He got acknowledgments of receiving his application and sometimes an interview. When he did go for an interview he seemed to fluff it all too easily. "You've seen our product but how will it be of benefit to anyone who uses our oppositions product XYZ, why should they change to ABC".

In all truth he had no idea but fumbled for a half decent reply. In due course he received a rejection letter. Never mind there are plenty more companies. He started to look at products more carefully and how best to compare the product range of each one. He was happy enough with his present role so there was no rush. After the wedding and the honeymoon the newlyweds had hardly any savings.

In fact looking back Geoff doubted if they had £100 between them. They knew that one day they would want to buy their own house so they must start to get some savings together. The first thing to do was to open a savings account and discipline themselves to put so much money away each pay day. It started to climb and when their statements showed a little added interest it gave them some encouragement. It was when he and Dorothy went to Crewe Green to stay with his family for a couple of nights that there was something of a turning point.

Nellie had to go out and asked Geoff to give the insurance agent who was due to call the premium book and money that she had left on the sideboard. When he came Geoff handed these to him. He wondered 'could this be the opening that he was looking for' "Excuse me asking but I've been wondering about getting into sales, I wonder what the chances of me getting a job with your company might be like".

The insurance agent who introduced himself as Bert said "I would have thought they would be pretty good. As a matter of fact I understand that one of my colleagues by the name of Sam, is thinking of doing something else and I believe he will be handing his notice in before long. So why not go to our office on Nantwich Road, in Crewe and ask to see the manager George Waite who can give more information" Geoff got his bike out straight away and visited the office As he got off his bike he spotted something shining in the gutter right outside the office. On picking it up it turned out to be a silver lucky charm in the shape of a horseshoe. He picked it up, put it in his pocket and has kept it ever since.

George Waite invited him into the comfortable office asked him to sit down to have a chat. Geoff said how much he would welcome getting into a sales job and it struck him that everybody needed insurance and that he himself was a policy holder as he thought what a good thing it was to have an endowment which would give his wife protection or a lump sum after a given period of time.

This went down well with Mr Waite who went on to say that Mr Newton was indeed leaving and that he'd had the agency for a few years but had not put in the effort and there was tremendous potential in the territory he was leaving which covered the central part of Crewe together with Coppenhall and Sydney.

Whoever took on the agency would have to buy the book at a price based on the amount of business that it currently generated. Geoff was terribly disappointed to hear that the books earnings at that time were £11.14shillings a week, and told Mr Waite that it seemed fruitless for him to consider this anymore as he was now earning over£16 a, so that was a third less than his current earnings.

"Yes I can understand that young man" said Mr Waite "and how long before you are earning £20 a week?"

"That is a few years away if the present rate of increases continues" "he replied "Quite so" came the reply "but suppose I told you that I could almost guarantee that if you come here you will be earning £20 a week within 12 months"

"Within twelve months! I find that difficult to believe, but how do I go on purchasing the book when I've practically no money and that which we do have is going towards a house"?

"You're right to be concerned BUT bear in mind that your earnings are open ended and it will be up to you to work at it. I can give you the assistance of an Inspector and the deputy manager who are both responsible to help agents to find new business. As for purchasing the book, you do not need to put any cash into it out of your savings as you can do this from your earnings and payments are spread over eight years"

It was a very thoughtful Geoff who made his way back home. So many things were going through his mind regarding what to do for the best. One thing was certain it would be quite a leap and he really must let Dorothy have her say.

"How did you go on" she asked as soon as he entered the house.

"Quite well really but it would mean a massive drop in earnings to start"

He told her everything that had been discussed with Mr Waite. She agreed the drop in pay would be a setback however she added "This sounds exactly what you've been hoping for and I'm sure that with my support and encouragement we will get by OK. Apart from which I can always find a new job in this area"

"Dunno about that, you would be the one to be uprooted from where you've always lived and Crewe does not pay the same wages as you'd get in Birmingham"

"We must be realistic about this though. I suppose one big thing we haven't taken into account is that the price of property in this area is considerably less than in Brum, furthermore we may have to ask Mam and Dad if we could stay here until we could afford our own place."

Dorothy suggested they sleep on it for twenty four hours before making a decision. It still niggled Geoff that he was happy in his work, his income was OK but he still had the burning ambition to climb the ladder of success but was hampered by having to get a qualification with the Institute of Housing. He did his job well and all that but he needed the letters behind his name to go on to the next step, and he also knew that he hadn't the academic mind or will power to tackle that.

After a brief discussion the following morning Geoff rang Mr Waite to say that he would like to pursue his application to become an insurance agent. Birmingham had been good to Geoff - he'd got some good pals including Geoff Bryant who shared the table with him when they were in the office. Everyone did their best to get Geoff to stay and not hand in his notice but he'd made his mind up he was making for pastures new.

CHAPTER 5 –
RETURN TO CREWE AND FAMILY

Nobody could now persuade him to stay on and so it was that they moved to Crewe Green, together with Fred. Being fiercely house proud Nellie would take a duster from the pocket of the apron she constantly wore around the house and flicked it over the furniture each time she went to answer the door. Dorothy asked her if there was anything she could do for her in the house. Nellie would find her a task to do, but immediately Dorothy had completed it Nellie would look at it and do it again .. properly! This upset Dorothy inwardly but she accepted that this was the way her mother in law was.

Dorothy found a job for herself as a clerk in a local laundry but the money was poor and the conditions not really to her liking so she made application for a vacancy in the Ministry of Social Security in Crewe. The eight pounds a week she earned was considerably higher than the laundry and more like the wages she'd earned in Birmingham and after twelve months satisfactory service this rose to ten pounds a week. A really good wage for a woman in those days.

Geoff made a start in his new role. His work week now started on a Friday morning which turned out to be the busiest of his working days. Sam Newton accompanied Geoff on the first week end giving him a satchel, the collection book the rate book and introducing him to all the clients.   This was repeated on Saturday when they finished around 1pm and again on Monday when the collections were completed at about 3pm. The books then had to be balanced with the money that was paid into the office cashier on Tuesday between 9am and 12noon. On paying in for the first time George Waite called Geoff into the office for 'training' "This" he said "is the rate book which tells you everything you need to know. You call at a house, introduce yourself and tell them that Table 29 is extremely popular. You ask their age. Let's say that they will be forty at the next birthday. Then say that by saving half a crown a week you will receive £20 in 5 years time and £22 five years later, but in the meantime you will be insured for £60 plus bonuses.

There you are nothing to it ! Study the rate book and you'll soon get the hang of things " That was it ! Geoff's training took all of ten minutes, now all he had to do was to put it into practice! He arrived home - took his rate book indoors and studied it for a while before deciding that it was no use sitting there just looking at the blessed thing. Better do as the man said and put it to the test. What poor souls can he practice on he wondered. He did not want to go into the town centre and make a fool of himself on the patch that would yield the best results., So he made his way to SYDNEY a small pleasant village on the edge of town. He propped his cycle against the front hedge and duly knocked on the front door. He heard a vehicle pull up on the road behind him but paid no attention to it. A lady opened the door to him, "Good morning I'm from the Co-op". He started but she had turned to go back into the kitchen calling to him "I want two pints of milk, half a pound of butter, some carrots and." Geoff wondered what the devil she was going on about until he realised that the vehicle that he'd heard was the Co-op travelling shop. They both had a laugh over it, but Geoff wasn't here for a laugh he was here to do business. He had his rate book open, a proposal form and pen at the ready. She gave him a fair hearing but explained that she had plenty of cover for when 'the old man clogs it' But she did say that there was a newly married couple living at the farm just down the road and they may be interested.

Geoff thanked her and called at the farm. They were interested. He completed the proposal form and collected the first months premium. Jobs a good'un he thought. His confidence received a boost.

It was on a Tuesday in May when Geoff went to see George Waite. "Mr. Waite" he said "do you recall that when I first came to see you that you said I could be earning £20 a week in twelve months time? "Well I've come to tell you that you were wrong I've been here just under 6 months and for the last two weeks I've earned a little over £20. So thanks for the faith you had in me, I now want to be nearer £30 when the twelve months are up!

"Well done old chap you are doing well: incidentally I have some more news for you that may be of interest. Mrs Waite and I have lived in the upstair flat for a few years and we've decided that as my retirement is looming we should buy a bungalow. We've now found one that we hope to move into in about six weeks. If you want the flat I'll recommend you to head office.

If he wanted it! He couldn't believe his ears. Dorothy and Geoff went to see what the flat was like and fell in love with it straightaway. It was completely self contained on the first floor of this detached building. The entrance into a small hallway was on the side of the property and led only to the stairs. At the top to the left was the dining room/sitting room which was a long narrow, but cosy room. At the far end was a door which led into a nice sized kitchen. Also off the landing was a good size bathroom with a avocado suite. There was a very wide hallway which had off it a pleasant, light lounge with a large casement window which went from floor to ceiling and was about eight feet high and occupied the whole of one wall. Both rooms had a coal fireplace. Although it was a lovely room the lounge always seemed to be cold no matter how big a fire was made up. There were two rather large bedrooms at the front of the flat overlooking the main road and a row of shops on the other side of the road. Geoff used the room on the left as his office and the other was to be their bedroom. There was a third bedroom which was up a very short stairway which was small but adequate. A modest well kept garden at the rear was welcome together with a good brick built garage which also served to store the coal. When the Waites moved Geoff, Dorothy, Nellie and Bill all went down to do some decorating. With that out of the way it was time to get some furniture. They agreed to buy the two easy chairs off the Waites that were in the sitting room: so decided the first thing of importance was a bedroom suite and a television. There was a good well established warehouse in Crewe, the owner of which Bill socialised with and he kindly allowed the newlyweds to go and choose whatever they needed. In so doing they made some welcome substantial savings.

At the time that they moved in there were no supermarkets but there were some good quality grocery shops. They all offered similar products but mostly they had something that was unique to them. At Woodvines there was a delightful aroma of ground coffee not just in the shop but outside as well. Another was renowned for the bacon that he sold from a local farmer. Yet another had two huge blocks of butter on marble slabs one Danish and the other New Zealand. The proprietor would cut off a chunk of the preferred one, slap it on the scales and always managed to get the correct weight to within a fraction of what the customer wanted. Dorothy selected a shop called Wheelers who were directly opposite. Mr Wheeler always wore a ultra clean white apron and a straw hat. Dorothy would drop her order off into his shop prior to going to work and picking it up at around 5.30 when she had finished work. She would alight from the bus and her order would be ready. Mr Wheeler would then take the bags across the road and walk with them to the entrance to the flat. Sugar was weighed out from a sack into substantial blue bags that were neatly folded down and sealed. Tea bags? Whatever on earth are tea bags? Tea was normally packed into quarter pound packets and would be stacked neatly on to the shelves. Bacon? Certainly! what thickness would you like. Anything from 1 to 10, 1 was extremely thin and 10 was as thick as anyone would want, four or five were probably the most popular. Whatever: it really tasted like bacon should, none of the tasteless pre-packed rubbish. Nor did it shrivel up as it lost all the water that's injected in it as it was in later years. Large round blocks of cheese were on display with their rinds would be cut into wedges by a special cheese wire, weighed and popped into your bag. Many of the grocery shops would boil their own hams and display them alongside their bacon and suspend them from hooks in the ceiling. If you wanted your order delivered they would have a boy who could earn extra pocket money by making these deliveries on a cycle that had a large tray on the front exactly as David Jason did in OPEN ALL HOURS.

Geoff and Dorothy had been born into an era in which men went out to work to earn a living and their wives stopped at home to do all the household chores as well as the cooking. Going out for a meal was something special and something of a rarity. So the men folk would give the wife housekeeping money. Normally from this she would buy all the foodstuffs, the fuel and all cleaning needs. So as this was the 'norm' for most families Geoff and Dorothy agreed on her receiving £5 a week for food and milk and her clothing. Geoff thought this was rather indulgent of him, but she was a wonderful wife so he didn't begrudge it. "You'll never guess it" she said to Geoff one evening "Mr Wheeler apologised because my weekly shopping with him has gone up to £3. 15 shillings and 7 pence". Apparently she had said to him "Good gracious Mr Wheeler things are getting so expensive these days I do wonder where it will end !"

Things were looking up: they had a nice home and Geoff's earnings were creeping up steadily thanks to the assistance he had from the inspector and the deputy manager as well as his own efforts which meant going out canvassing during the day and frequently having to go in the evenings to speak to the husband and wife when they were both at home. Dad had decided to treat himself to a new car so he offered Geoff his old 1950 Ford Prefect. As he had recently passed his driving test Geoff jumped at the idea and so gladly purchased LKK 220. They could now visit Dorothy's parents without having to go by rail. The journey took them almost an hour and a half. This was in the pre-motorway days which would cut out some of the towns like Stafford and Cannock.

Dorothy was not too happy about the kitchen decoration and suggested that this was a job that they should prioritise and that she had seen some wallpaper that she liked in Riley's window. "How many rolls will it take to do it" she asked Geoff.

As he wasn't sure he measured the walls and they took them to Riley's to make the purchase. Geoff decided he would start to decorate the following Wednesday morning. He painted the woodwork, prepared the walls and was pleased to have it all completed by Thursday afternoon. Dorothy was pleased with the finished job, so all was well.

A couple of weeks later Geoff had a few evening appointments so decided that rather than wait for Dorothy to prepare a meal when she got home from work that he would cook himself egg and chips. Having prepared the potatoes he put the chip pan on the stove, and while they were cooking he went to the garage to fill the coal bucket. On returning he was shocked to see smoke in the living room, he dashed to the kitchen where through the black smoke he could see flames leaping around on the stove. Not knowing what to do he opened the window grabbed the chip pan and hurled it out. The smell was awful and his decorating was ruined. The black smoke slowly disappeared but the new wallpaper was thick with horrible black grease. He cleaned up as best he could, went to the phone box to call Dorothy to tell her what had happened so it would not be too much of a shock for her when she got home. As Dorothy said it was a stupid thing to do, but it could have been a lot worse.

Their friends Jeff and Eileen had now bought themselves a dog and as both of them loved dogs Dorothy and Geoff decided to get a cross Sheepdog puppy which they called Smudge. He was mainly black, brown and white. He had a lovely temperament but was quite spoilt by the two of them.

Geoff had always been something of a worrier: sometimes he worried over the most trivial of things but one evening Dorothy asked him what the matter was: was there something troubling him. "Well yes there is " he said "I've had nothing to worry about for so long that I suspect that there must be something pretty horrible waiting to happen for me to worry about I wonder what it is!

"Oh for goodness sake: whatever it is we'll get over it so don't be so silly" It was about this time when Dorothy announced that she was pregnant. Geoff was thrilled with the good news "Oh, I'm so happy" he said "well done. I wonder if it will be a boy or a girl"

"Well yes it will be one or the other. Does it matter?"

"Not at all, when is it due?"

"The doctor said it will be towards the end of September"

Geoff was now thinking and worrying – we will lose Dorothy's earnings, we've got a dog to feed, can we really afford to have another mouth to feed and clothe?

He was so happy with Dorothy's news that he didn't say anything to her, but he got pen and paper wrote down his income and then the outgoings: arriving quite quickly that the outgoings were higher than the income. The only result this could possibly have according to Charles Dickens character Mr Micawber was misery !

Geoff did look on the bright side – if it was a son or a daughter it really didn't matter one little bit.

But with a boy he could buy him a train set and have some fun and later a football. With a girl it could only be a doll which wasn't quite Geoff's cup of tea.

It was a Wednesday afternoon in August when they decided to take a stroll across the local golf links. They followed the course of the brook which ran gently on one side of the links and talked about possible names. If it was a girl Geoff rather favoured she being called Jennifer but this got a resounding NO from Dorothy simply because of the way it was used for some character of that name on the radio "Jennnnnnnnnnn. iff.er . So the name they both agreed on was Jacqueline. In the event of a boy it was easy: he would take the name of his Grandads – ROBERT and WILLIAM – so that was settled.

They went back home for tea feeling pleased with their decision.

There was an evening football match that Geoff had arranged to see with his mates Kick off was 7.30 which meant that he'd be home around 9.30.

He went up to the flat where he was greeted by the waggy tail of Smudge but where was Dorothy? Geoff called out but there was no reply . he found her with her head under the blankets and moaning like mad. "Whatever is the matter" he asked. "I feel absolutely dreadful, my stomach is aching and I feel so sick"

He offered to fetch the doctor but she wouldn't hear of it saying that it would pass if she could get a good night's sleep. Geoff got himself a drink and a bit of cheese and biscuits before going to bed. Smudge went to the bedroom with him and curled up under the bed where he normally slept. Dorothy was still groaning and still in pain but she still refused for Geoff to get the doctor. However it was approaching 4am when she said she thought she may be having the baby.

PANIC STATIONS!. Geoff hurriedly threw his clothes on over his pyjamas and told her he was going to ring the doctor – no arguments. The phone box was about a hundred yards down the road. He rang the number and dashed back home. Before he had reached the top of the stairs the doctor pulled up at the front. Geoff took the doctor to the bedroom where Smudge came from under the bed growling as he did not approve of having his beauty sleep disturbed.

On examining her the doctor said to Dorothy that she should be in the nursing home now as she was quite advanced. He turned to Geoff asking him to get him some hot water. Geoff filled the kettle, boiled the water emptied that into a bucket, refilled the kettle and put it on to boil, He went back to the bedroom with the partly filled bucket and told the doctor he would top it up as soon as the kettle boiled. The doctor looked at him "Good God man. I only wanted a cupful to sterilise the thermometer .. do you think she's going to have the baby here?"

Well in all truth yes he had thought that but kept quiet.

"Have you got a car" asked the doctor. Geoff confirmed that he did.

"In that case take her straight away but don't go fast or you may have to make the delivery yourself"

It took them about 15 minutes to make the trip to the CLIFFS Nursing Home which was a splendid Black and white building set in a pleasant rural area. He pulled up at the front door where there was a bell-pull which made a loud clanging sound when activated. Someone came quite quickly and took Dorothy off and advised Geoff to phone later to see what developments there were. The days of the father being invited to attend the birth were, thankfully, quite a long way in the future. Geoff looked at his watch it was 5.15am. Getting back home he returned to his warm bed and fell into a deep sleep. It was 9.30am when he came to – the sun was shining – the birds were singing and it was August 27th 1959. He went down to the phone box, rang the nursing home and was told that Dorothy had given birth to a baby daughter at 5.30am – 15 minutes after her arrival. Geoff immediately phoned Dorothy's parents who were delighted at the news and said they would go and see her at the weekend. He then let his folk know. He was not a bit surprised when his mother said "In that case get rid of that dog"

Dorothy was in the Nursing Home for the best part of two weeks. It was a pleasant run out and Geoff was absolutely thrilled to see this tiny bundle that apparently weighed in at 5lbs 2 ounces.

He met up with another of the new dads and after visiting they would often pop into the local for a couple of quick drinks which Geoff found pleasantly relaxing. In those days it was accepted by nearly every new mum that they should be 'churched' at the earliest opportunity after the birth. Nellie made it perfectly clear to Geoff that Dorothy would not be allowed into her house until such time that she had gone through this ritual. There were about six new sets of parents who agreed that they would all go together to the local church (Wybunbury) for churching at the same time. Basically it was an opportunity to say "Thank You God for the gift and safe delivery of a baby" Geoff felt it was rather a shame that in later years this practice did not seem to take place.

Geoff was rather concerned that Smudge who they had somewhat spoiled may not take too kindly to the new arrival. On reaching home Geoff took the baby up to the flat in the carrycot which he placed on the table. He then picked Smudge up to take a peep at the baby. His tail wagged with apparent glee at this new arrival and tried desperately hard to give Jacqueline a welcoming lick, but that was forbidden.

Nellies concerns about having a dog were unjustified as it turned out and, when she got to the stage where Jacqueline could crawl, she could pull his tail, clamber all over him and he enjoyed this new addition and the added attention for after all he was no longer 'the baby'. Never once did he even growl. Although it was a premature birth by about four weeks she had all the world to grow in. It was a hot summer and her black pram was constantly adorned with a white sunshade. She slept solid for twenty-three hours a day each and every day, and always, but always outside in the garden. This went on into the winter when there were occasions when the snow had to be taken off the pram. The girls who worked in the office below the flat would go into the garden at their tea break or lunchtime peer in and make the noises that women do at the sight of a baby "Oooh Aaaaah Coo-oo" and so on.

She was baptised at St Andrews Church in Crewe. What a good turnout there was for Jacqueline's first special occasion. Grandparents, uncles, aunts, great aunts, great uncles and a host of family friend. All bringing some delightful gifts for a little girl. Dorothy loved to take her out in the pram every day. She often met other young women taking their offspring out and naturally stopped to chat and compare notes of the goings on. One particular person she got to know well was Marion who had a little boy of similar age to Jacqueline by the name of Timmy. The two children got on quite well with one another and were now beginning to say a few words. Jacqueline took quite a while before she mastered saying Timmy but in the main she knew him as Pimmy which was good enough for them both. After her bath in the early evening she would have her nightie on and go to bed. A variety of soft toys all had to be in with her. Dorothy and Geoff enjoyed reading stories to her once she was settled down, her favourite by a long way was Red Riding Hood. She lay, thumb in mouth, taking in every word. When they reached the part where the wolf gobbles up granny she was absolutely petrified as Dorothy or Geoff made the appropriate actions and she dived under the sheets. So they came to the decision not to do the actions any longer as they didn't want to scare her but she insisted on their play acting. Although there were many other stories in the book they didn't interest her so much and she could not get enough of Red Riding Hood. One bedtime Geoff jokingly said to her that it was about time she read to them. She opened the book and read it perfectly well, and she was still twelve months away from starting school. Geoff thought this to be too good to be true so he pointed out different words on the page and she hadn't the faintest idea what any one of them were. She had learned the story word perfect and even knew when to turn the page.

Inevitably the day came when she had to start school and fortunately she was much better behaved than her father had been and went without trouble. Going to school she met more and more children and added to her string of friends. One little girl called Rosemary was a year older than Jacqueline and lived close by. When they played at her home they used the shed as a pretend school. Rosemary was the teacher and Jacqueline the pupil. After a while it became noticeable that Jacqueline was playing less and less with her. It came to light that Rosemary would ask Jacqueline a question which if she got it wrong 'teacher' Rosemary would give her a smack. Geoff showed her how to look after herself and this included how to punch. At first it was more of a tickle than a punch until suddenly she gave him a right good biff. "That's it" said Geoff "now go and find her and if she gives you a smack you hit her just as hard as you hit me"

She skipped away down the backs, met Rosemary gave her a real punch that sent her home in tears. Job sorted – no more trouble from her and they continued as mates. Things were going well with Geoff, he was making decent money but he found himself in something of a cleft stick situation. He still longed to be in a job that supplied a company car but the money many of the companies were paying was less than he was earning. However a lot of his work involved going out to evening appointments when the husband and wife were at home to make joint decisions. Every Friday he worked from 8.30am to 8.30pm and Saturdays were from 9am to 2pm. He applied for sales jobs that were advertised and was invited to interview, but he found another drawback. Himself! He found that he did not interview very well: he was ruthlessly honest with himself after the interview and analysed where he had gone wrong. Basically he knew too little about the company or the products to which he had applied. With this in mind he planned a formula for rectifying this. Dorothy announced the good news that she was pregnant and the doctor told her that it was due early April. He was right, a baby boy was delivered on 7th April 1963. What were they to call him? There was no debate – no problem. They both instantly agreed that he would be named after his two Grandads. So enter stage, Robert William , two strong names. This went down well with both Grandads and they are names that somehow really suited him. He was totally different to Jacqueline as he needed a minimum of sleep. He was born at Easter time and again it was about two weeks confinement for Dorothy. Geoff decided that he would use this time to decorate. What a lovely surprise it would be for her. They had decided that the best place for his cot would be in the room used as the office. Pink for girls and blue for boys so Geoff bought a tin of blue Walpamur and did that first. Now for the living room: He decided he wanted to do something different to the norm. He wanted something special. On one wall he had paper with a rock pattern to go on the chimney breast and the walls on either side of the chimney breast were to have a floral pattern. On the short walls at either end of the living room he had a paper with a pattern of leaves. On the long wall opposite to the fireplace was a hunting scene. This was bordered by a mock oak panelling paper. A total of five different papers. Dorothy, he thought, would be enthralled by this wonderful use of his imagination

He told the girls in the office how busy he had been while Dorothy was lazing around! "Can we come round to have a look at your handiwork" they asked Geoff readily agreed; so in their tea break they went to make an inspection. He had a feeling that his design might be a bit too advanced for them, but he was interested in their reaction. "Does Dorothy know what you've done " asked one "I told her I was decorating but obviously she doesn't know how I've done it. I want it to be a surprise for her home coming"

"It will be that alright" they said in harmony.

Friends, family and neighbours had been so generous with Easter eggs for Jacqueline that Geoff was finding it difficult to find space for them all: some went on the table and some on the court cupboard, it was all quite overwhelming. He set off to visit Dorothy who asked him how the decorating was coming on. He told her it was all finished and that the office girls had been in to see it and how surprised they'd been. Dorothy said how much she was looking forward to getting home and seeing the handiwork.

On arriving back in the flat he was warmly greeted by Smudge whose tail was wagging harder than ever and he had a distinctly happy look on his face. When Geoff went into the living room he could see why: there was not a single Easter egg in sight Smudge had eaten every last one, silver paper and all.

And they say chocolate is no good for dogs – don't tell Smudge for he suffered no ill effects at all.

Jacqueline was left with her grandma while her dad went to pick up Dorothy and Robert. He could hardly wait to see the pleasure and delight on Dorothy's face when she saw the imaginative decorating.

Opening the door with a flourish Geoff said "There you are my dear what do you think of that?" He was right she looked amazed "Good heavens above! What have you done" "Don't tell me you don't like it then" said Geoff "the girls from the office said you were in for a surprise" "Well that sums it up very nicely it's a surprise alright, a bloody awful one: whatever possessed you to do this? I can't have anyone in to see this it is dreadful"

Geoff was mortified all his hard work for absolutely nothing. They went out as soon as Easter was over, Dorothy chose the wallpaper and Geoff had to set to and do it all again in a much more uninteresting way.

It was lovely having us all back at home thought Geoff. Jacqueline was thrilled to have a brother even though she now had less attention. Robert however demanded attention for on the stroke of midnight without fail he would yell, yell and yell all night long or at least until 6am when he would drop off for a couple of hours.

Although it affected both of them it was Dorothy who normally got up to him night after night as Geoff had to be up earlier to make a living. He was taken to the doctor who said there was absolutely nothing wrong with him and that they would just have to put up with it. Grandma Leese said that he will be like that until he is two years old. Somebody else said that a teaspoon of whisky would do the trick but someone who overheard this said it would addle his brain. So in the end they could do no more than let nature have its way Geoff did get up in the night when Dorothy was weary with having done so regularly, and he turned him on his tummy on the bedroom carpet and walked him around wheelbarrow fashion.

It didn't help and he wanted more of that as he thought it great fun. One night Geoff was quite worried. He and Dorothy were really worn out with the relentless yelling. This particular night Geoff went to him picked him up together with his mattress to a height between two and three feet then dropped the whole package back into the cot. Robert went quiet – very quiet. So Geoff went back to bed and Dorothy asked him how he had managed to quieten him so quickly. They both lay awake listening there wasn't a sound. Had he harmed him? It was Dorothy who said that the peace was marvellous, but is he still OK. They both went to his bedroom and immediately they peeped into his cot he yelled as usual. He was perfectly OK and they were so relieved.

Jacqueline had been quite a good talker from a early age but there were bits that she took a long time to get right. A memorable one was "Fuf wants wuffi" which translated into Smudge wants a drink of water. Robert was much slower with his talking and when eventually realised that his mouth served another function other than eating and drinking he developed a language peculiar to himself. Or more correctly to himself and his sister. What was complete ga-ga to to his parents Jacqueline interpreted whatever he said so he could get what he wanted through her. It got so bad that Dorothy and Geoff decided that this could not go on or the lad would never learn. So with that they ignored his requests. It was Jacqueline who completed his speech education for when he asked for something in his language she would get it and say to him 'cake' or 'drink' or whatever it might be. So he then copied her and before long the problem was solved. Roberts baptism was also well attended at St Andrews and the afternoon was spent having nibbles and drinks in the flat.

Geoff was feeling that his chance of getting a company car were fading, so he saw George Waite and asked if he could have a loan based on the business he was now doing to get a new car. This was agreed to and he bought a brand new Ford Popular registration 691 NVT. He sold his old car to a client who had never had a car previously. They were an older couple and said to Geoff shortly after they had purchased it that they hadn't realised what mad heads there were on the road these days. "D'you know we decided to have a trip to North Wales on Sunday and we were doing 35 miles an hour and cars were overtaking us ! overtaking us and we were doing 35! Geoff wondered if they meant this was in a 30mph zone but no it was on a major road near Chester Ah well thought Geoff they'll learn.

It was approaching Christmas when Geoff cut his finger on some broken glass: Dorothy was putting on some iodine and a bandage when Jacqueline saw it and began screaming at the sight of blood. She was so upset and almost hysterical but her dad assured her that it didn't hurt and would soon be alright.

They were sitting quietly enjoying an evening watching television, having a couple of glasses of cider together with a box of chocolates when there was a rumble from the grate and down came some burning soot. Geoff jumped up, got some water to put on the fire. As he did so they heard the clanging bells of a fire engine. Geoff said "Sounds as though some poor beggars worse off than us - there must be a real fire somewhere" No sooner had he finished than there was loud banging on the door. On answering the knock he was flabbergasted to be pushed to one side by a couple of firemen trailing a hosepipe. "Had a phone call to say you had a chimney fire" said one. "I've put it out there's no problem now" said Geoff. But they clambered up the stairs, went into the living room, covered it with protective cloths and proceeded to hose up the chimney.

"When was it last swept" asked one "Don't really know" was the reply "We've not been here long so we've never had it seen to"

"This is quite a short chimney so you are best to have it swept at least twice a year in future"

"Well thanks for coming so quickly and dealing with it so efficiently, but we'll heed your advice, will we be charged for this service" asked Geoff. "No it's on the rates" was the reply. They had it done six months later and intended to have it swept prior to Christmas but Geoff had left it too late - all the chimney sweeps were booked up. However the enterprising Geoff decided that he could do it himself even though he had no brushes. So he found a good Holly bush with plenty of berries which they wanted for their Christmas decorations. He tied a couple of his lengthy garden canes together and fastened on a clump of the holly. He then proceeded to push this up the chimney. It did the trick the soot came down and most of it was caught in the protective covering he had placed over the grate. Well pleased with his efforts he retrieved the home- made 'brush', but only one length made the return journey. Luckily there was easy access to the chimney via the large casement window in the lounge which opened on to a flat roof above the office. So he clambered up and put his hand into the chimney pot and pulled out the holly which was much to the amusement of several passersby who had stopped to look in amazement at what he was doing. He gave the audience a quick wave as they clapped their hands.

At Christmas both sets of grandparents came loaded with gifts. They had Christmas dinner and were enjoying a drink by the roaring fire in the lounge when one of the grandmas asked Jacqueline who was now three what she was going to be when she grew up. Without hesitation "A nurse" she replied. Geoff and Dorothy were taken back by her response particularly after the 'bloody finger' experience. History shows though that she became a state registered nurse and never did anything else until she retired at the age of 60.

Christmas was such a lovely time and it was good to have both families together opening gifts – having a few drinks and nibbles and catching up on family affairs. After their guests had left Dorothy and Geoff felt that they were now able to relax snugly by the fire and look back on a very satisfactory day.

Geoff had to go to make a business call in Ludlow Avenue regarding a prospective client who needed a quote for car insurance. He was quite impressed with the situation of this small post-war built estate which was close to all amenities but also had the added advantage of being in close proximity to pleasant countryside. A corner house took his eye which had a For Sale notice in the front garden. That he thought is a place in which I could live. Although they were happy with the flat it would be far better to buy a place of their own and build up some capital as the value of property was on the rise.

He was also concerned that if he did find another job the tenancy of the flat would be in jeopardy. He told Dorothy of his discovery and asked her if she would like to go and see it. The estate agency was just across the road so they went across to find out a few details. He rang the owner and arranged a viewing for the next day. Mrs Heath was the vendor and she turned out to be German. A pleasant lady who gladly showed them around. The house seemed to be just what they wanted. Being on a corner it had a 88feet frontage, a garage, three lawns a well kept garden with what the Estate agents leaflet described as an orchard which turned out to be in the narrow bottom of the garden which had a few raspberry and blackcurrant bushes. Some orchard Geoff thought . However it was pleasant and had plenty of room for the children to enjoy themselves.

The asking price was £2500 and Geoff said he was prepared to make an offer there and then, but she said that she would consider offers but this must be done through the estate agent.

Discussing it on the way back Dorothy said that she was impressed with the house and the location and would be quite happy to live there. Without further ado they went to the estate agent made a offer of £2300. After a little haggling they agreed on £2400. That meant they would need a deposit of £240. Wherever would they find that sort of money? Geoff fervently hoped that he could depend on the Bank of Dad. On going to see Bill and Nellie about a loan it was Nellie who said "£2400 I don't think that very wise, that's an awful lot of money to have to repay with the added interest. It's going to be a rope round your neck for the rest of your lives" "But" retorted Geoff "that estate is fairly new and the properties were being sold for £1200. Now it's double that What other way is there of doubling your money in so short a space of time. Just think at that rate the house would be worth £4800 in just a few years time. Bill agreed that it did make sense to buy a place and this seemed to be what they wanted to do so promised to withdraw the cash from his account in a couple of days time.

He kept his word and Geoff took the deposit to the estate agent who calculated they would have to pay £12 each month for 25 years which came to £3600 approximately. The family moved in at rather bad time for both children had measles and had to be kept as much as possible in the dark. Fortunately Aunt Annie agreed to look after Jacqueline for the day and Nellie had Robert whilst things were sorted out. They were very lucky to befriend Mrs Foster who lived in a bungalow directly opposite. She turned out to be an excellent neighbour who often popped across for a cuppa' It turned out that she had been married to Charlie who for all his working life had been a cleaner of steam locomotives in the engine sheds. They had lived in a terraced house in the town centre. His money was poor so his wife suggested that they turn the front room into a fish and chip shop. Charlie agreed to this and the business flourished. So much so that when he retired they bought their bungalow for cash as well as completely new furniture. They had been in residence for only a short time when Charlie died.

It was around this time that the British coinage was changed from £ .s. d (Pounds, shillings and pence) to decimal coinage. It wasn't a massive change to the majority of people but basically the imperial pound was 240 pennies to the pound but the new pennies, which were considerably smaller were worth 100 to a pound. But a new penny was worth approximately twice as much as its predecessor. Quite confusing for a while. Mrs Foster, though, decided that the old system was far better, with the consequence when she went shopping the retailer had to translate for her. Dorothy though did rather a lot of shopping on her behalf in return for her looking after the children when it was necessary. Over the years Mrs Foster had got rather mean with herself and was upset one day when she met Geoff. "Just look here" she said to him revealing a rather nasty and painful bruise on her leg. " However did you do that"? Geoff queried.

"Oh I had to get out of bed in the night and it was so dark I couldn't see where I was going and walked into a bedside cabinet"

"Mrs Foster you should get yourself a bedside lamp to see what you are doing"

"I've got one - but last quarter my electric bill was over two pounds so I want to economise"

"Your health and welfare come before money you really should not walk about in a dark room, it's asking for trouble"

Whether she took his advice or not Geoff never knew. What he did know was that when she died her son who had not been near her for years inherited everything his mother had worked hard for. Rumour had it that he blew the lot in short time. Both children went to Pedley Street school, which later became the Railway Police HQ in Crewe. By and large they played really well together but were now building up a circle of friends from school as well as the neighbourhood. When he could Geoff enjoyed seeing the children round the garden and joined in the games, particularly football.

Summer holiday's were something the family looked forward to. The favourite destination being Llandudno on the North Wales coast a resort Geoff had been familiar with since childhood since his Aunt Annie had worked in the Queens Hotel on the promenade for several years and knew her way around the area very well. They bought buckets, spades and a dozen flags which would decorate the sandcastle that Geoff planned to build with the children. Having booked in to the boarding house they went down to the promenade. It was a pleasantly warm day and the fond parents were looking forward to seeing the reaction of the children when they had their first glimpse of the sea and to them having donkey rides.

Grandma Thomson had made some beautiful clothes for Jacqueline including a delightful emerald green dress which she was now wearing together with her frilly knickers as well as a eye catching ribbon in her wavy hair.

Llandudno was a place very much favoured by the elderly both for holidays and a desirable place to retire to. So Jacqueline trotted along ahead of her parents. All the elderly ladies who were sitting on the seats along the prom were watching her skipping along. "Oh just look at that pretty little girl" "Isn't she a little cutie" "Ahh bless her she's the belle of the ball" and so on all along the prom. Dorothy and Geoff were very proud knowing that this was their daughter they were talking about.

"Come on Jacqueline" called Geoff "let's go down on to the beach and have a paddle in the sea then see the donkeys"

But NO! She was quite content to show off to an adoring audience. She was loving it. Geoff picked her up and they went down the steps to the beach. Jacqueline screamed her head off whilst Geoff took her shoes and socks off and went to put her down on the sand. But all to no avail. The screaming got louder and more prolonged. They were fighting a losing battle so let her get on with her own devices. Once back on the prom she gave a huge smile and went parading along in front of the tanned, elderly ladies who started off again "Oh, isn't she sweet" "I've never seen such a lovely dress" "She's really gorgeous" Jacqueline was in her element.

Robert was totally different, he loved the sand, the paddling, the donkeys and building sandcastles. Fortunately Jacqueline gave it a try the next day when it was cooler and there were not too many elderly ladies around. Jacqueline was quite a diddy little girl when she was invited to be a bridesmaid to Janet Dorothy's friend of several years.

Janet's dad, Reg was a self made businessman who had made money after the war as a metal merchant. He also had a thriving builders merchant business and a farm at Lapworth Grange where they now lived. In addition to his business activities he was a Conservative councillor on Birmingham City Council. There were no 'airs and graces' about him, he was a down to earth Brummie who told you straight what he thought.

Dorothy and Geoff had been invited to the Grange on occasions prior to moving to Crewe. They once went to the birthday party of Rowan the family dog where a seat had been placed at the head of the oval shaped dining room table for Rowan who had his own plate with a very special birthday cake. There were about ten guests who were led by Reg in the singing of 'Happy birthday dear Rowan' It was a bit silly but it was great fun.

Dorothy and Geoff were, like, Jacqueline thrilled to bits by Jacqueline's role. She was by far the youngest of the three bridesmaids and she looked so proud as she followed Janet down the aisle to the altar. The reception was in a massive marquee on the larger of the lawns. When Robert first spotted it he said "Just look at that big wigwam" ! A band had been hired for the event and Central Television had a crew sent down to film it. All very nice indeed. and costly !

Whenever the family were out in the car Robert could always spot witches hiding more often than not in trees. Try as much as they could nobody else could see anything even resembling a witch.

Robert had awful trouble with his throat so was taken to see the doctor who said that he needed to have his tonsils out as soon as possible and asked if we would be prepared to take him to North Staffordshire hospital at a moment's notice. This they readily agreed to as he really was suffering. In view of this Dorothy suggested that they forego a regular holiday in favour of a weekend in London. They went down by train and found Bed and Breakfast accommodation at a rather poky place adjacent to Kings Cross station. They had their main meals out at anywhere that took their fancy and seemed not to be over the top on price. It was in one such place that Robert chose to have a curry. He'd never had such a thing previously and both Dorothy and Geoff doubted if he would like it and tried to get him to have something different. However he refused all the alternatives. He was warned that he must eat it all up because he would get nothing else if he didn't have that. Their efforts were to no avail.

He gasped when he tried it. It was obvious that he was not going to eat it. Hard luck Rob but you were warned !

On the return journey the train stopped at Stafford. As they waited for it to pull out Robert got excited "Look, look there" he said "there's a crowd of witches getting on the train". "For goodness sake don't be so silly there are no witches around here" "But there are, there's loads of them and they are getting on this train" "Oh your imagination is running riot" said Geoff. Just then along the central corridor about forty nuns walked by looking for their reserved seats.

"There you are; told you"

"Robert, witches have broomsticks they don't need trains" said Geoff "They are Nuns who are religious ladies and do a lot of good by helping the less fortunate" Robert would have been about ten when Geoff asked him if he would like to go and see a football match. It was a pre-season friendly between Crewe Alex and Stoke City who had some well known players in the team.

After the game Geoff asked if he would like to go and see the Alex play on a regular basis. "No came the reply I want to go and watch Stoke City"

Geoff had been a Stoke fan in his younger days so decided he and Rob would attend the home games. For a small lad it was difficult as the ground level was quite a bit higher than the lower area of the paddock so each time they had to take a box for Robert to stand on. Did his interest going to the matches continue? From then on he seldom missed a match. As he grew in independence he went to most of the away matches and had a home season ticket which he still renews every year and he's now in his fifties.

Jacqueline's education was progressing and she went on to the local High School for girls and then on to College. She did well getting 'A' levels in Psychology and Sociology as well as CSE's in English language and literature, Cookery, History, Human Biology and Sociology as well as, and rather amazingly, with Arithmetic.

Both Dorothy and Geoff were completely amazed when she announced that she had decided to make Nursing her career. This was the girl that had shuddered at the sight of blood, but had announced at the age of three that being a nurse was all she wanted to do. Well done thought Geoff who never really knew what he wanted to do in order to earn an honest crust until much later in his life.

Having made the necessary enquiries she discovered that she could not start SRN training until she was eighteen.

Dorothy and Geoff found it rather surprising that she wanted to be a nurse but came to the conclusion it was probably in the genes for both their families had quite a long association with that calling.

Jacqueline and Robert were not at all afraid of work. Until such time as she could go for her nurse training Jacqueline took on a temporary role as an assistant in the local branch of Woolworths.

Robert had to help earn his keep by taking on the task that Geoff hated doing by cleaning all the shoes in the house. This was a task that he conscientiously did each Saturday morning. It was made clear to him that once the job was done he would receive his pocket money. One Saturday his pals called for him so he asked for his pay before he went out. However Geoff knew that he had not done his work and refused to give it to him. So Robert did the job and then had to catch up with his pals. Geoff was very self disciplined and recounted the time when he had been a young teenager who wanted to go on a day trip to Rhyl with a crowd of his mates. He had asked his dad how he could earn some cash in order to do that.

Bill had taken him outside and pointed to a hedge consisting of holly and hawthorn which ran the length of one side of the garden. It was about 100 feet long and the best part of three feet wide - on the other side was a public right of way, it was 8 feet from top to bottom. "I want you to bring that hedge down to a height of six feet and as soon as it's done I'll pay you"

Geoff was quite tall but he needed long step ladders for this. In addition he had two saws, a pair of shears, long and short handled pruners..

He could see this was a mammoth task that lay ahead of him, but made his mind up that he would get the job done as quickly as possible to receive his reward. He dashed home from school each day, took off his school uniform and as it was a warm summer put on a short sleeved shirt which offered no protection from the thorns. At the end of each session Nellie had the job of removing any thorns from his arms and apply iodine. He gave up seeing his mates as he realised that should they get any rain it would delay his progress, and as he had absolutely no money he must carry on. He completed the work with just days to spare.

Bill inspected the work and said "You've done well son, a first class job. I'm proud of you. You've earned this, spend it wisely" and with that he handed his son a ten shilling note (50 pence).

Geoff was overjoyed. My gosh he thought I never thought I'd have this much. The lads had a super time in Rhyl, Geoff treated himself to three rides on the Dodgems, but refused to roll any pennies down a chute to cover the squares in the hope of winning more money because he knew the odds were stacked against him and he had worked too hard to throw away hard earned cash.

Geoff had built up the business on his insurance book and his earnings were increasing rather nicely. He was offered the opportunity of promotion to inspector: this would have entailed him going out with the agents canvassing for new business on their behalf. He would have received a regular but rather low wage plus fairly generous bonuses on each sale made But his heart was not really in it and he still yearned for a change in direction.

He had almost finished paying for his insurance book which by this time was worth considerably more than what he had paid for it. If only he could find a suitable job he would have quite a nice little nest egg when he came to sell the book.

CHAPTER 6 –
A FRESH CAREER

The local weekly CHRONICLE newspaper normally carried a very healthy number of Situation Vacant adverts which Geoff perused regularly. The paper had recently been bought out by the Thomson Newspaper group headed by Lord Thomson of Fleet who was expanding his newspaper empire and according to a advert they were 'Looking for sales people to develop the advertising from local retailers by showing them how local papers can be a very effective tool in increasing their turnover and consequently their profits"

This, Geoff thought is for me – working for the local newspaper – company car – decent salary – progressive national company – he really must apply for this. He sent his letter and received a prompt reply asking him to attend for interview in the CHRONICLES head office in Bridge Street Chester on 22nd December at 2.30pm. In those days there were no parking restrictions so enabling him to park right outside the entrance. The receptionist asked him to wait a moment and she would let them know that he was there. Minutes later he met Alan Crofts who introduced himself as the Advertising Manager and led him into the boardroom. There were about eight men sat at the boardroom table and Geoff was invited to take a seat opposite to them. The person who was to conduct the interview introduced himself as Barry Hawkes.

In his experiences of being interviewed Geoff had come to the conclusion that there would be one vital question which could sway things in his favour – the trick was spotting it.

Barry asked a number of personal things and then it came. "Mr Pritchard tell me why after seven successful years in insurance you would want us to consider you for this vacancy which has no relevance to insurance what so ever"

Geoff looked him in the eye and replied with confidence "Mr Hawkes I can see exactly where you are coming from, however I do disagree with you some what. People buy insurance to cover against certain possible hazards that may happen in the future. Similarly retailers should be aware that advertising is a form of insurance for the immediate betterment and protection of their trade that will help them to expand their business through increased turnover and bigger profits. Those who don't advertise would be the losers."

Geoff could hear a distinct rumble of approval from around the table. He knew he had scored a bulls eye. They thanked him for attending, he thanked them for seeing him. He felt rather pleased with himself on the return journey.

Dorothy asked how he'd gone on. "Not too bad at all" was the reply. He'd had too many disappointments in the past to build their hopes up too much. It was Christmas Eve when the letter arrived from the Chronicle . It read "I am pleased to advise you that your application was successful ."This really would be a Christmas to celebrate.

Both sets of parents and Dorothy's brother Stuart arrived at Ludlow Avenue on Christmas Day. As usual they were loaded with presents mainly for their grand children plus the inevitable chocolate bars for Smudge. Geoff was thrilled to tell them about his new job which would provide him with a company car and that he had already given his notice in to the Cooperative Insurance Society. He knew his new work would be a challenge, but he felt physically and mentally ready for the days that lay ahead in his new career.

He sold his insurance book to a recently retired professional footballer by the name of Tim Coleman who as a right winger (7 Shirt) had made a name for himself by scoring seven goals in an away match for Stoke City against Lincoln City.

He was a very pleasant man and accompanied Geoff on the insurance round to be introduced to the clients.

But as far as Geoff was concerned insurance was now part of his history and whilst he had been relatively successful he must look to the future.

Thomson Regional newspapers were media leaders in training and before you could venture into a shop you had to undergo a week's initial training. The course he was on was held in Watergate Street Chester and was scheduled to start at 9am. Most of the inductees were from other newspapers within the Thomson group based from Inverness down to Reading so they had to be found local hotel accommodation, whereas Geoff who lived almost 30 miles away had to travel in daily. Three of the other inductees were, like him, newly recruited to work for the Chronicle group.

On driving in on the first day he realised that he had misjudged the timing of the journey which resulted in him entering the classroom almost five minutes late. Geoff excused himself to Barry Hawkes who was to conduct the course. Barry's first words were "That gentlemen is the end of the first lesson" Geoff couldn't believe that they could have had a lesson in that time, but they had and as Barry explained "The first lesson is NEVER be late for an appointment. Had you (pointing at Geoff) arranged to meet me, as a client, at 9am I, indicating himself would have gone. There can NEVER be an excuse for being late.

The course got under way: everyone was supplied with a training manual, drawing pad, pen, pencil, ruler. There was a mid morning coffee break followed by lunch at 1o'clock. The class was due to re-start at 2 o'clock but it couldn't because again somebody was missing until 2.15 and that was the tutor Barry ! He came in rather red faced., "Sorry about that chaps but the lift got stuck between floors" "Barry your first lesson was there are no excuses for being late" came a chorus from those present except for Geoff who thought it best if he remained discreetly quiet. Geoff could see that the training manual was a wonderful publication that started off by asking the very simple question "What is newspaper advertising?" and the answer was "Newspaper advertising is PROFESSIONAL salesmanship in print" Barry himself had a excellent record of success in selling advertising in the newspaper industry. He stressed to the class right from the start that you are not Space Salesmen, but professional highly trained sales people who sell high quality advertising in order to achieve an objective. That objective was to sell top grade advertising In order to attract and hold the attention of a sales story whilst a desirable action or reaction is achieved.

Barry then put to the group "Why do people buy local newspapers".

Easy "to keep abreast of what was going on in their locality"

"Correct" agreed Barry "so in that case who is your main competitor"

Most of the group named other papers in the area. "No" said Barry "You will be competing with the editorial staff of your newspaper. They are skilled highly trained writers who know how to attract potential readers to read the stories they have written. In which case YOU must write copy that will attract the readers to the ads that you are placing in a way to detract them from the editorial stories" That was something that Geoff and all the other trainees had not considered. "And we do this by writing the most important part of any advertisement, and that is the headline. Most retailers would answer that by saying the name of their shop is the most important. What they see as important is having their names as large as possible at the top of the ad, but suppose the name is JOHNSONS and you go along with that, then you are doing them no favours but simply throwing their hard earned cash away. The name is important but how much better it would be if it read for example "LADIES ! Latest Spring Fashions at Lowest Prices, now available at JOHNSONS.

He then handed round adverts that had actually appeared in the paper the previous week and asked the group to re-do the advert, keep it the same size but make it more professional and give it a bit of oomph.

It was fun, it was demanding and it was exciting. Writing the body copy, showing the prices, the sizes and very importantly not just saying what the product was but what it would do to improve the life of the reader.

Barry pointed out that an advertisement was something intangible, so it was no use at all for a salesman to walk into a prospective retailer and say 'Do you want to buy an advert' because nine times out of ten the answer would be NO. "So" he asked "How can we turn this intangible into a tangible product? It's easy. We do it by preparing a layout, and you don't have to be an artist to do that. As a salesman you set yourself an objective. You consider what size ad you think the prospect should have. You settle for a 8inch double column for a cycle shop and draw it up to size – now you want a headline, an illustration from the artwork books your newspapers subscribe to, put in the price, the retailers name, address, contact details, and hey presto you've now got something tangible that your prospect can hold. He may ask how much it's going to cost him If he does BINGO he's as good as bought it. "This size would be £20 but I could adjust by making the ad smaller or bigger would that be satisfactory Mr Prospect" He may not say yes straight away but at least you've got a talking point and remember there's nothing he likes to talk about more than himself, his business, his products, so you are on a winner. Don't forget to tell him that there are discounts available on your rates, subject to the amount of his prospective spend over a year".

The training was over and it was Frank one of the other inductees who was to work for the CHRONICLE who said to Geoff. "Well we all know what to do, but it's different putting it into practice in a shop rather than in a classroom" Geoff thought this was rather a negative attitude but replied "I'm sure that we will all benefit from what we've heard this week and we'll learn as we go along" Alan Crofts came into the room and said that he hoped we had all benefitted from the course. Now it will be up to each sales person to use the training and expertise to good effect in order to meet the monthly targets.

He advised his new sales team which area they would each be responsible for Gareth and Fred would each have a territory in Chester, Frank would be in the Mold office. Mabel would be in Mid Cheshire and Geoff would cover South Cheshire of the territory based in Crewe and Nantwich.

The first project that they were to produce was a Farming Supplement which would be published at the end of March. Advertisers could go into the whole group of newspapers or into individual ones at the appropriate rate. The editors of each paper within the group had prepared a list of all prospective clients within their area. This was a very big aid to the sales staff and was an initiative that Geoff was to use on his territory in the future.

"Finally" said Alan "you will be pleased to know that your cars are ready to be picked up from ABC Motors. Good luck to all of you and I'll be in touch to see how you are progressing"

A company car at last ! I've done it thought Geoff! I've actually got a company car! He pulled off the forecourt of ABC Motors and headed for Crewe. He hadn't gone far when he found himself struggling to get out of second gear. No matter what he did it refused to go up to third. As he struggled he completely fluffed it and came to a halt right by a bus stop which had a fairly long queue. He didn't want to be seen struggling with the car so he rolled the window down and asked for directions to Crewe. "Take the first right, keep straight on for a hundred yards to a roundabout and take the second exit"

At least it gave Geoff some respite and had calmed his nerves, he slipped into first gear, then second, will it won't it? Yes it went into third and then into fourth, never to give him any more trouble. On reaching home the family went outside to see the new red Hillman Imp. Geoff said that he would take the old car (691NVT) to the new owner. Jacqueline and Robert said their goodbyes with a flood of tears they had loved that car.

Today, thought Geoff is the start of a new life – not just for himself but for all the family – there was no need to put money on one side to get a new car or even the tax and insurance and probably no petrol either. But we'll wait and see all he had to do was to be successful, and if he wasn't after the good training then he would only have himself to blame.

However it was now Friday evening and that's his night at Crewe Bowling Club.

It was Bill who had suggested when they had moved into LUDLOW Avenue that Geoff might like to join the club which was strictly for men only. He had played Crown Green Bowling on various local bowling greens with his mates and had always found it a rather pleasant way to spend an evening. So he relished the idea of becoming a club member. The bowling green was considered to be one of the largest in the area. It was in a lovely setting barely a five minute walk to his home. Bill was a pretty good snooker player, he had a good eye and had the ability to work out shots that his son would never have thought of. As time went on Geoff in turn introduced several of his friends to the delights of the Bowling Club, and they initially made Friday night the one night in the week that they would meet up. This particular evening he was relaxed and thrilled to tell them of his new job and his company car. The drinks were on him tonight, or at least the first one was! He went home contented, Dorothy was so pleased for him having seen him achieve his ambition. She knew he would be successful and gave him her full support, Alan Crofts had advised Geoff that he would visit him in the Crewe Office on Monday morning as soon as he possibly could and that it would be a help if Geoff could have a list of prospects ready prepared. Not only did he do that he also prepared a sales pitch that he thought may be suitable for the Farming Supplement. He had one attempt at it, put it to one side, made a cup of tea and relaxed for a few minutes: he then got a fresh sheet of paper and wrote out a sales pitch again. He rather surprised himself when he saw that his second one contained items he had not put into the original pitch. With this in mind he went out to cut the grass then returned to write out a third sales pitch: he was glad that he did for things came into his sub-conscious that were not in the first two. He now looked at all three and did a fourth and final script which he was not going to change.

He wondered if the others at the Chronicle were doing the same thing. He rather doubted it.

It was around 10 o'clock when Alan Crofts arrived at the Crewe office "Where's your office" asked Alan.

"As yet I haven't got one. I just have to find a space which at the moment is the corner of some else's desk, which is not satisfactory so I hope it gets sorted out quickly for all our sakes"

Alan and Geoff though were more interested in getting a few sales under their belts rather than worry about a desk and chair. The first call Geoff had planned was to a Fordson Tractor dealer. Alan said that he'd never met the people from here but had spoken to them on the phone quite a lot so he would lead the way and show how it should be done. The entrance to the dealership led immediately to the receptionist. Alan introduced himself and said that he would like to see Mr Johnson who came straight away. Alan told him of the planned supplement specially being done for the benefit of the farming community. Mr Johnson said that it was a good idea, but in view of the fact that he could not get enough new tractors to meet the current demand he didn't want to aggravate the situation and add to the waiting list so thanked them for calling and saying perhaps next time. Alan said he quite understood and that we would keep in close contact. They went on to the next few prospects without making a sale although some required a call back.

Alan returned to his office in Chester, Geoff went home for lunch but had the feeling that they should have done better with Mr JOHNSON. He would have to figure it out. The rest of the day went pretty well. He decided that there were so many prospective advertisers on his list that it might be an idea to select some of the prospects upon whom he could use his own technique and the script that he had written up. The first one he chose was a tractor repair company who were based at a farm in a rural area about six miles away. The name was PRITCHARD TRACTOR SERVICING. (no relation)

When he got there he could see no one around. He ventured into the small wooden building – no one - He called out, "Good afternoon – anyone here"

"Yes I'm under this bloody tractor what is it you want"

"Well I was hoping you could spare me a few minutes as I am from the Crewe Chronicle and we are publishing a special supplement at the end of March which is aimed at making the farming community throughout the county aware of the many services that are open to them. In your case I would suggest that you consider taking advantage of this at the very competitive rate I can offer you".

"I haven't the time to leave this bloody job so you can come down here and show me what you can do for me"

Geoff thought this wasn't covered on the course., but he was not going to miss this chance. He went down. Mr Pritchard explained he could repair any type of tractor and he would like to get some extra business so that his son could eventually join him in the business. Geoff said he would find an illustration of a tractor to include in the advert. Mr Pritchard wiped his hands down his overall, thanked him and asked him to keep in touch. His first advert! Only a titch, but it may go on and grow.

Geoff was still niggled that Johnsons had not booked a space. So he returned with an idea. "Mr Johnson you said that you could not get enough Fordson Tractors to meet the demand, but I see you have many used tractors on site, supposing we were to advertise those but emphasising that you cannot supply new Fordsons because they are so reliable and competitive to buy that the demand is increasing, so if you are a farmer with any make of tractor who is looking ahead the very least you can do is to put your name on our waiting list so as to avoid disappointment when they do need to change"

"Hey that's a sound idea.   Yes I'll do that but not too costly"

"OK thank you, shall we say between about fifty and sixty pounds"?

"That'll do nicely, but no more"

Geoff sorted out the copy and prepared it for Mr Johnsons approval.

"Great" thought Geoff "I knew I could do it"

The staff in the Crewe office were a good crowd and made Geoff very welcome. Most of them were office bound but they all did one thing in common which was to attend the counter when anyone went in to place a classified advertisement. These were usually linage adverts and were charged for by the number of words. They ranged from cars to be sold privately to household items that were no longer needed.

The office manager was Bill Newman who, Geoff soon found, out was something of a character having overall responsibility for the commercial section but his main function was involved with the circulation of papers. The bulk were delivered by van to all the newsagents in the area every Wednesday afternoon. Bill would then have a stack put into the boot of his car and deliver any extras that the newsagents required. He also wrote out the billboards which he placed outside newsagents shops. The only other man on the commercial side was Ron Southall who had been employed by the company since he'd left school.

The editorial staff occupied the first floor offices. It was all very friendly and the local editor, Colin Roberts said that he would give Geoff any support that he needed. What he needed more than anything was office space or at least his own desk. He found the ideal place, which was adjacent to the front door and was used purely as a dumping ground for any unsold papers. When he investigated he picked out some at random , they went back up to ten years and were not in any particular order. A very adequate room being used as a dumping ground. His discovery coincided with a visit from Mr Adam the Managing Director who asked Geoff how he was settling in. Geoff said that he'd found this storage room and that he felt it could be used as an office for himself. Mr Adams took a look and immediately arranged for work to be done. The company handyman came the very next day. Not only did he clear out the mess he redecorated the office and much to Geoff's surprise and delight made a most superb desk which ran the length of one wall. A new telephone line was installed which was solely for his use. He was thrilled with this new set up and soon got things organised as he wanted it. Although they were in the communications business their own internal communications left a great deal to be desired. The pagination of every edition is governed by the amount of advertising being carried. The greater the volume of ads the more editorial stories and pictures can appear, consequently the number of pages varies from week to week. The same principle applied to the Farming supplement, but no one had explained this to Geoff who just went on selling without advising the admin people of the progress that he was making. He thought rather than give individual sales he would give them the lot in one go as it would seem more impressive and he was out to impress. In those days papers were nearly all printed by letterpress using hot metal and not the off-set printing which was introduced later. In consequence lead printing blocks were needed from most advertisers. These he kept safely in cardboard boxes.

Almost every day Geoff had a phone call from somebody in admin telling him that the lads in Chester were doing really well with the supplement whereas the Crewe and Nantwich sales were looking abysmal. Geoff told them not to worry, everything will turn out OK. Then days later Alan Crofts rang "I'm amazed that you have done so little on this supplement you have the prime area and the fewest bookings and we are going to have to put this to bed in the next few days - I'm really disappointed".

Geoff said he would take his bookings over the following day.

He loaded boxes of lead printing blocks into the boot of the car and made his way to Chester.   He staggered up the stairs under the weight; proudly entered the department saying that he didn't know what they'd been worried about as he proudly announced that he'd sold over twelve pages of paid for advertising and a lot of it was at the premium rate to go through the full series of the papers. The rest of the team had barely sold that much between them.   Geoff was on top of the world, but when it was explained to him that the editorial people would now have to find a lot more material to fill the extra pages which brought him down to earth. If only they had explained this before - but he had been too eager to boost his ego. Never again did he do anything like that.

Not only was the supplement a great success but Geoff managed to get quite a few of the advertisers into the papers on a regular basis. In most cases he introduced them to a contract scheme whereby if they took so many inches of advertising each month they would qualify for a decent discount. Most of the advertisers welcomed this and signed the contract.

When he was on insurance Friday had been a long arduous day. Now he could finish at 5.30, go home have his steak and chips and then join his mates at the Bowling club for bowling, snooker and round off with playing various card games. He was in Nantwich on Friday, a glance at the church clock showed it was 4.45. It was a twenty minute drive to Crewe, then phone Chester with a report on his days activities and be home shortly after 5.30.   But life was feeling so good to him he decided he would make just one more call As he had always enjoyed fishing he decided to give the fishing tackle shop of Alan Patterson a call and give him the benefit of his expertise.

He walked in, explained his mission. Geoff's timing could not have been worse. For in walked a man with his young son. "A shillings worth of maggots please Alan" he said. Geoff stood to one side as he watched the wriggly assortment of coloured maggots put in his container and the bob piece rung up on the till. As they left two more walked in on a similar mission. Between customers Geoff had managed to get in a few relevant points but out of courtesy stood to one side while the customers were dealt with. It was now 5.30 – never mind he thought this can't go on much longer, but it did. Was it worth the wait? You bet it was, Geoff wasn't going to hang around all this time and not make it worthwhile. He booked him for all the remaining title corners, also known as earpieces on the front page for the rest of the year, and as an added bonus he signed a contract as well. Alan more than fulfilled his contract, and he turned out to be a really good person to know. Geoff arrived back home at 7.45. He showered, had his meal but arrived at the club much later than normal.

Geoff was enjoying his success. He liked to think that he was pretty good at self motivation which was better than the 'big-stick' attitude adopted by some in senior roles which could have a worsening effect.

He was honest in his own self criticism, sometimes so much so that he actually depressed himself. He thought back to a few years ago when he expressed the desire to get into a sales job to an Uncle through marriage who told him "You are too miserable a looking buggar to sell anyone anything"

Geoff rather agreed that he did have a more or less permanent serious look. In fact he had an aversion to people who seemed to have a perpetual smile on their face. No one Geoff thought exemplified this more than a certain 20th century Prime Minister.

Geoff came to the conclusion that there was no single word that describes what makes a good salesman, but he realised that empathy was a highly desirable asset to possess. Usually he could put himself in another person's position and ask himself what he would do if he faced their same circumstances. What would he do if he was a shop proprietor and somebody came in to sell him an advert in the local paper? Would he buy it? Will it cover the cost and give him some profit no matter how small that may be?

One thing he did conclude was that if those circumstances arose and he did not buy then he would never know if it was going to be beneficial. In any event he would want to feel assured that people were going to read it, that they approved of the illustration that they liked the headline. Will readers react favourably?

Geoff realised that people are all different but with various attributes that are very similar. We all like to think that the people who try to do business with us appreciate us for what we are and that we all have our little idiosyncrasies. As he went on his different business calls Geoff tried to find out a little about the likes and dislikes of his potential clients - had they any family, did they play any sport or what they did for relaxation, what was their favourite holiday resort. All manner of things he thought useful he jotted down and kept in a small note book for future reference. It could prove useful in the long term.

Geoff was perplexed some months after the Farming Supplement had been published when the general manager of one of the major tractor dealerships in the county who had signed a agreement to advertise each month greeted him with "I've decided not to take an advert this month" In the past he'd always had a printing block at the ready to hand over. Geoff decided very much against saying anything about the agreement as he wanted Mr Morgan to take the advert because he wanted the benefit it could bring and not because he'd signed a paper. Geoff had to put his thinking cap on. "Well Mr Morgan I would have thought this was an excellent time to get your message across. because blah blah"

"No, I'll give a miss"

"This is leaving the door open for your competitors"

"No I'll give it a miss"

"Would it help if I just put it in the local edition?

"No I'll give it a miss"

Geoff had a dreadful but distinct feeling that he was not going to get the ad. Playing for time and looking for divine inspiration, Geoff asked if he had any objection to him having a smoke. "Not at all – go ahead" said Mr Morgan "Thank you" said Geoff and withdrew a packet from his pocket "Do you use them" he asked as he opened the packet of fags and held them out to Mr. Morgan. "Well actually, yes I do" came the response "by the way this new block arrived yesterday can you put it into the usual papers for me please"? as he was speaking he handed the block to a flabbergasted Geoff. This charade was enacted each month. If Geoff asked for the order he got a 'No' By getting out the cigarettes he got an immediate YES ! Amazing in later years Geoff did wonder WHAT IF smoking bans had been in operation at that time would he have made a sale?

The Thomson group of Newspapers was renowned for providing probably the best sales training in the newspaper industry. There were many provincial morning and evening newspapers as well as the weeklies that were owned by the group which stretched from Inverness in the North to London in the south, Newcastle on Tyne on the east coast and Cardiff to the west. The Chronicle group was over 200 years old but had never had a team of trained advertising sales people. Now things were different and there were two advertising departments: one to sell Classified advertising the other to sell Display advertising on the news pages. Each department was set a monthly target. These were loosely based on the volume of the same month in the previous year and where possible followed the trend of the current year. Each month the department would have a target to meet which was agreed by the Managing Director and the Advertising Manager. He in turn would then assess the potential business of each territory. A target was set for each salesman. A bonus would be paid if the team target was met and bonuses would be paid to those sale staff reaching their specific target. Everybody who made their target would have their name on the Thomson Target Club which consisted of all sales staff within the Thomson Group. Inevitably, like all leagues it could only be topped by one person. There was no monetary gain in doing this but it was a most prestigious and much coveted position to be in.

Alarm bells were ringing in Nantwich. The town had a number of good family run businesses many of which had been in existence for generations, but it was strongly rumoured that a supermarket chain had aspirations of opening a branch in the town in the near future. Geoff came to the conclusion that it would be in the interest of these small shops to band together to at least try and keep the inevitable at bay for a while longer. So he indented the graphic design studio to come up with ideas so that the local food retailers could show solidarity and advertise their personal services and quality to the local inhabitants.

"YOUR LOCAL, LONG ESTABLISHED, FRIENDLY FOOD RETAILERS OFFER FREE HOME DELIVERY AT NO EXTRA COST", was the heading to the page and spaces were available for the retailers to advertise their individual shops. Geoff arranged a special price provided that they agreed to run this composite page each month. He prepared his sales pitch about showing solidarity and reliability plus years of experience and quality to the public.

It went down rather well, he was pleased with the reception it got and felt confident that he was on to a winner. His early optimism was somewhat thwarted when one his prospects said if Archers go in I won't, others would go in but only if they could be at the top of the page, yet another would say yes to this providing his ad was put in upside down. Geoff couldn't believe what he was hearing so he hit on the idea of hiring a room in a local hotel and getting the prospective participants together. He would give a brief presentation and then try to get their co-operation and put any grievances behind them. The hotel agreed to this and said they would not charge for the room hire as their contribution to making it a success.

But it was to no avail "I wouldn't want to be seen in the same room as him"

"If that bastards there I won't stay"   "I must insist on being at the top of the page"

"I don't want any association with him"

Geoff admitted defeat.   The supermarket did hit town several months later and several of those small retailers disappeared almost overnight. That was Geoff's first main failure. He hoped there wouldn't be any more. But there were.

Top: The wedding of Dorothy and Geoff at Erdington Parish Church on 27th April 1957.
Below Left: Dorothy and Geoff on honeymoon in Bournemouth.
Below right: Jacqueline helps mum with Robert, her new brother.
Bottom Right: Geoff puts Robert in his pram.

Above: The Roberts and Pritchard family enjoy the moment in the grounds of St. Michael and All Angels Church, Crewe Green following the wedding of Gareth and Jacqueline.

Below: Robert and Julia are married in the sunshine of Cyprus.

CHAPTER 7 –
AT YOUR SERVICE

At this time Barclays Bank were launching a new idea of shopping with credit cards.

They booked a half page advert giving details of their project on the understanding that the newspaper would approach all the retailers who had agreed to offer this facility with a view to them taking a small advert. The bank supplied a list of participating shops.   One of these was Bennett's Dry Cleaning company who had a few branches in the area. Mr Bennett readily agreed to taking part. A few weeks after the promotion had appeared Geoff went along to Mr Bennett to see if the advert had been successful "Yes it was OK, I did quite well from it" said Mr Bennett,

"but I did have one chap who came in with a load of cleaning who queried if he would be charged a fee for using the card. When I told him no he asked how then does the bank make any money out of the card, so I told him as the retailer I had to pay a percentage of the transaction to the bank for using the facility. In that case said the customer I won't pay with the card, but I will give you cash and you deduct the percentage you would have paid Barclays from my bill. Deal done. Result a happy customer, a happy retailer and a happy Geoff because Mr Bennett signed an agreement to advertise every month. Everyone was happy. But oops what about Barclays?

Bennett's stuck to the agreement and quite frequently were happy to pay the premium rate to go on the front page.

The advertising sales staff were expected to make 12 calls a day. In practice this could sometimes be exceeded but more often than not it would be nearer 10. With this in mind Geoff could see that the true potential of the area was not being covered properly and felt that a second salesman was needed. He had become quite matey with Ron in the office. In talking to him Geoff established that Ron would love to get on to the sales team. As most shops had a half day closing every Wednesday it was decided that all the sales staff should meet at the Chester office for a sales meeting or training between 2 and 5.30 pm each week.

Geoff saw this as a good time to speak to Alan about splitting the territory and give consideration to taking Ron into the sales team. Alan agreed that a second person would be an idea, but not Ron as he was only a young lad.

"Alan you took Ron on about five years ago when he was 17 how many times have you seen him since then? asked Geoff.

"I don't think I've actually seen him since he started but I do speak to him nearly every day" he replied

"He's a very ambitious lad, he's smartly turned out and he has a lot more knowledge about advertising than I had before I got this job so you really should at least give him some consideration. Suppose I bring him along next Wednesday and he can attend the meeting and you can see for yourself how ambitious he is and how much potential he has".

And so it proved. Ron was taken on to the sales staff and the territory was halved He got his company car, he also had a monthly target to meet, and like Geoff he had the all important enthusiasm. As time went by they worked well together, but it was interesting when one day around noon a very perplexed Ron came into the office looking somewhat hot and bothered, "Tell me something" he rather breathlessly asked Geoff "How the devil did you ever manage to sell advertising to that chap Mr. Morgan. I've never come across anyone who kept saying no to everything I said I feel completely worn out and inadequate and yet you got him in each month, I just do not understand how"

"Sorry, Ron I should have told you. But go back immediately after lunch, make him your first call – offer him a fag and just say 'now what about this ad' and he will give you a booking together with the block straightaway"

"Oh come off it" said Ron "that's ridiculous. Now tell me how you really did it"

"Ron what I've told you is almost unbelievable, but it is right" and he related how he had discovered this. "and Ron they don't tell you that one in the training manual. but do make it your first call this afternoon"

It was around 5 o'clock when Ron returned jubilantly holding a new tractor block as though it was a gold nugget: but it was better than that it was a sign of success. Ron still could not believe what he had witnessed.

Geoff was loving every minute of his work, so much so that he spent a fair amount of time at home in the evening preparing for the next day's onslaught on the local retailers. The newspaper group subscribed to a really good graphic design service called Metro an American publication which was crammed with illustrations for just about every sort of business enterprise from Ladies Beauty Salons to Monumental

Masons. It was issued monthly so kept abreast of all the seasons with relevant graphics – eggs – chickens – daffodils for Spring and Easter - a host of Father Christmas's, Robins and snowmen in December for Christmas.

If Geoff planned to see a shoe retailer the following day he would draw the proposed shape and size then cut out a piece of appropriate artwork showing footwear , write a suitable headline, indicate where the copy would go, insert name and address of the prospect and so turn an intangible into a tangible object that the potential customer could hold and see what he was getting for his money. These 'visuals' were fairly quick to do and were well worth the time it took to prepare. Being an American publication the illustrations were not always appropriate to the British market, but that didn't matter as they would serve the purpose very well as proved the case next day. "I really do not like that shoe" said the retailer, 'Sold' thought Geoff! the rest is just a technicality "Not to worry" he said "have you anything that you feel is more appropriate" "Yes I have, look this is much better"

"OK we'll use that one " said Geoff "Ah yes just look that fits nicely, I'll find a suitable spot for you in the paper and bring you a copy round on Thursday morning. Is that OK"

"Yes of course" came the response "I look forward to seeing it.

By this time the group had gone from printing letterpress which was all done by hot metal to off-set printing. This meant that the old lead blocks were no longer wanted and illustrations, drawings, photographs could all be reproduced directly from source. It also gave the opportunity to print future newspapers in colour. This was a major step forward in the newspaper industry and gave greater scope to the editorial people and certainly to the advertising staff. The future looked good. Geoff was getting to be something of a workaholic: he loved the work, he enjoyed the use of the car, had a reasonable salary but he also realised that he needed to relax more - both with his family and friends. They enjoyed going away for short weekend breaks with the North Wales coast and Blackpool all within easy reach and providing a relaxing couple of days. But he just could not resist booking in to a hotel then going out to find the office of the local newspaper to purchase a copy of their latest paper and acquire a advertising rate card.

Back to the hotel where he would get his pen and a ruler then suggest to Dorothy and the children that they go and sit on the front. Once the children had settled down to making sand castles he would measure up the size of each advert in the paper then using the rate card calculate how much advertising revenue they had in that particular edition. He then scoured the pages to see if there were any advertising ideas in it that his own group could use. If he saw something that attracted him he would stow them away in the boot of the car because he knew that at some time he would be able to make good use of them.

What a way to spend a relaxing weekend Geoff thought, but he was enthusiastic and he simply loved it. He'd always subscribed to the theory that if you don't enjoy doing something then don't do it. However in later years he came to realise that there must be an awful lot of people who simply cannot find any work, let alone any work that they really liked. In fact one of Geoff's contemporaries did say he did not envy the younger generation, many of whom could not find work of any description and that the current generation had never had it so bad.

Geoff said that he certainly didn't subscribe to that at all and asked him if he would sooner be an eighteen year old now or someone of the same age in 1939 when the best opportunity of employment was on the battlefield with only a 50-50 chance of reaching your 21st.   In the 1920's youths could get an apprenticeship fairly readily which quite frankly was a cheap form of labour until they came out of their time at 21 when they were entitled to men's wages but instead got the sack.   Geoff said that a lot of today's youth seemed to have the attitude that the world owes them a living.   Sadly the nanny state seems to be to blame for a great deal of this with too many handouts.

Geoff made a lot of friends at the Bowling Club which he discovered had members from all walks of life including managers from a major car manufacturing company, auctioneers, bank managers, the proprietor of a fruit and vegetable wholesale company, several school teachers as well as a wages clerk, a few bus drivers, a cook, several insurance men and retired people who had a wealth of common sense. Geoff was of the opinion it did not matter what people did or had done for a living what really mattered was that they were all people determined to enjoy the company of their fellow members.   Membership at that time was restricted to men only who lived within a fifteen mile radius, or worked in Crewe. The bar steward was appropriately dressed with a pair of black trousers a white shirt with a black bow tie and always carried a white linen cloth draped over his arm to wipe any spilled drink on the tables.   There were some exceptions as ladies were allowed in on a Sunday evening provided of course they were accompanied by their husbands.   Some of the ladies said it was totally wrong not to have lady members.   Geoff was of the opinion that there were plenty of mixed clubs and several organisations catering for women such as the Mothers Union and the Women's Institute which men would not want to be in, or indeed, would they be welcomed at. "So why object to this club being for men only?" Indeed he pointed out that when the club invited other clubs to have a friendly bowls match they did allow their wives to prepare the food – on the proviso that as soon as they had done that they should go home!!. Sexist ! Yes of course it was. But in reality the ladies rather loved it ! This was a time for him to relax.

He was a good listener and he was very aware that we can all learn from one another and this can pay handsome dividends if what we see or hear can be put to good use.

During the 1960's driver's could park their cars almost anywhere. Yellow lines were something for the not too distant future. Geoff's car was parked right outside the office door on High Street. It was around 10am when he left the office to get into his car. The road sweeper was on the opposite side of the road and as far as Geoff was aware he had never seen him previously. He laid his brush on the cart and signalled to Geoff as he walked across the road. "Hey there - do you work for the Chronicle" he asked.   When Geoff confirmed that indeed he did the sweeper was rather impressed. "Are you a reporter?" he questioned, to which Geoff replied that he was not, but that his role was to take care of the advertising on the news pages . "Well now" said the sweeper "what I want to know is why don't you have a section in the paper like they have in the weekend newspapers where they have small square adverts on pages they call BARGAINS BY POST" He went on to say that he read each one of them and they had all sorts of things like bikes that fold up, new sheds, pots and pans. You could have something like that in the Chronicle".

"That's an interesting thought, I'll look into the possibilities of that" said Geoff

"Thank you very much for the idea, we're always looking for fresh ideas". The truth was that to cover the country it was much more cost effective to use the national press than a mass of weekly papers, but it was food for thought. Returning to the office later in the day he talked it over with Ron. They both realised that there were more businesses in the area that did not advertise than did. All retail outlets had something special to offer or else they would not exist, and some of the shops that did advertise only did so perhaps once a month, possibly because of the cost, so something smaller could be used on the other weeks to keep things ticking over. They agreed that initially they would keep the spaces to a standard size of two inches deep by one column width and that they would sell that for a minimum run of four weeks and allow changes in copy if required. They also decided that to be effective it must occupy at least three columns of the broad sheet paper. They decided to call it AT YOUR SERVICE. Geoff indented the graphic design studio to produce an effective banner heading with two inch squares below to give prospective advertisers an idea of what they would be subscribing to. Retailers loved it and Ron and Geoff enjoyed selling it as the clients were getting high impact at low cost. There was a variety of such diverse businesses that it gave it a certain potency, a carpet shop, someone selling sewing machines, drapery, hair and beauty products, curtains, DIY products. It was made up mainly of businesses that had not advertised previously and it spread into the other newspapers in the group in, Chester and Mid Cheshire. It wasn't long before other newspapers in the Thomson group followed suit and were publishing the feature on a regular basis. It must have been quite a good money spinner for Thomson Newspapers. This had all happened because of a brief encounter with a totally unknown road sweeper who sadly Geoff never saw again, and those newspapers who took up the idea won't have had any inkling as to how it came about .

Working for any of the papers within the Thomson Group was tough, but fair. In house training was ongoing. Every Wednesday afternoon in that era was half-day closing for the majority of shops. Gareth had been appointed as Sales Supervisor, which meant that he was number two in the department to Alan. He was a good salesman and had previous experience with several well known companies including Avery Scales. He was a flamboyant character and could impart his knowledge in a clear and positive manner. So many advertising sales people seemed daunted at trying to sell big adverts. Geoff's philosophy was that providing you can justify it to yourself then let the prospective client tell you that it's too big or too expensive. He can do that on his own without any help at all. Gareth gave a brilliant illustration of this sort of attitude by relating a story of his time selling scales. He had gone into a small grocery shop in a tiny village in Mid Wales. The shop was run by a middle aged lady for whom a pair of scales that would weigh ten pounds of potatoes would have been more than adequate. However Gareth demonstrated various models including the top one which could manage a hundredweight. He suggested, more in hope and amusement that this set of scales which was the most expensive in the range would be absolutely ideal for her every need for years to come. To his amazement she agreed and said that they would be perfectly fine and YES she would have them. Gareth put the order through but he was a little disturbed that the lady had gone somewhat over the top. However, she took delivery, and Gareth made a point of going to see her a few weeks later with a view to changing it if she was not happy with her choice. On entering she told Gareth that she was absolutely thrilled and delighted with it though she rarely weighed anything bigger than two pounds of sugar. She told him that people were coming miles from the villages all around to see these massive scales, many of them had become regular customers and as she said "business has increased amazingly beyond belief".

Geoff found that there were several advertising salesmen who didn't think that advertising worked ! Good grief he thought if they think that they must be in the wrong job. The problem thought Geoff was not the product or the media it was the salesmen themselves. The prospective advertisers were better at not buying than they were at selling. "It's too expensive" "Tried it once and it doesn't work" "Nobody reads the ads" "I've never bought anything because of an advert and I don't think other people do either" Geoff did agree with those retailers who said that word of mouth from satisfied customer's was the best form of advertising, and of course it is - because it's free and it's a personal recommendation from a satisfied buyer.

So thought Geoff if your press advert brings in even one new customer that can soon multiply through his first hand experience so the value of an advert cannot be quantified in the short term. So this is a good reason to advertise regularly. In his experience several retailers seem to be disappointed when nobody says "I saw your ad in today's paper" Geoff would retort with "When you go into a shop to purchase a pair of socks or a tie do you say that you came in because you saw their advert in the local paper"? Maybe – but unlikely.

Advertising is an important arm of retailing as indeed are the window dressing and the personal salesmanship of the staff, but advertising is the one arm that is probably the most neglected by the smaller businesses, hence the reason that's why they remain small.

Gareth's role was discipline and support of the sales team as well as the in-house training and in-the-field training. Most days he would be with one of the members of the sales team accompanying them on their calls for that day. Prior to seeing a prospective client he would establish from the salesman what the objective of the call was. It may be to sell a six inch double column advert. After the sales pitch had been made Gareth would assess the salesman's performance making appropriate comments. These were known as kerbside conferences. At the end of the day he would give an appraisal of the day's activities. This covered everything from personal appearance, the cleanliness of the company car, the preparation for the day, the presentation standard, the sales pitch and the all important asking for the sale. These would be marked either A for good B being acceptable or C below standard. The whole thing was discussed with the sales person and then filed for the attention of the manager.

Each sales person was required to complete a DAILY CALL CARD this ideally was filled in after each call: it simply required name of prospect, size of ad sold, or reason for not buying and future action.   It was not a popular chore but used correctly it was a invaluable planning aid.

Training was essential. Every new member of staff underwent an induction course. The first thing was to introduce the newcomer to all members of staff within the department and what their roles were. They were shown where the toilets and the canteen were located as well as who ran the football burster. They were introduced to the managing director, the manager of each department and anyone they were likely to encounter on a regular basis. In the case of newly recruited salesmen they were given a training manual and spent the biggest part of the first week in the training room before they were allowed out on to their territory. They were then placed on a week's formal training together with new recruits into other Thomson Newspapers which took place in Newcastle on Tyne.

These courses gave a wealth of knowledge both in selling and preparing an advertisement. Geoff had found that many retailers would ask the question "How much should I spend on advertising" If it had not been for his training He nor most of his colleagues would have known the answer except for a vague "depends on your turnover" Many local retailers did not want to divulge what their turnover was but Geoff used the knowledge of the retail sales pound to good effect. The retail sales pound suggested that 11% of turnover was used to pay wages. Well there was only one way to find out and that was to test it. Geoff was quite familiar with a local retailer who had advertised once a month for several years. He had four ladies working for him in the business of selling fabrics for curtains and dresses, specialising in Irish linen. He was a very approachable sort of person. Ideal for Geoff's experiment.

At that particular time he thought the average shop worker would earn around £12 a week add on another £12 a week for his book keeper and £30 for himself. Total weekly wage bill £90 multiply this by 11 which was roughly 9% and BINGO the estimated turnover would be around £52,000 so accordingly he should be spending around £1400 a year on advertising. It was a simple, unsophisticated method. But did it work?

Geoff went to see Mr Williams the proprietor of the linen shop explaining what he had done. "I realise this is a cheek and I'm not asking you to give me any figures but are you prepared to tell me that I'm a long way off or pretty close in my assessment of your annual turnover"

"Yes go ahead I'd be most interested in what you've come up with"

"I reckon it's between £50,000 and £55,000"

"That's astounding" he replied. "It's more than pretty good. I know that you will treat in confidence but it's £56,500"

Geoff was thrilled that a few minutes thought and a simple calculation had produced such a close figure. However he thought it's done more than that - . it's shown one prospect that he knew what he was talking about and would give him extra credibility. The Retail Sales Graph also showed the twelve months of the year and the percentage of business each type of retail outlet would achieve for each month. So if the Annual turnover was £100,000 and it was agreed to spend £3000 on advertising then we should recommend that the retailer uses that same percentage of his budget indicated by the graph. If turnover percentage in February was 8% then you use 8% of the £3000 in that month (ie £240) and if it's 15% in November then you can recommend £450 . Some retailers thought it better to advertise when business was low, but as Geoff said "You can't buck the trend, and it's no use fishing when the fish ain't biting but maximise when folk are in a buying mood"   Geoff planned to use this to good affect before long for Mr Williams business. Horace Williams was what might be called a charming, old fashioned retailer who had a very pleasing shop just off the town centre. He sold good quality products, and was a very keen supporter of CREWE ALEXANDRA football club who seldom missed a home game. At the first call Geoff had made to the business Mr Williams made it very clear that the bottom right hand corner of the back page was his and nobody else's. Geoff agreed that he would honour that understanding, excepting on the weeks that he was not advertising. Mr. Williams hadn't too much option so agreed that was very fair. Once a month he had an advert that measured 4 inches deep over the width of two column. The copy always included the wording Irish Linen Specialists. The shop had a narrow frontage with the entrance set back somewhat which gave them extra window space. The door had a bell which chimed when anyone walked into the rather long shopping area. There were usually three or four assistants with tape measures over their shoulders who greeted everyone with a friendly smile. At the end of the counter which ran the full length of the shop stood Mrs Williams

"Good morning Mrs Williams" Geoff would say "and how are you"?

She would respond with "Very well thank you, I suppose you are here to see Mr Williams are you"?

"Well yes Mrs Williams I would appreciate that"

"Then one moment please whilst I see if he is free"

"Thank you very much"

She would now take a couple of strides to her left where there was a partitioned area that sufficed as 'the office' complete with a small desk and telephone. Mr Williams would have heard every word, but nothing must deter from the approved routine "Mr Williams " she would say "are you available to see Mr Pritchard from the Chronicle?"

To which came the standard retort. "Thank you Mrs Williams, Yes I'm always pleased to see Mr Pritchard, please show him in"

She would now take two paces to the right and say "Yes Mr Pritchard, Mr Williams is available and will be pleased to see you"

"Thank you Mrs Williams" and with that he would walk in to see the client. This was enacted on every visit without revising the script. We could all hear one another, but it was an old-world-charm routine that we went through.

The newspaper sales targets increased regularly and the training we'd received suggested that the most efficient way to meet these increases was to get regular advertisers to increase the size of their advertising. Sounds simple - but in reality it was not easy to get somebody to increase the size of the advert which they had been running for years and which had proved to be beneficial to them. However we could try increasing the number of adverts they placed over a twelve month period, and in many cases this worked well. BUT not with Mr Williams, who made it abundantly clear that his 4inch double column ad had served him well and they saw no particularly good reason to increase his spend. However Geoff thought there must be a mutually beneficial way to satisfy us both Then he had an inspirational moment. Why, why, oh why did he always insist on that same spot on the back page of the paper every time he advertised? Especially as his adverts were particularly aimed at the housewife whereas the back page was always the main sports page with reports on Crewe Alex which would have a predominance of male readers who don't give a monkeys whether he sells Irish Linen or toffee apples. It struck Geoff that his advert was probably for self gratification. He wanted his name to be on the sports page with his sporting heroes. The response to his advert was important to him but so was having his name on that page. His 4x2 advert occupied 8inches of space. So, Geoff thought, if he had a space one inch deep across the eight columns it would still be eight inches and cost just the same. A lovely man, but, Geoff thought, he was quite likely a vain man. He was spot on. Mr Williams loved the idea. On

Wednesday afternoon when Geoff saw the advert in the paper he knew that he had won. The next day he made him the first call. With a copy of the paper in his hand they went through the usual routine. This time Geoff changed his usual opening "Mr Williams have you seen the ad" he asked, but without waiting for a response added quite quickly said "I'm so sorry - you must be terribly disappointed with the result"

"Oh no" was the reply "I got my copy early this morning and I'm rather pleased with it" "Well I'm glad about that but personally I didn't think your name stood out as much as it should do, so I've asked the editor if he would allow us to make it half an inch bigger. If you are agreeable that would make a massive difference"

Mr Williams stroked his chin and looked thoughtfully at the advert. "Yes" he said "after all it's only another half an inch, so yes let's go for it next time". Half an inch isn't much but it meant that his advert had increased from eight inches to twelve inches and in Geoff's book that was a 50% increase.

Sometime later towards the end of the year Geoff suggested that it be increased by another half inch. He agreed , which meant that his original space had doubled from its original size. Yes – he was a lovely man, agreeable and perhaps a little vain. But who cares he was happy and so was Geoff.

Making target was never an easy task and called sometimes for a degree of ingenuity from all the staff. They would have brainstorming sessions on the different features they could do in order to entice retailers to advertise. Probably the most popular were SHOPPING IN HIGH STREET or FOOTBALL SEASON STARTS etc All sorts of Ideas were put forward, but the one that Geoff absolutely refused to be associated with was CONFUCIUS HE SAY etc. The idea was Confucius he say "me no like riding in rickshaw. The solution he buy a nice new car from ABC Motors. But Ron absolutely loved it, but then it was his idea. He sold a full page feature in no time. It was fun – it was imaginative and it helped make our monthly target. Well done Ron.

Geoff learned a valuable lesson from Gareth when they were double calling one day.

Geoff had a tendency to have a friendly chat following a successful sale. For example his notes showed that a regular customers daughter had taken her A levels some few months ago so he would enquire about her success. All this took time and sometimes led on to other topics.

On this particular day they went into CARTERS the JEWELLER where Geoff got on very well with George the proprietor. Geoff made his pitch, George liked the layout that was presented to him and with minor adjustments was happy to place the business. As soon as the business ended Gareth said "Thanks for the order Mr Carter, lovely to have met you. We'll go and process the order for you now" Geoff was rather put out by this and was about to say something when Mr Carter said. "Nice to meet you too Mr Thomas. That's the way I like to do business, Nice and brisk so that I can get on with other things"

So!! thought Geoff what he had regarded as a nice cosy after sales chat was in fact more of an intrusion into a clients working day.

Gareth made a point of this saying that Geoff did have a tendency to linger "Take my advice" he said "Get in, make your presentation and the moment he says yes get out" Geoff said that he felt uncomfortable with that, but would bear it in mind whenever he called to see MR CARTER.

Geoff though used his own discretion on the majority of calls but regretted having done so on one particular occasion. The prospect was far from being a regular advertiser and Geoff thought it was time he was back in the paper. He entered with confidence but not much hope so was pleased when the prospect immediately said that he'd been thinking about taking an advert in the paper so he was glad that Geoff had gone in. They sorted out the copy quite quickly and Geoff added a few pleasantries about the weather and holidays. The prospect said "Do you know while we've been chatting I've decided not to bother with the advert" Try as he might Geoff could not change his mind, and he never knew why, but wished he had taken Gareth's advice.

Jim Alexander had been appointed Sales Director of Thomson Newspapers by his fellow Canadian and owner of the group, Roy Thomson, who was to become Lord Thomson of Fleet. Jim had the wonderful combination of being a first class graphic designer and a brilliant salesman. Prior to coming to England he had been employed as a graphic designer by a newspaper in Canada . Jim believed in big bold ads, the bigger the better so when he received a brief from any of the sales staff he would design something a great deal larger than what they had indented for. Frequently this resulted in the sales staff returning to the office telling Jim that the prospect had liked the layout but it was too big. Jim got fed up with his work being turned down. "What the hell's up with you guys, I produce great ads that are far superior to anything you've ever had before and you can't sell the bloody things. What I'll do is go out and sell the blasted things myself". Not only did he design and sell the ads he also started advising retailers how they could make more sales. As an example he made a presentation to one department store and made a few observations to the proprietor about the stores layout.

"Do you know sir I came in here an hour prior to our appointment just to take a look around to see if there were any pointers that I thought may help you. You have a wonderful store with good quality items, your ladies wear department is easy to find and so is the menswear, but I didn't want anything from them I simply wanted a collar and lead for my dog, but you have no signs up saying Pets Accessories this way, but you have a load of signs pointing to the Exit. You must have high overheads in this store with rates and wages and it costs you money to get them in, so when they are in why the hell make it so easy for them to get out by having Exit signs all over the place. Keep 'em in - they may have come in for a new hat and coat but while they are here get them to buy a tin of biscuits or a new bike, but don't tell them how to get out."

The proprietor said that he was most impressed by the comments and that he would certainly look into it, which he did. Result EXIT signs were taken down, shoppers stayed in store longer and made more purchases. Turnover and profits increased and so did the advertising budget. He became a tremendous asset to the Thomson group. There were no airs or graces about Jim who had some wonderful stories appropriate to a sales team. One day he was attending a sales training group of newly recruited salesmen.

They were intently listening to what he had to say and Jim was stressing about leaving no stone unturned in pursuit of making a sale.

"You lot sat here need to be resourceful, sniff around a bit more, get into places you've never been before and you may well be pleasantly surprised at what you find. In fact in this room is something worth finding, but you won't find it sat on your arses. So get off your backsides have a good look around the room, don't miss anything and you can keep whatever you find.

After some searching one of the trainees tilted the chair he'd been sat on and found a five pound note Sellotaped to the bottom of the seat and so claimed the prize. Jim gave him a good natured rollicking "Good God man you've had your arse perched on it all this time and didn't know it was there. I wonder if there are any businesses on your territory that you didn't think it was worth going in to sell them an ad. If so go in and see what you can do. Remember prospects are good at saying 'no' so don't say it for them . and you may get a surprise as they could well say 'yes'. On another occasion he related a story when he was flying to Belfast. As he sat down the stewardess asked if he'd like a drink. "Thank you, I'll have a Scotch please" Before she had chance to go Jim was joined by another passenger. Jim turned to him and said that he'd ordered a drink and would he care to join him? "Thhhhhhank you verrry mmmuch" came the reply "I'd love a whhhhisky ppplease". As they enjoyed the drink Jim explained that he was in newspapers and was visiting the Belfast Telegraph. Are you going on business or pleasure he asked his fellow passenger.

"Oohhhhhhhh Immm gggggggggggoing for an inteeeeeerview with the BBC" "That's interesting us both being in media" said Jim "and what type of work are you applying for, camera man, accountancy"

"Ohhh nnnnnooo" stammered the man "I want to be an annnnnnounnceeer". Rather taken back by his response Jim asked "Do you fancy your chances of getting the job"

"Nnnnnnnnnnnnnooott really Iiii ththiiin theyllll give it to a Cccccatholic. Of course the point of the story was that no matter what or who you are you have to display initiative and overcome any adversity, be single minded enough to get your message across to your prospects and above all be optimistic.

Interestingly it's not just from formal training and experience that we can learn but from the most unexpected sources.   It was the day prior to Jacqueline's birthday and Dorothy was preparing for the party to which she had invited several friends, some were from her school and others lived in the neighbourhood. All the mums from around about had agreed that when the children had reached a certain age they would no longer have a traditional party. Jacqueline was coming up to that age. Next door were two sisters both of whom were a few years younger than Jacqueline so did not qualify to attend because of the age difference.

Geoff was in the house preparing a few games for the party when there was a knock at the back door, which Dorothy answered.   It was the girls from next door Alison and Keeley. "Oh Auntie Dorothy what a lovely cake. I suppose it's for Jacqueline's birthday she's so lucky having a mum who can bake cakes like that. It really is beautiful. Dorothy replied "Why thank you Alison, but I'm sure your mum makes you a lovely cake when it's your birthday"

"No she doesn't she has to buy one, you're so clever to do that. Unfortunately I'm too young to come to Jacqueline's party, but those who come will love that. Then you and Uncle Geoff will have a slice as well as Robert and Jacqueline's Grandma and Grandad. I think there'll be plenty to go round don't you Auntie Dorothy"

Geoff was taking all this in and could predict where it was going to.

Dorothy replied that she hoped there would be some left over.

"I think you're right Auntie Dorothy so with what's left you could cut two small pieces off one for Keeley and one for me" Geoff waited for Dorothy's reply thinking 'come on then my dear get out of that' !

She couldn't. "Yes I can do that for you" replied Dorothy.

Allison hadn't quite finished her sales pitch, "Thank you very much, if you wrap it up I'll call round for it the day after the party"

"Yes of course " said Dorothy

SALE ACHIEVED ! No nonsense no frills she was going to get some cake and just to nail it she wasn't going to rely on Dorothy taking it around. She'd do that. "Wow what a sales lady she's going to be" said Geoff "As soon as you answered the door she knew exactly what she wanted and how to get it. She could teach some of our sales staff a thing or two."

No matter what or who you are you have to display initiative and have the means to overcome an adversity, be single minded, get your message across clearly and above all be optimistic.

CHAPTER 8 –
SOME TOUGH CUSTOMERS

In order to measure success all Thomson salesmen were set a target by the advertising manager who in turn got the annual departmental target from the managing director, who, in turn would have been set the overall company revenue target by head office via the advertising controller. At local level the Managing director would have added a "little bit of insurance" into the figure received from above. Then the Advertising Manager would have added on his " little bit of insurance" Local targets were based on the volume figures produced for the same month of the previous year and then add on the percentage rise in advertising rates plus the ad managers "little bit of insurance".

All individual salesmen could do was moan and complain because their targets were far too high, but of course it didn't make a scrap of difference as you being the last link in the chain were stuck with it. All the salesman had a basic salary plus two sets of bonuses; one being for meeting his or her own target and the other was when the team target was met. Ron and Geoff worked rather well together, and whilst they were both keen and enthusiastic about their own performance they did help one another out when it was possible. As an example if either one was short of making his target the other would 'lend' the other an advert. So if Geoff was, say, £50 short of target Ron would 'lend' him a clients advert of that price if he was over target. This way they kept face and more importantly each got their bonus. As it so happened this was an agreement they hardly ever had to resort to.

Thomson newspapers had a system whereby each newspaper sent a copy of their newspaper to every other Thomson newspaper. As there were well over thirty papers it didn't take long to amass a pile of them. Many were morning papers and had little in them that were appropriate. Several though were excellent and well worth keeping. Those that were not wanted were kept on one side and a deal was struck with a local fish and chip shop who brought in portions of fish and chips in exchange for all the unwanted papers. Geoff and Ron did wonder if his regular customers ever puzzled over getting their fish supper wrapped up in the Belfast Telegraph or the Scotsman.

A great deal of the advertising was sold in editorially supported features. It may be on the opening of the fishing season, shopping in a particular road, the launch of a new car or where to head for on your summer holiday. On one occasion Geoff had a phone call from Miss Forster who had a very highly thought of Milliners business in Crewe. She was also an active voluntary member of Cancer Research. She had decided to hold an event at a local hostelry to raise funds for this cause and had a number of local retailers who were supporting her by having a stall at the venue. She asked Geoff if he could arrange to have some editorial to support her efforts and supplied him with the exhibitors who she hoped would buy advertising space in the feature. One of these was a ladies hairstylist by the name of COIFFURE FRANCAISE who had resisted every effort by Geoff to advertise in the paper. But this was different 'Yes he'd be glad to give support to such a good cause' He gave Geoff a good illustration of the style he would like portrayed in his advert and Geoff suggested that as it was early 1976 that they have a heading of GREAT NEW STYLES FOR '76.

They agreed the price and size of the advert and Geoff went on his way delighted with this breakthrough. As usual he and Ron went to Chester on Wednesday which was the day the Chronicle was printed. They were both pleased with the look of the feature: it was in a nice early position in the paper Miss Forster would be delighted. But Geoff was not at all pleased -- he was furious for the heading now read GREAT NEW STYLE FOR 7/6. Oh for goodness sake their lowest price was 3 guineas. What a botch up! Where's the overseer? How dare they make changes to my copy? He dreaded facing the client in the morning. How do I cope with this Geoff asked himself. It was the overseer who had changed it: he simply thought the / should have been between the two figures not in front of it. "In future don't bloody think. ask, ask me"

The next morning Geoff tried to phone Coiffure Francaise but it was continually engaged. After several attempts to contact the client Geoff turned his attention to other things. Minutes later his phone rang, it was Coiffure Francaise. Geoff recognised his voice and said "I'm so sorry" and went on to explain. "Listen Geoff" he said "you've tried very hard in the past to persuade me to advertise with you and when I do it's a real cock up, and I've explained to a lot of ladies this morning that it was an error by the paper. BUT I've learned a lesson and I do now realise that people do read the paper thoroughly. I'd like you to call in later in the day and arrange for me to have a regular advert in the Chronicle, probably say once a month" Can I call ! You bet I can! Thought Geoff. Wheew what a relief.

The nature of the business was such that each new day replicated to some degree the events of the previous day, last week, last month and even the previous year. Even so there were sufficient happenings to give a tinge of excitement which gave a new outlook or produced a fresh challenge. The sales staff were in fact somewhat competitive amongst themselves: each of them wanting to achieve sales figures that were at least as good, and hopefully better than those of their colleagues. In addition there was also the Classified Advertising Department which dealt mainly with Estate Agents, Situations Vacant and Car Dealers.

As strange as it may seem people who worked in Classified sales were the main competitors the Display sales staff had to contend with. Classified sales staff could approach any type of retail business whereas the Display team were not allowed to touch vacancy, property or used car advertisers. Geoff and his colleagues must stick solely to the retail trade. This did cause a little bit of animosity, but when the papers came out on a Wednesday they would forget their differences pop over the road, have a couple of drinks, a few laughs, and a bit of leg pulling together.

The reason for this was that the Classified advertising rate was higher than that of the Display department so management generally preferred the higher rate. There was though one exception to this NEW cars were news so it was acceptable that any new car advertising could be run on the news pages.

This meant that Geoff and his colleagues had to use a bit of initiative. One idea they came up with and used to good effect was to design a half page advert with a brand new car under a very bold heading which read:

This Brand New Car is yours for FREE (providing you buy the spark plug for £5400)

Take heed ! Always read the small print

Geoff was rather surprised when he took a phone call from the manager of the local Woolworths store who asked him to call and see him if possible that afternoon. It was mid November and Geoff was intrigued because Woolworths never advertised in the provincial weeklies. When he arrived the manager told him that he had a modest budget to spend on advertising turkeys for Christmas. The ad contained an illustration of a roast turkey as well as a coupon for would be purchasers to put their name, address, phone number and approximate weight of turkey they needed. Geoff was feeling rather self satisfied and managed to get quite a good position early on in the CHRONICLE. On the day the paper was published Ron looked at the ad and said to Geoff "What a bloody awful advert, a complete waste of money"

"Well Ron, come on tell me what's wrong with it"

"There's no address in it"

"Ron it's Woolworths everybody knows where Woolworth are"

"OK, let's go outside and test it".

At that time the office was somewhat off centre to the town and so there were not too many people around. Full of confidence Geoff went outside with Ron. There was an elderly couple just walking from the town centre to the car park carrying their shopping bags. "Right Ron this is it they'll know exactly where Woolworths are" "Excuse me I wonder if you could direct us to Woolworths please? asked Geoff. Beaming down at them in the full and certain knowledge that they would give precise instructions. "Woolworths – Woolworths? No I dunna know" replied the man "What abart you" he asked turning to his wife.

"Ah know where they are in the Potteries but I dunna know where they are in Crewe" Geoff looked askance, everybody but everybody knows where Woolworths are Geoff thought to himself whatever is up with these yokels? However he thanked them, looked at the beaming face of Ron and returned to the office. "Bloody idiots" said Geoff.

"They are not, but possibly you are" was the best Geoff could get out of Ron. However he did think to himself 'Yes you're right Ron that was the most basic error. Thankfully the Woolworths manager was over the moon with the response and asked for it to be repeated. It was, but this time with the address.

Gee thanks Ron!

Looking back Geoff often thought to himself how pleasurable it was to have so many good quality independent traders rather than all the supermarkets and multiples that were to come later, and further down the line nobody in their right mind could have envisaged buying on line. Why not? Simply because computers were still a long way into the future.   But that's what they call progress. Huddled over a keyboard, looking what to choose on a screen, press a button, fifty or sixty quid goes out of their account. So cold, so uninteresting and all so impersonal. If that's progress thought Geoff 'I dread to think what's around the corner. I may be old fashioned but I love it'.

His memories took him back to that wonderful, wonderful leatherwear shop that was in Nantwich and run by Mr and Mrs Pearson. The wonderful aroma that only good quality leather can have. A huge selection of suitcases, briefcases, handbags and ancillary products. Not cheap by any means but the quality shone through and the prices were always fair. All served by the most charming couple you could encounter, and they were not afraid to spend a decent amount on advertising, and they welcomed Geoff's help in the design and timing of their adverts.

There was only one department store in Nantwich. It was known as Stretch and Harlock. It was thought to have been established for over two hundred years. They had been advertising in the Chronicle for many years so Geoff did not have to do any hard work in order to sell the idea of press advertising. It was run by Kenneth Harlock and his sister who Geoff simply knew as Miss Harlock.

They were absolutely delightful, genuine people with whom it was a privilege to do business. Sometimes Geoff did wonder if his visits were something of an intrusion on their time. But they were such nice people they would never dream of telling him so. It was mid October when he went in to the store with a proposed full schedule of advertising for the Christmas offerings. He was well prepared with details of all the plans he had for them during this peak period. He had the dates that he thought they should advertise together with the sizes of the adverts, the costing and complete layouts including the headlines and body copy and just to put the finishing touch Geoff had prepared for the January sale advert as well. Geoff was a little apprehensive about how this would be received by Kenneth but he'd prepared well. "Mr Harlock I've taken the liberty of coming up with a schedule for your Christmas advertising. I realise it may seem a little premature, but I am aware that we are fast approaching the busiest time of the year when you will be wanting to concentrate your efforts into the daily running of the store rather than have me popping in and out at such a hectic time."

members could be proud of and in turn invite their pals along. He made contact with various breweries to see if he could negotiate better terms, but he knew that members enjoyed the drinks from the current brewery, and he did not want to dispense with their services. Another brewery offered them better terms but the original brewery promptly came up with an even better deal. So it all remained 'as you were' but with reduced prices. Jobs a good'un thought Geoff. There was a great deal of controversy when it was decided to enter one of The CROWN GREEN BOWLING LEAGUES It meant that the green was not open to members on alternate Monday evenings due to the league matches being played. Nor had anyone thought that the game was now becoming popular with ladies, many of whom were quite good bowlers who had managed to get into the league teams of their respective clubs. This meant the unthinkable - ladies who were in such teams would be allowed to walk on the hallowed turf.

Geoff was stuck with the situation: on the one hand it had deprived members of several Monday evenings on the green - but on the other hand it had increased the potential bar sales. It's right what they say 'You can't have it both ways' Geoff was accused of wanting ladies in the club as members, but nothing could have been further from the truth. He enjoyed it as men only and such venues were disappearing all too quickly. But in due course ladies were given the opportunity to become members. It was never quite the same from then on.

As the children were getting older Dorothy decided it was time for her to go back to work on a part time basis. At first she became a 'dinner lady' at a local school which she rather enjoyed with other mothers who lived close by. However she made a successful application to become a rent collector with Crewe Council. This gave her an enhanced rate of pay for her work on Friday, Saturday and Monday mornings. The children were growing up, as children do, and for a while Jacqueline had broadened her horizons to include the possibility of becoming a model which is the dream of many but the reality for very, very few. She had seen an advert for a company who were inviting young ladies to visit them at a hotel in Chester where they would be assessed for their potential in a modelling career. Geoff thought this sounded rather 'fishy' but he and Dorothy agreed to take her.

They were shown into a room where they met a pleasant young woman who told Jacqueline that she had wonderful potential and her prospects of being successful were extremely good. All she had to do was to pay £300 for a selection of various photographs that would be contained in a presentation pack. These would then be sent to various agencies and she would get her money back plus a great deal more in the next few months.

Jacqueline was thrilled. Geoff was dubious to say the least, but asked "Do you really think that her chances are that good"

"Most certainly, she will have the opportunity to make fantastic money"

"That's good to hear" said Geoff "so let's do a deal. You take the pictures for free and you take all the fees she earns for the first six months"

Geoff's generous offer was declined. "So" he said "if you are not prepared to take on such a generous offer it rather suggests that you haven't got the faith in Jacqueline's prospects or in your ability to find her work yourself. So thank you for your time but we must decline your offer"

Geoff was in Jacqueline's bad books as she was in tears for much of the return journey. A few months later it was shown up as a nationwide scam which thousands of girls had parted with their money and got nothing in return. On the plus side she was accepted into Salford Royal Hospital to become a State Registered Nurse. Geoff was so pleased for her but was really upset when he, Dorothy and Robert took her in the car one Sunday to start her training. They were shown the accommodation that the new intake would have. Apparently it had only just been completed so everywhere was spotlessly clean. Geoff wondered how long it would stay like that. It was fortunate that Jacqueline met up with Bernadette another girl from Crewe and they became quite good friends.

About twelve months after going to Salford the two girls decided they would like to find their own flat. Geoff and Dorothy thought it was madness as the rent was far too high compared with what they were earning. They tried to persuade them to stay in the nurses home, but they were adamant they wanted their independence. Jacqueline told her mum and dad that Bernadette's dad was paying his daughters share of the rent.

"Jacqueline I told you that once you were eighteen you would have to look after yourself and not to ask for any financial help. You have made the decision to move into accommodation that is far too high relative to what you are earning. But it's your decision and you can be sure that neither your mother or I will help with financing you. So money wise you are on your own".

At weekends when she went home Dorothy always packed a few sandwiches and some cake up for her to take back to Salford. With her training completed she found a job at Leighton hospital, Crewe It was then that she rather surprisingly said to Geoff "Thank you for teaching me a very good lesson in life by not helping me with my finances. The snack that Mum put up for me to take back I kept and ate them as a main meal during the week. And Bernadette had used her wages to buy new clothes through every credit card that was available at that time and had run up heavy debts. So I thought you really mean at the time but I now know it was a very sensible decision and I learnt the true value of money".

Eventually Jacqueline got married to Gareth Roberts, a fireman at Crewe Fire Station. They had two children Megan who became an occupational therapist and Matthew who sadly was diagnosed at a early age as being autistic. He works at one or two cafeterias as well as a large railway hotel. He is a cheerful lad and popular with the customers from whom he receives generous tips.

Jacqueline and Gareth are now both retired and take an active role in helping with various activities associated with autism and help to run a specialist swimming pool activities for the autistic. In 2017 Jacqueline was delighted to receive a invitation to the Garden Party at Buckingham Palace which she attended with her friend. Quite an honour.

Robert had gone to college and finished up with very creditable grades He found work in a railway warehouse before widening his experience and going into a variety of warehousing projects. He gained a certificate for warehouse management and also in Health and Safety at work. He met up with a delightful girl by the name of Lisa. They lived together for about ten years and then decided to go their own separate ways. Robert went as a Ski instructor in France for a while before returning home where for a little while he lived in the family home. He then met up with a young lady he had known since school days by the name of Julia. She had been married previously and had one son. They got married in Cyprus, but unfortunately Dorothy was diagnosed with breast cancer and the date she was given to go into hospital was the date they had arranged to get married ! Sadly Dorothy and Geoff thought it best to have the surgery rather than wait for several more months before the chance came up again. Although disappointed they were delighted to see how well they got on together.

Julia is the manageress in a local solicitors practice and Robert is Health and Safety Manager for a large national company.

A STEP UP THE LADDER

It was announced at a Wednesday afternoon meeting that Gareth Thomas had accepted a post with the Newcastle Evening Chronicle. Geoff was pleased for him and hopeful for himself. The following day he was asked by ALAN CROFTS if he would be interested in taking over from Gareth as the Sales Supervisor. Was he interested? Boy oh boy he certainly was more than he could describe However it would be a few weeks before Gareth left and Geoff wanted to go out with a bang and the opportunity arose on Friday when he phoned Roy Townsend at Breeden and Middleton in Crewe. Roy had been employed as a milk delivery rounds-man with the Co-op Dairy. He loaded up early in the morning and went on his round with a pull-along electric milk float. One place he delivered to was B and M situated in the High Street. They had a good name for quality televisions, selling mainly BANG and OLUFSEN range. As he rented his own TV from them he called in on a Friday morning to pay his rental and to leave their milk . On the counter was a pile of leaflets headed INTRODUCE A FRIEND TO OUR RENTAL SCHEME AND WE WILL PAY YOU £1.

Roy took a good few with him and dropped them off at houses where he delivered milk. A few days later he had four completed leaflets, took them into B & M and promptly collected £4. This went on and before long he had received £30 for his initiative. Mr Middleton left word that he wanted to meet this gentleman when he was next in. This resulted in Roy being offered a job in the store as sales manager.

He made rapid progress. One of the first things he did was to have the sales staff in and told them that he was hiring a large van from a local haulier called Lathams. This would arrive on Monday morning and they were all to help in loading as many TV sets on to the back of the vehicle as they possibly could. Once loaded Roy directed the driver to head for the town centre which had numerous streets criss-crossing one another. When they reached an appropriate spot all the staff took a TV set knocked a door and simply said "Good morning I'm from Breeden and Middleton and I'd like to leave this television with you to try for a week – if you don't like it we will take it off your hands, but if you would prefer to keep it you can do so for a rental of £1 a week". Only a handful of people turned the offer down and returned it at the end of the weeks trial.

Geoff found that one thing about selling advertising was that it called for initiative, perseverance but above all faith – faith in yourself – faith in the product. If you didn't possess these then, oh, boy it would be really hard work. Worse still though if you lack enjoyment it will show through and you just would not be successful. Nobody in any sales job can truthfully say that they didn't miss an opportunity. Geoff certainly did but such happenings were few and far between.

There was a certain ladies hairdressing salon in Nantwich who had never placed any advertising in the paper and Geoff was determined to change that. There was no way that he could foresee the problems it was going to cause. On entering the salon he approached the gorgeous blonde haired, elegant, receptionist and asked who he should speak to regarding advertising. The receptionist told him that she was far too busy at the moment to speak to him, but if he were to call back at another time it would be better. He did call back but failed to sell an advert to the proprietor. However he did discover that the receptionists name was Yvonne Ormes who before too long became Miss Great Britain, and was also to be a favoured contestant in Miss World.

Roy Townsend phoned Geoff and asked him if he could call and see him as soon as possible. Geoff took the short walk to B and M where the receptionist said "Roy's got someone in at the moment so could you take a seat in the waiting room - he shouldn't be too long, I'll get you a coffee".

There were a pile of trade journals on the table by which Geoff was sitting so he picked one up; as he did so a loose insert fell to the floor. Picking it up he saw that it was a publicity 'cheque' for £50 to any dealership which sold a certain number of that companies TV sets by the month end. Geoff was impressed as it looked like a genuine cheque, he picked it up wondering if a similar promotion could be used by B and M. Well he was in the shop and would be speaking to the man who could make that decision within the next few minutes.

"OK Geoff, sorry to have kept you, come on in" said Roy

"That's OK Roy as a matter of fact that little delay might prove to be quite invaluable" and he went on to explain about the cheque "You know Roy that's something we could adapt to the benefit of B and M, but instead of putting in a cheque we could use a false bank note which would be much more impressive to the readers than a cheque. I could get our studio to work on it without committing you to anything".

Roy liked the suggestion so Geoff arranged to have a half pager advert drawn up together with a mock £10 note which would be headed THE BANK OF BREEDEN AND MIDDLETON which then went 'Promise to pay the bearer £10 against the purchase of any television set in the Bang and Olufsen range valued at £100 or more' At that time £5 notes were blue so we wanted to make a strong similarity but to distinguish between a real note and our fake we made the value £10."Just imagine Roy when they open the paper this note will float down to the floor" "Geoff you've completely sold me the idea I love it. Let me see the final work and then we can fix a date for it to appear"

Geoff briefed the studio who thought it a fabulous idea and wanted to get the note a faithful likeness. It was the studio manager who asked what do we do about the Queens head. Somehow they didn't think Her Majesty would like to represent the Bank of Breeden and Middleton.

"You are so right" said Geoff "but I do think I may know someone who would be only too willing to replace Her Majesty. I'll ring her in the morning"

Prompt on 9'oclock the following morning he made the phone call,

"Yvonne how would you like to replace the Queen on a £10 note"?

Geoff explained precisely what they were doing and that there would be a modest fee for her. Yvonne readily agreed and suggested that he call into the shop the following day and she would have some head and shoulder pictures to choose from. The picture was sent to the studio who produced a great advert and a spectacularly good mocked up £10 note. Roy gave his final approval. A date for the promotion was agreed. Geoff visited the print works early on the Wednesday it was all due to happen. He didn't want anything to go wrong on this and would keep his beady eye on things until he saw everything coming off the press. Wally Bowden was the overseer in the print room "Hey Geoff, take a quick look at this note and see if it's OK before I get them all runoff"

"Wally" said Geoff "the note itself is fine but the blue is far too insipid" and with that he took a fiver out of his pocket saying that this was the shade he wanted. Wally's next attempt was much better so Geoff agreed they could now be run off. It just so happened that when any loose leaflets had to be put into any of the papers as they came off the press Wally had to have a team of ladies waiting at the end of the press to put them inside the paper. Wally seemed to enjoy these occasions as he went all round the building opening all the doors and calling out "If any of you ladies want stuffing then get down to the press hall by 2 o'clock" Wally was never short of volunteers! Geoff was absolutely over the moon with this promotion so he thought it would be a feather in his cap by sending it to Jim Alexander who was constantly looking for promotions of this kind so that he could pass on to other papers in the group.

The papers would have been on sale by the time that Geoff got home, and as Dorothy was going out that evening he decided it would be an ideal time to turn over a patch of land which he needed to cultivate. The ground was rather heavy due to prolonged rain but he was not deterred by that so he put on his wellies, grabbed his garden fork and a spade and set to. He had hardly made a start when Reg, his next door neighbour came out to the dividing fence.

"Geoff, can you change a fiver for me please I need some small change"

"Yes of course I can, I'll just pop inside but I won't be a minute".

Wellies off – slippers on - a quick dash upstairs found the necessary change – then went down stairs slippers off - wellies on and outside.

"There we are Reg – just check it over to see it's Ok" and with that he took the £5 note off Reg and put it in his pocket.

Reg roared his head off, you'd better look at that fiver he told Geoff. It was headed Bank of Breeden and Middleton !!

"Caught you good and proper there, mate, but it does look an awful lot like the real thing !!"

Indeed it did. Oh my – what have I done – all sorts of things conjured up in his mind. Nobody could be caught out by them he thought, but then realised he, himself had just been done over. Oh Help.

Geoff wouldn't dare to relate what had happened.

The following morning he was told that Woolworths in Chester had accepted one for the purchase of a packet of crisps and had given change to the customer for a five pound note. They, quite rightly, demanded the Chronicle to reimburse them. Luckily that was the only incident of the kind. Geoff was so thankful – one was bad enough though.

It was 8 o'clock on Saturday morning when there was a loud banging at the door Geoff peeped through the bedroom window it was Roy Townsend and his number two a chap called Ernie. Whatever do they want at this time of day pondered Geoff as he made his way to the door.

On opening the door Roy turned to Ernie and said "Well at least one member of the Chronicle staff hasn't been arrested then"   Geoff looked in amazement

"Arrested. Why should anyone arrest me, but you'd better come in and we'll have a cup of coffee."

"Geoff a terrific promotion but it's somehow backfired on us. I was arrested late last night by the Fraud Squad from Scotland Yard, and had to go to the shop to hand over a stack of those notes. The editor of the CHRONICLE was arrested at 2 o'clock this morning. He had to go into the print works where the artwork and plates for printing and all the leaflets they could find were confiscated."

Both the Editor and Roy had received a severe dressing down and were given strict guidelines about the misuse of Her Majesty's currency.

"But you Geoff, the instigator of it all" said Roy " slept soundly through the night.

I hope you don't get the sack because of this Geoff, but if you do I'll find you a job" "Gee ! thanks Roy would I also get a company car?

His response was unprintable.

Thankfully no other reports came in about any other retailer taking any of the B and M notes. However all members of the sales staff were issued with a set of pamphlets giving the very strict guidelines about the misuse of Her Majesty's currency.

RON had decided to go on to a new job with a large publishing group which produced an excellent range of trade journals. These were highly respected publications printed on a glossy paper and reproduced colour of a very high standard. Geoff was pleased for him but really sorry to see him go.

Gareth left to take up his new appointment and Geoff was to replace him as Sales Supervisor. Geoff's replacement was to be John Parker who was from Liverpool. He was an ardent Liverpool supporter and was very embarrassed when he was provided with a blue car. His mates would never forgive him as they thought he'd changed allegiance.

Geoff didn't want his successor to be unhappy and quickly found a red car which was used by one of the other salesmen who was quite happy to swap for blue. Geoff went to see Roy to tell him of his promotion but assured him he would keep in touch. Roy wished him luck and said "I bet you haven't seen one of these before have you?" and produced from his drawer what he called a pocket calculator and proceeded to demonstrate it. "Look all I do is enter 15 x 9 and it gives an immediate answer 135 isn't that amazing. Now you give me a figure to divide it by" So Geoff knowing full well that it would be impossible for a machine to do said "OK then, this will stump it try divide 135 by 141" Immediately up came 0.9574etc.

Geoff was baffled as to how such a small hand held thing like that could do such a calculation and very impressed when Roy said they only cost £15. Geoff said he would like one but hadn't any money on him. Roy told him to take it and pay him when it's convenient.

There were a pile of small paperback booklets on Roy's desk which were a mini course in the art of salesmanship. When Geoff said they looked interesting Roy said that he had no further use for them and that if he wanted them he could take them off his hands. "But" he said "read them tonight or you'll never read them" Geoff didn't heed his advice and didn't read them that night and furthermore he never did read them until several years later. Roy had a uncanny understanding of how our minds work. That's why he was so successful. He attended a presentation given in London by one of the leading television companies who were to talk on the importance of increasing sales in the in-home entertainment business. With everyone assembled there was an announcement that stated due to unforeseen circumstances the guest speaker was unable to attend. Roy stood up and said that he would be quite happy to volunteer to take the place of the speaker. He was taken unawares, had no notes, no preparation but went ahead and did his own thing at the end of which he received a standing ovation. One person who was present was the managing director of one of the Japanese manufacturers who congratulated him on a wonderful ad-lib presentation and invited him to Japan to do a similar presentation to Japanese retailers. With all expenses paid he did a terrific job and went as the companies guest to similar events on several other occasions GEOFF OFTEN WONDERED – WHAT IF ROY HAD NEVER RENTED HIS TV FROM B and M OR HAD NEVER PICKED UP THOSE LEAFLETS HOW DIFFERENT HIS LIFE MAY HAVE BEEN.

WOULD HE HAVE CARRIED ON WITH HIS ELECTRIC MILK FLOAT? Nobody knows the answer, but Geoff wondered how many of us see opportunities but don't recognise them for what they are?   Far too many he thought. In fact he realised that he may well have been one such person himself, for Roy, Geoff discovered, had many ideas on the subject of salesmanship, some of which were much before their time. He always advocated that the standard of salesmanship particularly in the retail trade was pretty abysmal: and this was something which Geoff agreed with him. In fact he was of the opinion that by and large most shop assistants rarely actually SOLD anything. If a lady for example walked into a shop and bought a loaf of bread and a quarter of boiled ham plus a box of chocolates the shop assistant could not possibly have claimed to have SOLD her anything , because the customer had BOUGHT them. If on the other hand the assistant had said we have some very nice cream cakes would you like half a dozen she would have at least attempted to get the lady to make an additional purchase which could result in a SALE and the assistant would have done a good job. So many missed chances.

CHAPTER 10 –
LOST OPPORTUNITY

Roy put it to Geoff that there was tremendous scope for opening up training sessions for sales assistants in the retail trade and asked him if he would be prepared to go in with him and run these courses in the evening. They were to approach local traders with a view to them sending staff on one of the courses. Geoff rather liked the idea but really couldn't see it being very lucrative so turned the offer down. He had to admit some years later that he was wrong and Roy had been right. As time passed by Industrial Training Boards were set up to cover all types of industries and training itself was to become an expanding market which could command very high fees. Not a good decision Geoff.

One of the main roles of a Sales Supervisor was to ensure that the sales staff were adequately prepared to reach and hopefully exceed their monthly target. It would have been ideal to have a meeting at the start of each day with all the sales staff gathered together and be able to show what they had planned for the day, then to meet again at the end of the day to see what progress each individual had made towards their objectives. Unfortunately this was not practical as the offices from which they worked were anything up to thirty miles apart. There was a general ruling for all Thomson Newspaper salesmen to be in the office by 9am and out on the road by 9.30 and not to return until 5pm and finish at 5.30pm.

Geoff always thought this was a rather ludicrous idea and management should trust the integrity of their sales staff by judging them on the results of their orders rather than the circumstances in which they were obtained. If targets were missed then that needed analysing and rectifying as necessary, but management should not be so dogmatic. Geoff maintained the telephone was a marvellous way to get from A to B in seconds rather than by doing the same calls on foot which could well take half an hour.   However the powers that be thought otherwise and ALAN would phone a branch office after 9.30 and if any salesmen were there he would remind them that they should not be in the office at that time "So get out now and don't come back until 5pm" and that is exactly what happened to Geoff who told ALAN that he should be more trusting and allow his staff to have a degree of initiative. "Listen Geoff, it's been proved beyond all doubt that the man in the field MUST I repeat MUST be out of the office by no later than 9.30. It's not up for argument or debate: that is the ruling so just obey it" and with that ALAN put the phone down. One of the ideas for a new car dealer that Geoff came up with was for the husband and wife to visit a particular dealership where having decided which car to purchase the wife would step on to a pair of scales and the dealer would deduct £1 for each one pound in weight the lady weighed. He'd had a rather amusing half page advert drawn up by the studio and headed for the local FORD dealership. The Sales Manager loved it. "Mr Pritchard I really like that, but one of the bosses from head office is coming to see me on Thursday so I'd like to get his opinion on it before I make any decision, but thanks for a fantastic idea"

"Glad it meets with your approval and yes I can come back on Thursday what time would best suit you"? queried Geoff

"Difficult to say but if it's OK with you I'd sooner bring him to your office and we can discuss it there but I would think it would be around 11.30"

On the Wednesday afternoon Geoff was at the weekly meeting in CHESTER, Gareth and Alan had gone through everything and concluded by asking if anyone had anything they wished to bring up. "Yes" said Geoff "I know full well about being out of the office by 9.30 but."

"BUT nothing" Alan interrupted "there are no BUT'S on this - you will be out of the office by 9.30 and not return until 5 o'clock UNDERSTAND"

"Of course I understood, a daft ruling but, yes I understand, and everyone here bears witness to the ruling - so OK - so be it".

Back home Geoff had a quick tot up; he was a few pounds over his target so he had a plan how to overcome ALANS fanaticism over the 9.30 ruling.

Next morning Geoff made a point of seeing the Classified salesman, JOHN HOWELL. "Hey John I'm going to do you a favour; I've been to see the FORD people with a rather unique idea and they are hoping to get here between 11 and 12 to discuss this with me. BUT I have to be elsewhere as it turns out so reluctantly I'm prepared to hand it on to you to go on the motoring pages instead of on a news page". John couldn't believe his ears: Geoff, of all people actually handing over an idea. He wasn't going to turn the offer down. This was a rarity so grab it quick thought JOHN. On arriving at CHESTER the following Wednesday Geoff was more interested to see the advert he'd passed over to John than his own ads. There it was just as he had handed it over to the classified salesman.

At the weekly meeting various things were discussed but right at the end ALAN produced a copy of the Crewe paper, turned to the classified motors and said to Geoff "Look at this half page FORD advert ! That's more suited to the news pages not classified how is it you missed out on getting it?"

Oh boy thought Geoff have you really fallen into it.

"Alan I'm sure that we all recall last week I tried to ask you if I could be in the office after 9.30, but you shot me down and told me there were no excuses for being in after that time. So in view of that I handed the bloody ad over to classified. But I'd made my target without it so it did JOHN HOWELL a favour.

The result was that the 9.30 nonsense was dropped in favour of a little bit of common sense and trust.

The AT YOUR SERVICE weekly feature was getting some amazing results for several of those advertising in it. A local printer contacted Geoff to enquire about the costing of going into it. Geoff pointed out that the feature had grown in popularity and more and more local firms had enjoyed success by using it that they had increased their advertising budgets, but we can accommodate something for you but suggested that initially they take a four weeks run as frequently anyone just taking one ad may not see any benefit. The printer sent some copy in and it was agreed to have a four weeks trial run. The paper was on sale on Wednesday, the printer rang Geoff on Monday saying that the advert had been so successful that he really could not cope with the extra volume of work it had produced after appearing only once, so please could we stop it.

Geoff pointed out that they had agreed a four weeks trial but in view of this he would stop the ad but hoped they would continue once business slackened off. The printer reorganised his set-up so that he could cope with more work. He advertised some six weeks later and continued to do so on a until cancelled basis. The printer was also good enough to write a testimonial letter which he agreed Geoff could publish in full or in part.

There was another call from a lady who asked if Geoff could call to see her as she wanted to help her two sons to develop their hobby into a paying concern. Geoff was intrigued and arranged to go that afternoon. When he arrived at the address it turned out to be a small cottage in the village of SHAVINGTON. The front gate opened on to a pathway which was about fifteen feet long and lead to the front door. On the right hand side were some well maintained flower beds with a little shrubbery in the background , but to the left was a couple of small garden ponds. All very nice thought Geoff as he knocked the front door which was opened by a lady who he thought would be around the sixty mark. "Mr Pritchard I assume" she said "I'm Mrs Davies so please do come in and I'll tell you what I'd like to do" "I'll get us a cup of tea and a homemade cheese scone if you like" she added "Sounds a delightful way to talk business" said Geoff "and what sort of business is it your sons are involved with"

From the kitchen she called "You've just walked past the business. They're into fish of course"

Geoff felt like a fish out of water. Whatever can she be talking about he wondered. As she returned with a pot of tea, two cups and the newly baked scones she said

"Did you not see the fish ponds in the front garden? They are their business FISH, Breeding fish".

"And that's the business you want to advertise?" asked the bewildered Geoff. "Yes they breed their own fish, but they haven't got an ounce of business sense.

I've told them they should advertise what they do, but they won't listen to a silly old woman like me, so I want to show them just what can be done. As I'm paying for this, what's it going to cost me?"   Geoff told her that it would be £3 for an insertion and that his advice would be to take it for four weeks. At the end of that time he would contact her to see if she wished for it to continue. She could change the copy as often as she wanted. Mrs Davies knew what she wanted to put in the advert but Geoff gave her some aid to sharpen the copy and promised that he would find an illustration of a fish to include. The ad looked pretty good in the paper and Geoff heard no more until the run was up when he contacted her again. "It's going nicely, had a load of enquiries, even the lads are pleased and we want to continue with the advert"

Geoff advised her just to keep it going as it is but if she wanted to change it then to let him know and further more he suggested she ran it every week until she told him to stop. Is that OK.?   Yes it was.

Geoff took a lot of satisfaction several years later because that cottage with a couple of small fish ponds was the starting point of what became a tourist attraction by the name of STAPELEY WATER GARDENS.

WHAT IF . . . that unknown road sweeper had not spoken to Geoff would those two small ponds have got any bigger? Who knows? Probably not.

Gordon Davies was a freelance photographer in Crewe who rented a small studio in town but also did a lot of work for the Chronicle. He and Geoff got on rather well and on one occasion he was over the moon as he had been invited by CLARKSON HOLIDAYS to go on a trip to Spain with Sandra Gough who was a firm favourite in Coronation Street as Irma Barlow. Gordon was to take publicity pictures for that company and their forthcoming brochure. Between them they came up with the idea of inviting 'IRMA' to do her holiday shopping in Crewe. She would not be paid a fee but Geoff thought that the participating retailers would happily give her something suitable for her holiday.

RON and Geoff eventually sold the idea to a dozen local shops and accompanied her together with Gordon. At a shoe shop she tried on a few pairs including one pair which were black and another pair that were white. So she had one of each on her feet and glancing from one to the other she said she really couldn't make her mind up which suited her best. Mike the retailer said "Take both pairs, then you can start a new trend by wearing one of each pair". Lucky lady.

It would be a strange world if mistakes didn't occur and the newspaper industry was no exception. Misprints were probably the most prevalent errors, but a real beauty occurred which was much to the embarrassment of Alan Crofts. When the Chronicle group went from letterpress to off-set printing it gave a great deal of benefits. First and foremost the old lead blocks were no longer needed as it was possible to reproduce a piece of artwork without having to make any blocks as everything basically was produced via a photographic process. It also meant that the paper could carry colour on certain of its pages including the front and back page. By and large the front page ads were taken twelve months in advance and because the demand for them was high and the position was so desirable it meant a premium rate had always been charged. But now these two ads went up in price as the group decided that front page adverts would appear in colour. In order to indicate where the colour was to be an overlay was put over the original advert showing what part should be highlighted in colour. It worked very well and Alan made himself responsible if the colour instructions were not given.

One of the regular front page ads was for a television company that at the time had about a dozen branches throughout the area. Eddie the overseer in the Print room had received the advert but no colour instructions so he went to see Alan who was up to his neck in completing a report for the Managing Director said to Eddie "Oh I'll leave it to your discretion I really must get this report done" Eddie took the simple way out and gave instructions for the whole advert was to be in blue.

When Alan got a copy of his paper shortly after the last paper had come off the press he was horrified to see all the wording was in blue and the headline read:-

CHEAPEST TELEVISION RENTALS IN THE AREA,
HERE'S THE PROOF IN BLACK AND WHITE.

Geoff went to see Mr Vernon Cooper the retailer involved the following day in order to apologise, but he saw the funny side of it and roared with laughter, but he was compensated for the error. If it made him so happy we should have charged him more! On another occasion Geoff visited a local agricultural machinery business which did advertise both on the news pages as well as in the classified columns. JOHN SMITH was the manager who placed the adverts and he had a receptionist/ secretary whose first aim in life seemed to be to protect John from anyone who was there to sell something: Geoff rather felt that she was over protective of her boss who at times appeared to be embarrassed by her efforts. On one visit John did say that he felt that his advertising did not seem to have the same pulling power that it once had. Geoff was concerned about this and said that the circulation was rising steadily and that was particularly so in the agricultural areas. But John was adamant and said that he had positive proof that it was not working as well as it used to and showed him the classified adverts he'd placed over recent months adding that he had not received a single enquiry, and asked "How do you account for that". Geoff looked at the ads "That's amazing the prices seem to be pretty good and you have a good range to choose from, I certainly don't understand it". However something struck him but he couldn't place what it was that was wrong for after all it was just a list of tractors showing the prices, the address and the telephone number. Geoff looked at the last advert that had been placed for John. He had a horrible feeling "John do you mind if I use your phone for a minute, let me see if I can solve this." "I'd be glad if you could" was the reply. Geoff picked up the receiver and said to John now read out to me the number that's in your advert" "6 3 3 1 3 3" Geoff carefully tapped in the digits. It was quickly answered by a bright young lady with "Good morning FOURWAYS TRACTORS" "Oh good morning" Geoff responded have you still got the Fordson tractor you were advertising for sale at £1500"

"I'm afraid not sir that was sold the other day but we do have a variety of used tractors. I'll put you on to one of our salesmen"

"Thank you but no it was just the Fordson I was interested in"

He put the phone down. "Mystery settled John that was FOURWAYS whose number is 633313, you've been advertising for the opposition, and John most errors in adverts seem to be with telephone numbers which for some reason so few people seem to check properly, but both the numbers are so alike it is easy to look at it without realising it's wrong" However as this is a classified advert it is outside my jurisdiction, but I'm sure they will compensate you for this".

Geoff found it rather amazing that somebody being absent from work could enhance his fortunes.   The local Co-operative Society had advertised in the Chronicle for several years more often than not they took an 8 inch double column every week. This thought Geoff was quite ludicrous as they had so many outlets in the area and were busy refurbishing an old store. The appearance would be transformed into a modern, appealing departmental store.

Geoff made contact with Mr. Irvine the Society's company secretary and suggested that they meet up with a view to talking about and possibly reviewing the Society's advertising policy.   Mr Irvine was a perfect gentleman and made Geoff welcome when he visited the office.   Although the outcome was satisfying and Mr Irvine agreed to take an additional advert on a weekly basis he did not want it as big as the current one. So Geoff suggested a 6 inch double column which Mr Irvine agreed to. Although disappointed he thought that was a 75% increase in the volume but it's not nearly enough to portray the right image of the largest retailer in the area. On visiting the Society's offices some weeks later he was told by Mr Irvine's secretary "I'm afraid we'll have to drop the advertising for now as Mr Irvine had a heart attack and will be away from the office for some time"

"I'm so sorry to hear that. I hope he makes a quick recovery - but is nobody deputising for him?" asked Geoff

"I'll see if our general manager Mr Barratt will be able to see you"

Minutes later he was ushered into Mr Barratt's office.

He was a warm friendly man who advised him that in future it may be better to see him rather than Mr Irvine.

"Do you know Mr Pritchard I have great plans for the development of the Society and would like to see them taking much bigger spaces in the paper"

'Yippee' thought Geoff that's what I like to hear. But said "with the size of this business you really could do with improving the image and probably putting on offers that other retailers would have a job to match because of your buying power, and I'm here to help you achieve your ambition."

Mr Barratt's eyes sparkled. They were at least on the same wave length Mr Irvine was back in harness quicker than anticipated. When he saw Geoff he told him that it might be best for him to continue dealing with Mr Barratt as it would relieve some of his own stress

"Yes it can be rather stressful" he said thinking to himself it will relieve mine as well!

Geoff was most surprised when he walked into the Bowling Club one Friday evening when Mr Irvine and Mr Barratt walked in. "Didn't know you were members" said Geoff. "We're not but our old club has shut down and somebody suggested that we came down here to see if we could join"

"I'd be delighted to propose both of you and I'm sure I'll soon find someone who will gladly second your application. Do you fancy a frame of snooker, it's my table now" asked Geoff.

They accepted the offer and Geoff said he would break. Horror of horrors the cue ball shimmered the reds, returned to the baulk area then on to the cushion and tucked itself gently on the back of the brown. Geoff had snookered his potentially biggest advertiser. "Bloody hell fire" said Mr Barratt "see what we're up against partner?"

Geoff was a stickler for conducting business in a business like manner and never used the Christian names of his clients always preferring the more formal method of address of Mr or Mrs. In the Club it was always by their first name.

Tom and Geoff came to an agreement whereby the Society would place a full page on alternate weeks and half pages on the other weeks. This was a terrific boost for Geoff but the only drawback was that he had to collect the copy from each departmental manager. Some had written on a variety of paper bags, some on wrapping paper and one on wallpaper. Geoff's task was simply to re-write everything in a more legible way and to indicate on a mock up of the page where everything should go. This was a job he did in the lounge at home. On the first week he saw a small piece of paper saying This week's Special!! Tate & Lyle Sugar 1/2 He had to find a spot for it but as it was Friday evening decided to go to the club and make amends later. He arrived back home just after midnight It was 1.30am on Saturday morning when he'd finished. It had taken longer to fit this one last bit of copy in than to do the whole of the original. Mr Barratt arranged with Geoff to see him every Friday afternoon between 2.30 and 3.00pm. When he arrived there were eight company reps to see Mr Barratt. Geoff thought to himself that he would be there for at least a couple of hours, but NO! Tom came to the door with the outgoing rep waved him a cheery goodbye and beckoned Geoff to go in. "Mr Barratt I'm afraid I was the last to arrive, all these gentlemen are before me" said Geoff

"Gentlemen" Tom beamed at the others "I'm sure none of you will not want to hold up the production of our local newspaper will you?"

Geoff was sure they'd all feel pretty sick, but rather unsurprisingly no one objected. Geoff always took a visual in for Mr Barratt who nine times out of ten accepted what he had suggested.

However completing the business was not the end of the session for his desk would be piled up with products that the different reps had left for him to sample "Geoff" he asked " have you got a dog?". "Yes we have a crossed sheepdog" he replied. "Well here we are then a box of Doggy mix for him, I hope he enjoys, and I suppose your wife likes chocolates" handing over a lovely box of chocolates, "and here's a pack of toilet soap to try. You can have these on the understanding you will tell me next week when you call what you thought of them".

Naturally he was delighted to be able to help a valued client in this way! When Tom was away he gave Geoff carte blanche authority to see the various managers and to make the decision on the best size of advert for them. Geoff told him he felt very privileged to be entrusted with that faith. Tom said that he could trust him 100% and if he had not done so he would have made a member of his staff to make the final decision.

Sadly this did not work out on one occasion when a certain branch manager by the name of Fox contacted Geoff to say that he wanted an advert for next week's paper solely based on BACK TO SCHOOL products which were mainly uniforms for the various schools. He had gone to the trouble of typing out every item he wanted to include in the advert, so everything was nice and legible. Knowing the theme of the advert Geoff had sorted through the artwork books and came up with suitable attention compellers, boys and girls in uniform with satchels around their necks and found a rather grand looking headline BACK TO SCHOOL imposed on a rather splendid looking school.

Mr Fox took one look and said "I want no pictures whatsoever, nor do I need anything with large print. Just simple straight forward copy"

Geoff pointed out that what he had been given would justify a half page advert. "Absolute rubbish" was Mr Fox's retort. "Ohh you can twist Mr Barratt around your little finger and he falls for all the rubbish you tell him, but don't insult my intelligence please and do exactly what I tell you – no more no less" "Mr Fox I have been entrusted by Mr Barratt to make the final decision on the size and manner of the way in which the adverts will appear, and I must stress that to put it into anything less than a half page will do nothing for your promotion or for the Cooperative store so my best advice to you is you really should authorise a half page and not to do so you are placing me in a very awkward situation". "It's not in the least awkward you will follow my instructions precisely" Geoff's retort was "Can we compromise on this? I will reserve a quarter page but will you allow a margin of flexibility and I will ask the overseer in the composing room if he can even squeeze it into a quarter page and if he can't to increase it accordingly?"

"You get away with too much since you've been involved in our advertising. Mr Barratt is somewhat gullible and you can get away with things with him: apart from which I have not authorised a quarter page. I know it will fit easily into 8 inches over three columns and that is the maximum we will pay for".

"It will hardly be legible" said Geoff "Mr Barratt will be furious when he sees the paper. I just hope that you will let him know of my suggestions that you turned down."

"In his absence I am in charge not Mr Barratt, if you do a single inch more I will not authorise any payment. Now I bid you a good day".

When Geoff saw the paper on Wednesday he was mortified. It looked even worse than he had anticipated. Who is going to get the biggest kicking when TOM sees this he wondered. Most likely it will be me he thought.

Tom returned to his office on Monday and the first thing he did was to phone Geoff "What the hell's this mess – I thought I told you to run whatever you thought was best – I can't read this and if I can't read it nobody else can".

Geoff listened to this justifiable tirade and then explained precisely what had happened. He was asked to go to the office straight away. On arrival MR FOX was already there and looking somewhat abject. Geoff started to feel sorry for him as Tom tore into him without mincing his words. He made it abundantly clear that in any future absences Geoff was to have the final decision irrespective of anyone else. What a wonderful situation for a salesman who had to reach ambitious targets to be in, but Geoff could truthfully say that he never abused that trust.

Another awkward situation arose shortly after that. Some of the hand written copy was practically indecipherable so if Geoff was able to do so he would spend a little time in Toms office going through everything and taking up any queries.

For some months DULUX paint stockists had been encouraged to highlight in their advertising and window displays that their range of paints were now available at considerably reduced prices. It was a promotion that seemed to go on interminably and generally you could purchase this brand for anything from 7/- to 7/10 and several stockists advertised this in the Chronicle regularly.

On looking through the Co-op's proposed copy one item read SENSATIONAL OFFER ! Due to our bulk purchase we can now offer DULUX paint at the reduced price of 8/3

Being Geoff's biggest customer he felt it was his moral duty to point out that this price would make the Society look ridiculous and it would reflect badly on any other sensational prices they may be offering in the future. Geoff thought it best to be a little diplomatic and asked TOM if this should be 7/3 rather than 8/3 and qualified this by showing Tom the previous week's paper to verify what he had said. Tom picked his phone up and asked for the DIY manager to see him straight away. The manager seemed to be under the impression that what he was offering was a reasonable price and in so doing received a few well chosen words from an angry Mr Barratt. "If you don't know what the competitors are doing it's a bleak outlook for us. If it hadn't been for Mr Pritchard here this would have made us look pretty silly" Turning to Geoff he said "Geoff change it to 2pence below the lowest price that our competitors are doing it at."

"Sorry I can't do that" Geoff said "I must not betray the confidences of other retailers, you and only you can decide what price to sell it at. Apart from which you wouldn't expect me to tell anyone of your proposed prices until the paper has been published".

Tom respected that and Geoff went away with the price of DULUX being advertised at 7/- for one week only. Now that was a real bargain.

It was around this time that Mr Barratt suggested that Geoff may like to serve on the local Co-operative board. He told him this would be doing him a tremendous favour and bring a bit of new life into a society that had somehow got in to the retail backwaters. He felt he could not do it without people who possessed some foresight and business acumen. Geoff was flattered but declined. It was not long after this that the Crewe Society merged with the NORTH STAFFS CO-OP and Tom did ask if Geoff would be prepared to take on the role of Advertising and Publicity Manager for the new expanded CO-OP. Geoff though was perfectly happy where he was, but said he would be delighted to co-operate in any way he could. When the new Crewe store was completed by the Co-operative Society they arranged for it to be opened at 12 noon on Thursday.

This gave Geoff a timing problem. As the paper was printed on Wednesday would it be best to advise them to make the main promotion the week prior to the opening or the one that would come out the day before?

The week before and some people might just remember but the day before may not be so suitable as many of the papers were sold on Thursday which could miss the event . The decision was made easy when he found out that the great KEN DODD had agreed to make the official opening. Nobody, but nobody, could forget about Ken Dodd so he advised the CO-OP of his thinking and they happily went along with that Even so Geoff was a little apprehensive as to his advice. On the big day at 10.30am there was hardly a soul about However an hour later and the roadways in Crewe were packed and it was practically impossible to walk on the pavements. Geoff was staggered and the event was a tremendous success. Dorothy was amongst those waiting to see Doddy and she was lucky enough to get one of his tickling sticks which she treasured for many years.

Ron had left the company and now it was Gareth's turn to take up his new appointment in Newcastle. This meant it was a step up the rung for Geoff. He knew that he'd had a good time on his territory and made several new friends from amongst the people he'd met and done business with. He was all too well aware that he had his faults and weaknesses but by and large he did well and spotted opportunities which others may have missed. He was also conscious that the success or failure of the sales staff would now be his prime responsibility. It was he who would have to organise the weekly training sessions and to bring in some variety to them to try and keep everyone bright and alert. The sales staff were expected to make a dozen calls each day and to record on a Daily Call Card the result of each of those calls. As an example 9.45 Bill Smith, Ironmongery 10cmx2, or FREDA's BEAUTY SALON see next Thursday. Ideally these cards should be filled in after each call whilst it was still fresh in the mind. In all truth not many of them did this. Some filled it in at the end of the day. The cards were then handed in to the sales supervisor who would check them over and analyse the success rate.

Gareth had been a very good classroom trainer and was a good motivator. Geoff knew he would be a hard act to follow in this respect so had, he thought, to come up with a few fresh ideas.

He would also have to sit in with Alan when interviewing for sales staff. He felt this would be interesting and probably the most important factor of all, for it was through them that the future of the company and his own future would rely. The one aspect of it that he was really relishing was double calling with the salesmen. His most important and immediate duty was to make sure that his successor was well briefed on the 'patch' Geoff had been responsible for and that he introduced him to the main advertisers and to let them know that he would be "keeping an eye on things. He needn't have worried because his successor was equally determined to make a name for himself as he too was ambitious.

The opportunity to recruit a new salesman came up fairly early on in Geoff's new capacity. One of the applicants by the name of ALF MASON was one Geoff would never forget as he could never recall anyone who came across better at an interview, He was brilliant, said all the right things and answered the questions put to him very professionally. At that time he was selling fire extinguishers and at the end of the interview he said to Alan "Mr Crofts I fear for your safety, for if there was to be a fire in this department how would you tackle it as you don't have a fire extinguisher?

Alan and Geoff had a post interview review: Alan saying it was a pleasure to have an applicant who was so cheerful, bright and showed initiative. Geoff was not quite so sure but could not highlight anything that was giving him doubts. However he was taken on to work from one of the branch offices. Before allowing him loose on the retailers in that area Geoff had organised for him to have an induction course.

Once Alan was working on his territory Geoff decided he would go double calling with him to see how he performed. It was worse than he had anticipated. He had no visual aids prepared, he certainly could not handle any objections that cropped up in a professional manner. After only three calls Geoff suggested that they return to the office and organise things better before going any further. Geoff helped prepare a few decent visuals and a more professional sales pitch. Really it was not Geoff's role to do this, but he had agreed to recruit him and was obliged to help him all he could to make a success of his career. Geoff was required to fill out an appraisal form at the end of the day. The form had the main aspects of the day from use of visual aids to the appearance of the salesman and were marked accordingly A for good, B for average and C below standard. Sadly Geoff found it difficult to mark anything other than C on the overall performance. The appraisals were then discussed with FAC who found it difficult to believe that his new recruit could have fared so badly. A few weeks went by before Geoff accompanied Alf again and he hoped that he would see some improvement, but he didn't. Again Geoff found it difficult to mark him with even a solitary B. Geoff told FAC that he really thought this chap would never make the grade but in fairness to him he suggested that FAC spent a day with him to see what he thought himself. This FAC agreed to do the following week. FAC got a totally different impression and told Geoff that he'd had a good day with him, and on one aspect of the appraisal had given him an A. Geoff was dumbfounded how could there be such a massive difference and wondered if his marking was too severe. He made a point of having another day with Alf and found that there was absolutely no improvement whatsoever. It was then that a suspicion crossed Geoff's mind. "Alan" he asked FAC "when you went with Alf did you tell him in advance that you would be going with him" "Yes of course I did I wanted to make sure that he hadn't gone out before I got there otherwise it may have been a wasted journey" "Alan" said Geoff "Go with him once more but don't give him any warning: simply turn up at 9 o'clock and go with him for the day".

FAC did just that and on his return said to Geoff "Do you know that was a complete disaster I really can't understand how he has slipped so badly I've marked him with all C's. Why such a change"?

"The change Alan is that I never give any advance warning of my intention to be going out with him but you in the past have given him a week's notice. A week in which he could prepare himself reasonably well, and probably selected his calls by seeing people he knew would be advertising. But if you are not convinced get one of the experienced lads to go out with him - Malcolm would do very nicely". But FAC was convinced by what he'd seen: so it was goodbye Alf Mason. Geoff felt that whilst the sales team were in pretty good shape they would not always be around: some would move on to other work, others may want promotion and have to go to another centre in order to achieve this. Newly recruited sales staff should have the opportunity to see where they stood relative to other members of the sales team. Geoff had heard of a system used by the paper in Edinburgh and so got permission to go and see how it worked. He spent a couple of nights in that lovely city and returned with enthusiasm.

On his return on Monday morning he gave Alan a briefing on what he'd discovered and told him how well it worked. Geoff got the OK from Alan to introduce a similar system. A large blackboard was introduced that took up most of the wall at the back of Geoff's desk. This then had a ladder that was made up of steps representing each member of the sales staff. Their names were shown on the board together with their target for the current month and a third column showing what percentage of their target they had achieved. The left side of the board was taken up mainly with the features which were in the pipeline for future weeks. So nobody could be in any doubt as to what was going on.

Whatever the sales staff may say not one of them liked being at the bottom of the list as this showed the lowest percentage towards their target at any given moment. At first it was not popular with the sales staff but it worked and each of them saw the benefits.

When Geoff first joined the sales team it consisted solely of men but things were slowly changing. All the telephone sales staff in the Classified department were women and they seemed to be very successful. Even so it came as a bit of a surprise when Geoff walked into the office one day and Alan was talking to a young lady who he introduced to him as Elizabeth. Apparently she had worked for a while in the Classified department but rather fancied working in Display advertising. She was good looking, smartly dressed, well spoken and showed initiative by having gone to see Alan rather than wait for a situation vacant advert to appear. We had more of a general natter rather than a formal interview and both Alan and Geoff agreed that she could well be a useful asset. On starting she went through the normal training. After a brief spell in the MID CHESHIRE area she took over a territory in Chester.

She fitted well into the sales team, was very popular with the staff and normally managed to reach her monthly target. She was quite vivacious and was never afraid to express her opinions. As she lived a fair distance from the office she took her vegetarian lunch into work. This usually consisted of a raw carrot and a raw mushroom. Likewise Geoff found it more convenient to remain at his desk but much preferred a steak and kidney pie. "Do you realise Pritch that you've got the rotting flesh of a dead animal lying in your intestines"

"Yes I do" replied Geoff "and it's absolutely gorgeous"

Two major landmarks in the Chronicles history took place in the 1970's when the Crewe Chronicle celebrated its centenary and the Chester Chronicle celebrated it's bi-centenary.

Various activities were to take place at the appropriate time and Geoff's involvement was to produce celebratory supplements for both papers . He decided that if the sales staff were to reach their monthly targets they would be concentrating on that too much to be able to sell into a special supplement as well. He explained this to the sales staff and that in order to do this he was taking Liz off her territory for the next month and divide her usual calls among them. Sales made by Liz or himself would be credited to the appropriate sales person so they would not lose out It worked out well and they managed to sell sufficient advertising to produce a 36 page supplement.

For the Chester paper he did the same thing but using Frank Ledger as his Co-salesman instead of Liz.   So in May 1975 they produced sufficient advertising to justify a 40 page supplement.   (Both supplements were broadsheet format) Elizabeth was a great asset to the department and Geoff was rather upset when John Thomas the Circulation Manager was appointed by the Managing Director to organise the special events for Chester's bi-centenary event and requisitioned her to assist him. Her new role, for which she was well suited gave an opportunity for Jon Moseley, who had been appointed to work in the paper planning section, to fulfil his desire to get on to the sales staff. So as they would lose Liz for up to twelve months this would give Jon a good grounding.

The arrangement was that he would work on paper planning during their busy period and on the sales team every Thursday and Friday. Geoff explained this to Liz and asked her to clear everything from her desk by 5pm on Friday so that Jon could move in on Monday. As she had not done so Geoff went along to see her in her new office and asked her to remove everything later in the day. She had not done so on Monday, Tuesday or Wednesday so Geoff stormed off at her "Those bloody drawers of yours are still full so get everything out today without fail" But fail she did. It wasn't fair on Jon who was anxious to settle in to his temporary role but couldn't do so properly until the desk was vacated. It still hadn't been done by Friday. Geoff was livid: no more was he going to beg with her to carry out this task. She was only a couple of doors away and she'd had ample opportunity. Without further ado Geoff told Jon to get a black bin liner. Geoff opened each drawer and unceremoniously deposited the contents into the bag which JON obligingly held open . . . pens, pencils, ruler, lipstick, tissues, some odd coins, a mirror all were dumped into the bag.

Frank was seated at his desk "Geoff, she'll be absolutely livid when she sees what you've done, I hope I'm not around when she comes in"

"Frank as far as you're concerned it will be far better for us all if she's livid rather than me. Now come on Jon get your stuff into this desk, it's all yours".

Geoff and Elizabeth had a pretty good relationship by and large even though both of them could be bloody minded BUT as Geoff said "I'm the one with the stripes" He would never pull rank on her but this time Geoff felt she had gone far too far to test his temper. So he tied a knot in the top of the bag and attached a A4 sheet of paper and on it wrote "I've done the bloody job for you – now get rid of it. On Monday morning Geoff had hardly got settled at his desk when the door burst open and Elizabeth marched in with fury written all over her face. She strode over to Geoff's desk. "You bastard, you are a complete and utter bastard". Nobody spoke as she turned on her heels and left slamming the door to behind her. At lunchtime Geoff felt as though he needed to resolve the situation because she was still a valued member of his sales team so he went to Thornton's and bought her a box of chocolates which he knew she loved so much. He attached a note with the words 'Sorry – but !! ' He left them on her desk and later in the day she again went to see him. She looked at him saying "I still think you are a bastard, but I still love you and thanks for the chocs" Good relations were restored.!

Geoff had always impressed on the sales staff the importance for them writing out copy instructions very clearly so that no one could be in any doubt about the wording as mistakes can cost money as well as embarrassment. This was emphasised when he was in Northwich one Friday when a car pulled up and the driver asked the directions to FRANK BALLANCE MOTORS. Geoff said that he could direct him there but he was based about 15 miles away in Nantwich. The driver had a copy of the paper with him and it did quite clearly say NORTHWICH. It was a classified advert for used cars and the salesman had put N'wich and the compositors had translated that to be NORTHWICH Result: a dissatisfied reader: lost revenue : an unhappy advertiser. And why? Just because somebody couldn't be bothered to put the letters a n t instead of a ' Frank Balance like Geoff was a member of the Bowling club where they met that evening. Frank cheerfully accepted that it was a silly but genuine error and even more cheerfully accepted the offer of a free ad.

On another occasion when Geoff was in the Northwich office one of the reporters answered the phone and asked him to pass her spectacles which she promptly put on and made copious notes. When the call ended she took the specs off. Geoff was surprised to see that the specs had no lenses and asked what use they were. "Oh" she replied I can see perfectly well but I do need them for hearing!" What strange folk we are. Life is full of incidents and colourful characters, and every living person has a story to tell, if only they would take the time and trouble to write. Geoff was in the Bowling club one evening when he got talking to Ernie a member who had been in the teaching profession all his life and told Geoff that he had applied to take early retirement. He went on to say that in many ways he would miss seeing and listening to the kids but he felt it was time to sit back and enjoy the remaining years of his life pottering around in the garden and writing a book of his memoirs and in particular the hundreds of humorous happenings he had experienced with the children over many years of teaching.

A few months went by and Geoff enquired how the book was coming along only to be told that he hadn't started yet, but he could think of so many stories he really didn't know where to start.

"Ernie, don't make a conscious effort but get yourself a note book and jot them down each time something comes into your mind. Just a couple of words that will jog the memory is all you need. The order doesn't matter. Then during the autumn and winter months look at your notes and enlarge on them. You don't really have to recall a child's name or the time it was said – it's what they said that's important. If you can't recall which child it was then make a name up. It's the anecdote that people will find amusing – who said it does not matter one scrap."

Geoff persisted over the months but Ernie always found a good reason not to have made a start "But I will do" he always said. Then one day it was announced that Ernie had died. He was a lovely man but all those wonderful stories he could have told died with him. Sad, for now we will never know or enjoy his memoirs.

It is said that you can't mix business and pleasure. However this was something that Geoff couldn't fully subscribe to, and conversely found them to be useful bed fellows at times. Geoff got quite a lot of pleasure from his work, perhaps at times it was rather too much. One person with whom he got along with very well was Jim Bentley who was the publicity manager at CHARLESWORTHS on Hightown, Crewe.

On Saturday mornings in the 1940's Geoff had to cycle to Charlesworth's. At that time Geoff's home did not have electricity so they had a radio that was powered by a 'dry' battery and an accumulator that required recharging every week at a cost of sixpence. The 'spent' accumulator was left for recharging and the one deposited the previous Saturday was taken home.

On this particular visit Jim Bentley told Geoff that they had been talking about producing a company 'news sheet' to distribute throughout selected areas and he asked Geoff if the Chronicle would be prepared to print it. He replied that not only could they print it but that he would be delighted to take a week's holiday to undertake the project and write some or all of the articles.

He realised what a truly wonderful wife Dorothy was when he told her that he had undertaken to do this project for Charlesworth's and not only did she not object to his decision but thoroughly endorsed it. Actually the undertaking took a lot less time than he had anticipated so that he and Dorothy could have pleasant outings with the dog around places that they had not visited previously. In fact on the day that the News Sheet was to be printed they went together to the Chronicle office with all the artwork and whilst the composing room got on with the job they had a lovely trip down the river Dee.

CHAPTER 11 –
I'M IN CHARGE !

Geoff was rather surprised when Alan Crofts called him into the office to tell him that Eric Lowe the Display Advertising Controller had been in touch to say that things were pretty bad at the Stockport Express (another Thomson newspaper) and that Eric had advised the powers that be at Stockport that Geoff Pritchard at Chester was most suited to sort things out for them. So the next morning Geoff went over to see what it was all about.

A new MD by the name of PETER WISDOM had just been appointed but was unable at that time to leave his current post in Middlesborough. Peter's predecessor had gone completely against the policy of Thomson Newspapers to have two separate advertising departments so had merged Display advertising with the Classified advertising Department. Result a massive shambles!

Having two ad departments meant a little bit of competition with each other which had worked well at every other newspaper in the group. But 'No' someone who should have known better really botched things up.

Geoff was asked by Peter to go to Stockport for six months and come up with recommendations to rectify the situation. In return he would be offered the job of Display Advertising Manager should Geoff wish to take it up.

Geoff could see this was one hell of a challenge but looked forward to seeing what could be done.

He arrived at the office a few minutes prior to 9am. As he walked in the receptionist told him there were two policemen wanting to see him immediately in MR FIDDLERS office. "Where the devil do I find his office and furthermore what is he" He was told upstairs first door on the left and he's the Financial Director.

On entering MR FIDDLER said to Geoff "Not a good start for you being wanted by the constabulary"

"Are you aware" asked the sergeant "that it is illegal to carry advertising in newspapers on behalf of Bookmakers?"

"I'm aware that there are very strict limitations on such advertising but it's not necessarily illegal"

"You cannot say things like our odds are better or even quote the odds"

"Quite right sergeant. But just let me point out that this is my first day in the job and as yet have not found out where my office is so please come to the point of your visit"

"Sir, one of the papers in your group is the Salford City Reporter which carries an advert on the front page for a local bookmaker most weeks, and it must stop"

"Sergeant I will look into it today and see for myself. I'm sure you are right but I want to see which member of staff actually handles this. If it's illegal we will stop it but if the client would like to use our paper to further his business I will see to it that any future business he does with us is legal and honest, so now please excuse me I have people waiting to see me."

With that he left the office to find out where his own office was and to get on with the job.

He walked into the department to be greeted by a salesman who introduced himself as MIKE SMITH. Geoff knew the name as he was constantly the one and only name in Stockport that ever appeared on the THOMSON TARGET CLUB.

"Nice to meet you Mike your name is always on that bloody list. Well done and keep it up"

"Sorry but I won't be doing that as I want to give you a month's notice as from today I've got a job with another newspaper group"

"In that case Mike leave whatever you are doing and GO NOW . I'll get a cheque to pay you off in lieu of notice Nice to have met you – sorry to see you go – but go now to accounts I'll phone them to authorise it"

"But I'm part way through selling a feature."

"Mike forget it. You don't want to be here so I don't want you here just go".

It was not yet 9.15am "What a bloody start" thought Geoff.

Now he was to have the privilege of meeting TREVOR LIVINGSTONE who had joined from another TRN newspaper and was acting as temporary Sales Supervisor. Geoff's first impressions were that he was a fat, idle, good for nothing but he was stuck with him for now at any rate. He was introduced to a dark haired girl by the name of RITA who seemed quite content to sit at her desk chewing the end of her hair for the biggest part of the day.

There were four newspapers within the group. They were The STOCKPORT EXPRESS, The MACCLESFIELD EXPRESS, the WYTHENSHAWE EXPRESS and the SALFORD CITY REPORTER.

Each paper had its own advertising and editorial staff and its own local office.

His first impression of the staff was that they were a bunch of losers. The first thing he must do was to see if they really were alive. Geoff spoke to them all and said that on Wednesday they would meet up at a local pub called the Hollywood at 1 o'clock when they could have a couple of drinks and a bit of lunch – all on expenses of course. Geoff was delighted to see that the two from Salford as well as the two from Macclesfield seemed to be more alert and aware than those based in Stockport. In fact they seemed to have a fair bit of enthusiasm about them.

Following the lunch they trooped back to the main office where Geoff interviewed each one of them separately. It was a well worth exercise. The two from Salford both seemed keen. The one who had accepted the advert from the local bookie was told that if he wanted to advertise in the future he would have to follow the very strict guide lines. Unfortunately this was not acceptable by the client so the business was lost. Shortly afterwards that same company chose to advertise on television and seemed to grow rapidly.

The two salesmen from Macclesfield were totally different types. SAM GREEN was the senior man both in age and length of service. He was not far off retirement age and had been a thorn in the side of Geoff's predecessor, Eric Lowe. Well thought Geoff he's not going to be a thorn in my side, We'll just see how smart this guy is.

Sam made it abundantly clear that he was doing Geoff a great favour by coming along to the lunch and the interview as he had so many and much more important things to do. In fact he told Geoff that he was not just a salesman but he was actually the Advertising Manager of the Macclesfield Express and further that CHRIS WILDING followed HIS instructions and nobody else's including Geoff's.

Geoff made it extremely clear that it was he and not Sam who was the Advertising Manager of the Stockport, Wythenshawe, Salford papers AND MOST DEFINITELY THE Macclesfield paper as well. But Sam was having none of it He was the ad manager. Him and nobody else. Furthermore he claimed to have a letter at home confirming that. Geoff said that OK if he did have such a letter he may as well put it on the fire for it had no relevance today.

"Further more Sam If I want you to start each day by being here in Stockport at 9 o'clock every morning you will be here or face disciplinary action. If I want you here every Wednesday afternoon you will be here promptly or face disciplinary action. I see you are not far short of retiring just see to it that I don't spoil your retirement by giving you the bloody sack. So get one thing straight I am the advertising manager of the whole group, so now get back to Macclesfield and do not ever tell Chris what he has to do. He is quite capable of looking after his own territory and if he fails he will have me to answer to and NOT you."

Did it all work out for Geoff? Up to a point, yes it did, but Geoff accepted that Sam had been here a long time and given good service. He was well known in the area, and a useful golfer and he was near retiring age. However it worked well on the Stockport staff because they could see that if Geoff could be harsh with an old-timer that he wouldn't stand any nonsense from them.

One person that Geoff did feel sorry for was NED DAVIS who as the Classified Sales Manager had been thrown in at the deep end when it had come to the amalgamation of the two advertising departments under the jurisdiction of the previous MD. He was a nice guy who seemed to have had a raw deal. He was helpful towards Geoff and helped out particularly with the recent history of events at the Express. He was heartily fed up at having been messed around and had made his mind up that as soon as he could he would be opening up his own newsagents business.

Rita told Geoff that she could see what he was trying to do at Stockport and said she did not feel that she was up to the standard that he wanted in his sales team. Geoff actually agreed that she was going nowhere so wished her good luck.

There were some big decisions to be made at the Stockport Express, Geoff knew what some of them were, but it was difficult at that time to liaise with the Managing Director as he was still at Middlesbrough.

Geoff phoned Peter Wisdom with an update of the goings on in Stockport but advised him that getting rid of staff was easy, replacing them was much more problematical. This is especially so in Stockport which is on the fringe of the second city to London in terms of media. All national newspapers and commercial TV stations had a sales force in Manchester offering much higher salaries and company cars. Mr Wisdom did not take much persuading to agree to make provision in the budget to get all outdoor sales staff a company car. With this incentive now in place it would make recruitment of a higher standard of salesmen much easier.

Furthermore Geoff introduced a good bonus scheme which meant that sales staff could make a better living. Recent history showed that a number of former salesmen at the Stockport Express had secured similar positions on the Manchester Evening News. Now, thought Geoff, let's reverse the situation. It happened almost immediately JOAN LONG worked for the Evening News and made application to join his team. Geoff could see that she had great potential and offered her the lucrative town centre patch. She was well connected with the local media world and introduced her pal VERONICA WILD who worked for the Daily Express. Geoff happily recruited her and whilst she was good she never, in Geoff's opinion was not as good as Joan.

Geoff needed to recruit a Sales Trainer and a Sales Supervisor. Eric Lowe was asked to look out for a suitable candidate for the role of Supervisor and he would put out a few feelers for the position of Trainer. Terry Livingstone was told by Geoff that he no longer figured in his plans and advised him to look around for something more suitable. Terry had anticipated this and told Geoff that he had found a supervisory role with another newspaper outside the Thomson group. Geoff wished him well and thanked him for what he had done at Stockport.

FRED STEVENS a classified salesman for the Chester Chronicle had built up a good rapport with Geoff when they had worked closely at the Crewe Chronicle. Fred begged Geoff to give him the chance at Stockport as trainer. However Geoff did not rate him as management material and turned him down.

Rather surprisingly to Geoff, Fred set up his own advertising agency in Crewe and did extremely well. He was a very likeable person and very popular with the Motor Traders in the area so did a heck of a lot of business with them. Well done, Fred thought Geoff who did have a couple of people up his sleeve both of whom were based with the Chronicle. He thought he would 'test the water' and speak to Liz who was delighted to hear from him and went to Stockport for an informal interview. She would be quite brilliant in that role but Geoff could foresee problems.

He pointed out that it was a lengthy run from Chester to Stockport and she lived on the Wirral which was even further away. Could she assure him that she could be in the office from Monday to Friday by 9.o'clock EVERY morning.? Difficult.

Would she be prepared to move home from the Wirral to Stockport? Not likely.

She would have done a good job: they could have been a good team; but she made the decision "Thanks for seeing me Pritch, but no I could not promise that". Geoff approached John Craft who for all his faults was a real enthusiast, a good motivator and was determined to climb the ladder. Geoff's approach to him was not welcomed by Alan Crofts and there was quite a stink about it when Eric Lowe was involved. He told Geoff he should not be poaching staff and that he should go via the recognised route of speaking to him first. But John was not a favoured person with Alan Crofts and it was doubtful if John would have progressed at Chester. So Geoff had secured his services and he gladly moved his family and home nearer the office.

It was MICHAEL MANWELL who Eric Lowe suggested to Geoff would make him a decent Sales Supervisor. Mike was based at the TRN Group in Merthyr Tydfil. He not only came for the interview but also brought along his newly wedded wife. A nice couple and Geoff was pleased to offer Mike the job.

CHRISTMAS was approaching all too rapidly and the Davenport Theatre was giving advance notice of their seasonal pantomime. Geoff contacted the manager of the theatre to see if the Stockport Express could 'borrow' some of their panto stars.

Geoff explained that his sales team would approach a variety of retailers in the area and he would arrange for the 'stars' to visit those shops where they would have their picture taken with the retailer. These would then be included in a feature within the Express so giving the theatre, the pantomime, and the stars greater exposure. They loved the idea so much so that it became a regular feature for the following Christmases. The first year the stars were Cannon and Ball, another year it was Windsor Davies and Don Estelle who both starred in the long running comedy. "It ain't half hot Mum". They were accompanied by Anne Aston who was in the Golden Shot with Bob Monkhouse. Another occasion they got the great Ken Dodd.

Things were going well for Geoff and his team who were now settling down nicely. Most of the sales staff met their targets regularly and enjoyed bulkier pay packets. Geoff thought that there was, though, a slight problem between Mike and John.

Although Mike deserved his promotion which brought him to Stockport he always felt that John was the more dominant character. Just to give an example. Mike was to go on a course in Newcastle on Tyne. He was to prepare a session based on any chapter of the standard training manual. He practised his efforts on Geoff who made one or two suggestions as to how it could be improved. Eric Lowe who was conducting the course asked Mike to make his presentation to the group after which Eric congratulated him on making a first class and interesting job of it.

Some months later John was to go on a similar course and Eric asked Geoff to make sure that John prepared well for his presentation . Geoff had a phone call from Eric after the course. Apparently when he asked him to present his talk John told him that he knew the training manual so well that he had no need to prepare anything and invited Eric or any other member of the class to tell him what they would like him to talk about. Like Eric said "Geoff he's a good bloke but he's still an arrogant little buggar".

Eric was a much different character to his predecessor who was a heavy drinker, heavy smoker and a fearless gambler. Eric much preferred finding venues that offered food, music, and a variety of entertainment. One such place was a Greek restaurant where the food was not particularly good but the drink was lavish. He was really upset when the drinks bill far exceeded that for the food.

The year prior to Geoff going to Stockport the accounts showed that they had lost around £73,000 in trading. In Geoff's first year the paper still made a loss but it was down to about £10,000. The second year there was an improvement as well as a profit. Not a big profit, but a small profit is better than a big loss. Geoff was pleased to see that the figures for Display advertising were up quite dramatically.

The profit would have been greater but the National Union of Journalists (NUJ) decided to call the editorial people out on strike, so they could only produce skeleton papers for a while.

Geoff had high hopes that he and his team would have done enough to qualify for the much coveted award for the best performing Display team. Sadly the trophy went to the Sunday Sun in Newcastle, but Geoff received a congratulatory letter from Eric Lowe saying it had been a close run thing between the winner and the Stockport Express, but the Sunday Sun had lost a few issues due to union trouble.

The following year it was the Stockport Express that won the trophy thanks to the continued success of the Display advertising Department ..

The SALFORD CITY REPORTER celebrated it's centenary whilst Geoff was there. Having been closely associated with the Crewe Chronicle centenary as well as the Chester Chronicle, bi-centenary celebrations this was a sub-standard affair. Quite frankly it was far from being a memorable occasion. Geoff understood that Salford born film star Albert Finney was one of the invited personalities, but did not turn up. The Salford MP came along but made it clear from the outset that he would not be wearing formal wear: Geoff was, however, pleasantly surprised that he did not turn up in overalls, but a smart lounge suit.

Geoff was more than disappointed when he had a phone call from Eric Lowe to say that one of the daily papers in the group had heard good reports about John Craft and wanted Geoff's permission for them to interview him for the job of Sales Supervisor at Hemel Hempstead. Although delighted for him Geoff was not happy for himself or the rest of the team as he had become such an integral part of the department. Geoff dug his heels in and told Eric there was no way would he let him go as easily as this. However Eric reminded him that he had 'poached' him from Chester and really could not stand in his way of making career progress. Eric, as always was right. John had done a good job in Stockport - Geoff had benefitted from his time with him so reluctantly he had to give way. John interviewed well and was offered the job, which of course, he took.

Craft was a good name for John and he lived up to what Geoff always called him Crafty, and he didn't let him down on his last day. Geoff said to his secretary, Jean that he could not understand why Crafty had brought a huge suitcase into the office on his final day. Everyone had personal possessions in the office but Geoff's would have fitted well into his briefcase quite comfortably. John went into Geoff's office to say his farewells, leaving his case in the corridor.

"John, bring your case into the office someone will fall over it there or worse still somebody might even pinch it, and we wouldn't want that would we?

He reluctantly staggered in with it. "Whatever can you have in there" queried Geoff.

"Purely personal things a couple of pens, pencils, ruler, you know the sort of thing"

"No I don't actually, John – I find it quite intriguing to think what personal possessions anyone can have been keeping in the office" said Geoff.

With that he cleared everything off his desk saying "Now John put your case on the desk and let's have a squint at what is inside to make absolutely certain that you've not missed anything".

He struggled to lift the case high enough to put on the desk.

Geoff then invited him to unlock it, but John said he couldn't remember where he'd put the key. To which Geoff retorted "As you've only just locked it I suspect it won't be far off. So find it quick and then unlock the bloody thing "Guilt was written all over Johns face which had a hint of perspiration. "Look Pritch mate you surely don't mind me taking my training manual and some of the notes I've made whist I've been here?

"Come on Crafty, the games up. Now for the last time let's have a look what's inside". It was crammed with the company training manuals which were worth about £25 apiece. When they were taken out and returned to the cupboard he did possess one note book, a couple of pens and pencils a ruler and a rubber.

"John you know what they say - what holds a lot can hold a little -Oh dear me such a big case and all you really needed would have fitted into your pockets" "Now on your way and thanks for what you've done and good luck for the future".

With that he went. "Thank goodness I took his car keys off him this morning or that would have disappeared as well" he said to Jean.

Somewhat surprisingly Geoff received a phone call precisely one minute after midnight on New Year's Eve for several years from John Craft who always said the same. " Happy New Year Pritch mate I learnt more from you than anyone else in Thomson Newspapers and if it hadn't been for you I would still have been tramping the streets of Chester. Thanks mate and a Happy New Year to you, your wife and family".

Geoff was extremely touched by this tribute from John who at one time had been a sergeant in the Military Police in Northern Ireland and had witnessed many atrocities in the course of his duty. Hard as nails in some respects but at heart a real softy.

Geoff had enjoyed being at Stockport but in a totally different way to his enjoyment of working for the Chester Chronicle. At Chester everyone had pulled together with one purpose, and one purpose only in mind - the betterment of all the newspapers in the group. Geoff recalled the occasion which typified the Chronicle when John

Long was the Managing Director. John called a meeting of all line managers and their number two's in his office at three o'clock that afternoon.

When they were assembled he said "I wonder if any of you can enlighten me as to what use I am to the company?"

Everyone looked at each other not quite sure where this was leading: then he said, "This morning I was walking through the composing room where I spotted Geoff who said to me 'Good gracious not seen you for a long time' to which I replied Geoff I've been working in Belfast for the last six months" "But I was in the office at around 8.30 this morning and at 8.40 the Father of the Chapel came in to say Joe the odd job man hadn't put any toilet rolls in the loo what are you going to do about it?"

"It so happened that Joe was unwell at home. But for not being able to get into work and ten minutes after his normal start time he was being missed. But me - the managing director who hadn't been in the office for six months hadn't been missed by the number two in display advertising and it came as a surprise to him to know I'd been absent for six bloody months. So it does beg the question who does the most useful job - Joe who is the lowest paid worker or, me the big chief who has the top salary , the best company car and a generous expense account. Gentlemen with that in mind I'll close the meeting but ask you to go away and think it over".

Very profound thought Geoff and it reminded him of the unknown road sweeper in Crewe who had been responsible for bringing a lot of advertising revenue. But his name would never be known, Sad.

Whilst Geoff enjoyed a degree of success at the Stockport Express he was more involved with all aspects of the department rather than just the selling of display advertising. He had less time to get personally involved with the advertisers, however there were one or two incidents which he found challenging and played a major role in. The first concerned the major Ford Motor Car dealership which was called Gordon Ford a company which might be best described as pretty vigorous and forward looking . Geoff thought they would be open to an idea he had in mind which would be ideal for the commencement of the new football season. The territory salesman was put in the picture by Geoff and an appointment was made to meet the Managing Director of the dealership.

Stockport County at that time were in the lower reaches of the four football leagues. Although they were a reasonable side at that level their chances of beating any team from the top leagues were, to say the best, not at all good: in fact they were pretty awful. When they met up with the MD Geoff suggested the Gordon Ford dealership might like to consider giving each of the eleven County players and their manager a brand new Ford car should Stockport County win the FA Cup. The dealership managing director said it was a terrific idea but even though County's chances of winning the FA cup were practically zero there is always a possibility that they might just do that. So although they liked it they felt it was too much of a gamble.

Geoff agreed but pointed out that he had done some research and that the betting odds of County pulling it off were 1000 to 1 against such an eventuality. So if the cars cost £5000 each and just by some chance County were to win Gordon Ford would have to be paying out £60,000. However if the company were to place a bet of £60 at 1000-1 and County did win it would be covered by the winnings.

They liked it and booked a large ad to promote their generous offer. Nice bit of inexpensive publicity. Job done – everybody happy. Sadly County didn't even manage to win the first round. Hard luck lads, Geoff did his best for you. It was you who messed up! Percy Thrower was the gardening expert during the 1970's. He was on the Television, the radio and newspapers. Everyone, but everyone knew who Percy Thrower was. Geoff had an enquiry from the Brookside Garden Centre at Hazel Grove. They did very little advertising, but they were having an open weekend event and wanted what they referred to as a really good promotion. They wanted a bumper weekend and had prepared numerous very good special offers on plants, shrubs and garden tools. Geoff went along with the area salesman Harold Fawcett. It was an impressive garden centre and notes were made of the splendid 'this weekend only' special low prices. The gardening fraternity would love this. One of the attractions they had, if you can really call it an attraction, was a life size cut out model of Percy Thrower. Initially Geoff thought this would be of absolutely no interest whatsoever. Some thought was needed: especially when Geoff and Harold sussed out that they would be happy to take a full page advert, and even possibly a double page spread. At that time the Stockport Express was a broadsheet newspaper. Geoff had a look at the leaflets they had all featuring the image of Percy Thrower. He gave a quick sketch on his layout pad indicating where the picture of Percy would be and then in large print he put MEET PERCY THROWER in the largest and boldest typeface but in small print between MEET and PERCY THROWER he wrote 'the cut out model of'.

The management at the Garden Centre were over the moon. Just what they wanted and agreed to take the double page spread which included all the special prices of the plants and equipment they had in stock.

Geoff and Harold were invited along to the event but Geoff declined as he said travelling five days a week from Crewe to Stockport is a bit wearing so he rather enjoys his weekends lazing about at home.

Monday morning Geoff was really looking forward to speaking to the Garden Centre to see how successful everything had been. But he was pre-empted by the local police constabulary. An inspector told Geoff that the police could not cope with the volume of traffic that hit Hazel Grove that weekend. Buses were held up and some had to take a detour: cars were parked where cars should not have been parked and everything was pretty chaotic. The inspector was not a happy man. "Well inspector we all have our problems and mine was to get as many people into that Garden Centre and that was what we achieved" said Geoff and then rang the Garden Centre to see if they were pleased. "Yes absolutely unbelievable" was the reply "many thanks".

There were strong rumours going around that the Stockport Express and the Stockport Advertiser were going to merge. This was brought about by the emergence of several free-sheets opening up all over the place. They had low overheads and were to prove a real threat to traditional local newspapers. Geoff was tempted to join the National Graphical Association (NGA) who would be all out to capitalise should redundancy money be available. After a brief spell the announcement was made and Geoff made it clear that he wanted out. He picked up a fairly healthy cheque, purchased his company car for a very favourable rate and joined up with a free distribution monthly newspaper in Didsbury that wanted to turn it into a weekly publication. It was not by any means the best decision that Geoff ever made, but it was a decent paper and the proprietor was a journalist on a left wing national newspaper who had ambition and was trying hard to establish his newly opened newspaper. Some years earlier Geoff had been given advice which he hadn't really taken seriously at the time and that was - Never, ever work for a working class person because they will envy you any success you may have and will be only too happy to dispose of your service once you've helped them to achieve their project. And so it proved in Geoff's case.

Having helped build the business the proprietor told Geoff he was going to make him redundant as he would have been working with the company twelve months tomorrow, and by making him redundant TODAY he didn't have to pay him a penny in redundancy money.

"Smart thinking hey?"

"Very smart" said Geoff "I must say I admire your socialist principles. You should use it in the rag you write for, they'd really love that."

Now Geoff you are on your own!

CHAPTER 12 – GEOFF GOES IT ALONE

Geoff was not at all sure what he was going to do. He was into his fifties - the children were finding their own independence and were not so reliant on their parents. He could of course join the masses who seemed to be content to draw the dole for the rest of their lives. That, though would not be for him. He saw the situation as a challenge and was determined not to submit to what seemed to be the easy way out. Was the answer staring him in the face he wondered as he scanned the adverts in the Daily Mail.

COFFEEMAN, The company are looking for franchisees in various areas of the UK for full details contact: etc etc. Geoff phoned the company who suggested that he might like to speak to one or two of the current franchisees to get an insight into what goes on. He was given the name and phone number of a gentleman who lived only a short distance away by the name of Pat Norcross. On making contact Geoff was invited to his home for first hand information. It turned out that Pat covered some of South Cheshire and North Staffordshire including the Potteries. Pat told him that it was not a difficult sell as each franchisee had a marked territory and installed a pour 'n serve coffee machine into restaurants, hotels, offices and so on free of charge on the proviso that they bought all the ground coffee they needed from them. The coffee was of a good quality and users never really had any cause to complain. He also said that he did very little in the Crewe area so if it would be any help Geoff could take that on as part of his area. A very generous offer.

Dorothy and Geoff were agreed this was something which would be of interest so they made arrangements to visit the company's HQ in Bournemouth.

After their visit, Nick, one of the directors came to Crewe and helped Geoff to launch the new enterprise. Geoff was now COFFEEMAN-CHESHIRE.

It was fun - he went to prospective clients, put a machine in – made a cup of coffee and hey presto like any other business some said Yes some said No. But as time went by he got recommended by satisfied customers and he soon made a decent living, BUT. There was always a BUT in Geoff's life and whilst he enjoyed his new business he felt there was something pretty big missing in his life. He knew what it was – the thrill of advertising – the pleasure he had in seeing his work in a newspaper. Nothing could really replace that.

However there was one other thing he did. He bought a catering trailer – the sort of thing you see in lay-bys serving cups of tea and sandwiches. He had a tow-bar put on the car. Then purchased, bread rolls, butter, tea, coffee, sliced ham, sliced cheese. He got licensed as an itinerant trader and whoopee he had a fully fledged business. The next morning he took trailer and contents together with Dorothy and found what he thought was an ideal spot on a lay-bye on the road between Nantwich and Woore. Dorothy entered the 'cafeteria' and Geoff announced that he would be back at around 3 o'clock to see how she was doing !! "You're not leaving me here surely - what are you going to do"?

"Listen pet – this is your enterprise I've got to go and see some coffee customers – you'll be alright – but if you sell everything up before I get back just take the 'OPEN' sign down and sit inside. Good luck".

With that he hopped into the car and waved her a cheery goodbye. He kept his word and was back at 3 o'clock.

"Sold out, pet?"

"No I've not sold out – nobody has even stopped to buy a single cup of tea"

"Never mind darling – better luck tomorrow"

"You are joking! You are not having me out here again" "It does take time to get any business going my darling – tomorrow could be totally different".

Dorothy reluctantly did go for another two days during which she sold one cup of tea for 50pence. She'd had enough, Geoff had had enough so advertised 'the business for sale' It was bought by a Scouser who had recently been made redundant. Geoff wished him good luck as they happily saw their 'establishment' towed away.

Also without worrying about bread rolls and cups of tea he could look to building on his dream of his own advertising agency.

The COFFEEMAN business was going quite well and it brought in some badly needed cash. All franchisees paid the same for the coffee they purchased from Bournemouth but were at liberty to sell it at whatever price they could get for it. Prices varied marginally depending on the blend required. Geoff found that the Viennese and the Kenya were the two best sellers so didn't bother offering any of the other blends that were available. He could buy the Viennese for £21 for a box of 80 sachets and found no trouble at selling it for at least double that price . As each sachet made around 12 cups of coffee that meant that in theory a coffee shop could make 960 cups of coffee, and if they sold it at 50pence a cup they could make about £420 profit on a solitary box. In practical terms there was normally a certain amount of wastage, but even so there was a decent profit to be made. However there was a drawback which Geoff found rather aggravating: at the end of each month franchisees had to complete a simple return to head office. This showed the number of boxes of each blend sold and the cash total of all sales. Of this total 10% had to be paid to Coffeeman as a part of the franchise agreement. One morning Nick rang from Bournemouth to say he was pleased with the progress that Geoff was making. However he was concerned that many of the franchisees were not sending their end of month cheque and this could have a serious effect on the future of the business. Geoff said that he could understand the reluctance to pay as he felt that it took the shine off the business, so why not charge more for the coffee up-front? So instead of charging £20 a box plus 10% of the selling price charge £24 or £25 per box and dispense with the need to take 10% of the selling price, so the franchisee keeps the gross profit.

"Brilliant" said Nick "such a simple way. brilliant" So it was introduced almost immediately.

Advertising was a totally different ball game. Geoff realised that he would have to take extreme care in taking clients on and recalled a case when he was working for the Chester Chronicle. A well-to-do looking man in his forties went to see Geoff and said that he had just completed some tricky renovation work on CHESTER CATHEDRAL and wished to advertise in the Chronicle. He went armed with some rather impressive photographs of the cathedral and said he would like to include some of them in a advertisement in the hope of attracting work from local companies.

He said that in order to do it justice he felt that a full page in full colour would be fully justifiable as it would lead on to a massive input into his business. Geoff pointed out that he would be delighted to help but did he realise that the cost of that would be near £1000.

"I can justify that expense" said the prospect and so a few days later the ad appeared in the Chronicle. The advertiser was thrilled – so much so that he took Geoff to a slap-up lunch. He asked if there were any other papers in the Thomson group in Cheshire or Lancashire that would be interested in running the same ad and how much would it cost. Geoff said that the closest one was in Stockport and they had papers in Macclesfield and Salford as well. He promised to make enquiries for him and let him know in due course.

However it never happened! The Chronicle accounts department had had his cheque returned a couple of times and then it bounced away like a rubber ball.

Geoff contacted the man concerned who had the audacity to say that the advert had not brought any decent response and flatly refused to pay up. It later transpired that the work he had done on the cathedral was trivial and he had blown his role out of all proportion. It was bad enough the Chronicle losing so much on a bad debt – it would have ended Geoff's aspirations once and for all. So great care had to be taken.

Hazel Buckley had been on the sales staff at Stockport until she had taken redundancy when she joined a packaging journal. She phoned Geoff one day and said that she had a client who was a former school pal of Geoff who would like to meet up with him again. It transpired that the pal, Derek Foster was now the managing director of Rowlinson - Wirebound - Containers based at Wardle and placed advertising regularly in the journal Hazel worked for.

Geoff was delighted to renew the acquaintanceship and even more delighted to take on their advertising. With a spend at that time of around £12,000 it was not a big account, but it was quite a prestigious one. More importantly it was a division of a much larger group and their credit was good.

Geoff needed the service of a good graphic designer and contacted Terry Mullen who was an ex-Chronicle employee and running his own design studio in Chester. The initial work that Terry did was really terrific and Rowlinson's were well pleased. The trouble was Terry was based in Chester so not really close enough to hand. Then Geoff had a very lucky find: a freelance graphic designer who did not like canvassing for work but who was brilliant at what she did. Jean Crocker worked from home and was able to devote most of her time to doing work for Geoff. She was quick, imaginative, did high quality work and her charges were modest.

Geoff was an avid reader of newspapers and in particular the local paper, the Crewe Chronicle. It was a Wednesday evening when he was reading the Chronicle and said to Dorothy, "We must try and remember this; somebody is having a sale of Leather Jackets and Gents Suits at The CREWE ARMS on Sunday between 8am and 6pm we'll go along to that, prices start at £49 that's very reasonable.

On Saturday morning Dorothy wanted to go into Nantwich. As they drove past The Crewe Arms she said "That sale's on now, we may as well go and see what they've got. Geoff was looking for a new suit so this was ideal. It turned out to be run by two retailers from the Preston area. Robert sold the leatherwear and Stuart the suits.

Geoff pointed out that their advert said the sale was on Sunday, yet here you are on Saturday. "Yes" said Robert "the newspapers are constantly making a mess of our ads, which really affects our sales very badly".

Geoff told him that he ran his own advertising agency and it may be an idea for them to meet up as he would take full responsibility for getting everything right, providing them with proofs and dispatching the copy to the appropriate newspapers. It was suggested they meet up in Lytham on the following Wednesday afternoon. Geoff was given a list of the various venues they had for the next few months. They also gave him a list of newspapers that they used for each sale. It all seemed to be going quite nicely when Stuart decided he was going to restructure his side of the business and bought a large van which he had fitted out to hold the vast majority of his stock and then went to sell it on the continent at a variety of venues he had in mind particularly in Germany.

Although Geoff missed his business it worked out rather well for him. Robert decided he was doing far more business at the one day sales than he ever did at the shop in Preston. As a result he left the manageress of the shop to run it on her own and he decided to have a one day sale at a different venue every day of the week.

He was spending between a minimum of £200 and £550 a day on each sale. This was a dream come true for Geoff. Most of the newspapers paid an agency commission of 15%. Geoff managed to squeeze an extra 5% out of most newspapers by paying up front. Robert was the best payer Geoff could ever wish for. If Robert had a sale on Monday Geoff invoiced him on the same day and would have his cheque by return post so he was never out of pocket.

Geoff quite frequently got a call from Robert in the early part of the morning.

"Geoff I'm on my way to the sale but I've forgotten where the venue is!! All I can tell you is that I'm at a crossroads in Derbyshire and I don't know whether to take the road to Sheffield or Chesterfield"

"Robert you are going to Chesterfield where you have booked in at the Midland Hotel".

Another day "Geoff I'm in Hunters Lodge in Crewe but I've forgotten to bring my full length mirrors with me. Can you take the mirrors off your wardrobe and lend them to me for the day?"

"Robert NO, no, no I doubt if I could take them off and I almost certainly would never get them back on if I did, but I will see a pal who has a menswear shop in town so I'll see if we can borrow them for the day"

By a little bit of luck that particular retailer had just bought new mirrors and was about to dump the old ones so he didn't want them back.   So Geoff gave them to Robert who gave him £20!   A real bargain ! Good value !

Geoff counted up the number of days Robert had held a sale without taking a day off, and was surprised to see at one stage it was 285. Each day he would start off from Preston and go north to Dumfries or east to Grimsby, south to Hereford or west to Bangor city and any place in between. He always made a point of being at the venue by 8am and not leaving until there was nobody waiting to be served. He usually arrived back in Preston between 9 and 10pm. On one occasion he had to take his lady friend, Lorraine, dancing when he got home! He parked up the drive way and when he got back someone had drilled a large hole in the side of his van and stolen every leather jacket he had in the back. He never saw anything of them again. However he was such a good customer his suppliers gave him extended credit in order to help him recover. Geoff also did his bit by arranging for the newspapers that he had used most frequently to allow Robert a free advert for his next sale. This many of them agreed to. But being free it meant a loss to Geoff as 15% of zero is not enough to live on!

But he did get back on his feet - it had been a demoralising experience. Sadly after one sale he had rather too much to drink, got caught by the constabulary and lost his licence.

Rather surprisingly he was a qualified solicitor, but gave up the law in favour of selling leather jackets. A lovely man who had a good business. But sadly no more.

Geoff could never get thrilled about advertising for car dealers as they were all pretty much the same. However the launch of a new dealership in the area was something of a challenge. Normally Car dealers had healthy advertising budgets and so they were not to be ignored entirely. A new Nissan dealership was to open up on Macon Way in Crewe. Geoff discovered this when the foundations were being laid so wanted to make himself known and the service that he could offer. The general manager was DAVID MOLLARD and he and Geoff 'hit it off' right from the start. Geoff enlisted the aid of Jean Crocker and they compiled some really impressive 'teaser ads. These were accepted by David and helped to secure their business for some time. In those days Nissan appeared to have quite a ruthless way of handling their managers. Even so it came as a great shock to Geoff when he made his usual

Thursday morning visit to the dealership to find that David was no longer there and there was a new general manager at the helm. Geoff explained who he was and what his role was for the company, but somehow nothing seemed to be registering with this chap. Geoff sorted out his immediate advert and added that he had the most terrific and unique idea to promote the business and that he would be back within the week to discuss the idea with him.

Geoff left without a single thought of what he could do. So he would have to come up with something pretty quickly or his services would be dispensed with before long. He had the awful feeling that this 'new broom' really might want to sweep clean, and thought unless he came up with something good he would be history. What he needed was a plan and it must be a plan that might, just might, make him indispensable. Now it was an ideal time for the skills of Jean Crocker to come to the fore. Then BINGO it came in a flash of inspiration. Geoff phoned Jean and told her there was a huge degree of urgency about this project and would help fulfil her creativity of something in the cartoon style at which she excelled.

Basically she drew up a series of adverts numbered 1 to 12 each depicting a stage of building your own car. Each ad in the series had the words "How to Build Your Own Car" The first was a desolate piece of rough ground with piles of steel girders, a mountain of breeze blocks, people standing around with surveyor's equipment and the suchlike. The copy was sparse saying something like "First purchase a large piece of land, then obtain planning permission from the local authority, buy the building materials, hire a bulldozer etc. Finishing with the tag line There must be an easier way to buy a new car."

The next week the story line developed and so on for the next twelve weeks. They loved it at Macon Motors and more importantly so did the readers. This meant that Geoff would keep the business for at least the next twelve weeks. But as predicted they had got used to seeing him around so he kept the account alive.

Geoff was introduced to a former soldier by the name of Jim Davies who took an interest in several military organisations such as the British Legion and the Royal Engineers Association. He was very devoted to them and organised many money raising events. He approached Geoff to see if he could help him to produce a programme for a particular function he was organising which was to be held in Queens Park, Crewe. Geoff said that he would be delighted to produce a programme for such a good cause. He would get advertising support from local traders, plan the programme, arrange all the artwork, the typesetting and printing free of charge. However he would receive the revenue from the advertising for his business. Jim was over the moon. It wasn't a hard sell for Geoff mainly because it was a limited print run so he could only charge an appropriate rate. But the finished programme looked good and Jim was thrilled to bits as he was able to donate the whole of the proceeds from the sale of the programmes to his good cause. It had been an easy sell for Geoff but not a very lucrative one, but over a period of time he did produce similar programmes for Jim simply because it was helping him to maximise on the event. Geoff did manage to find a few rather good accounts with local retailers in a variety of trades including a Kitchen and Bathroom store in the Potteries, Double Glazing companies, a rather large department store in Newcastle under Lyne, a building contractor who had a decent sized housing estate he was developing in the Haslington area. This led to advertising in the Chronicle as well as a few thousand leaflets and brochures.

Some of the work, in fact too much of it, was spasmodic, for when a developer has built and sold all his properties his need to advertise has gone with them. It was around this time that Geoff got what turned out to be his biggest break. A modest 6cms deep by 3 columns wide advert for ARROW LOANS appeared in the Crewe Chronicle classified pages every week. Parts of the advert were barely legible. The sales person who looked after this account was not keeping a close eye on what was appearing. Geoff decided this might be a good opening for him. He doubted if the ad was costing any more than £60 a week, but small and regular is better than none at all. Geoff phoned the number shown in the advert which was answered quite quickly.

"Good morning, I wonder if you could tell me who is responsible for your advertising"?

"Yes I am - my names is JOHN ARROWSMITH"

"Mr ARROWSMITH, my name is Geoff Pritchard and I run my own advertising agency based in Crewe. I do believe that I could improve the looks of your advertisement, possibly even making it a little smaller but more 'punchy'. How would it be if I got the studio to come up with an idea that I could present to you without any obligation whatsoever".

"I've had some of the big Manchester agencies to see me in the past and none of them have come up with anything special so I think you'd be wasting your time. However if you want to come on that understanding ring me when you have something to show me and we'll take it from there".

"Well thank you Mr ARROWSMITH, you've given me a chance to prove myself now it's up to me and if I fail then quite frankly I don't deserve your business"

Geoff was going to leave nothing to chance. He didn't think there was very much business for him in this, but he wanted to prove his worth. With that in mind he went to see Terry Mullen who thought Geoff was mad going to all this trouble for a relatively small ad.

"Terry" said Geoff " I want to take this with all the typesetting done ready to go to press, you are right it seems crazy but whether I get the business or not I will pay you as soon as I collect the finished job: so you won't be out of pocket. Now when can you have it ready for me to collect?"

Unfortunately due to a bank holiday weekend and a glut of work it would take about two weeks to get it finished. Never mind thought Geoff. Longer than he'd hoped for, but he knew it will be a winner.

Two weeks later Geoff returned to see the finished work. It looked fantastic. It looked bigger but it wasn't – Terry had performed a miracle. Geoff handed over a cheque to cover the cost and was on his way.

An appointment was made with MR ARROWSMITH for Friday afternoon at 2.30.

There are some very rare occasions in life when as soon as you see a person you know that you are going to hit it off together and this was one such time. MR ARROWSMITH sat at a very imposing desk. He had with him his business partner who he introduced Geoff to by the name of MARY. She was a good looking, well dressed lady who took the seat to the right of MR ARROWSMITH, who said "Right now - down to business". Geoff very carefully took the folder that was holding the advert from his briefcase. "Here we are, you will see that the heading is stronger and the logo more prominent, the table is clearer and on top of that we have made it six centimetres deep instead of seven, which will save on the weekly costing"

John said nothing, but studied it carefully.   "Well what do you think of it MARY?"

"John, I really think it's a terrific improvement"

Geoff could feel himself 'glowing' inwardly, these people were very decisive and he had come up with a winner.

"Yes we'd be happy to run that but I don't want it any smaller than the original so can you adapt it accordingly?"

How strange thought Geoff, most clients usually want to make it smaller, but who am I to argue over that? "Yes of course I can do that, I see that you use the Crewe Chronicle every week, I expect you advertise in the Northwich Guardian as well do you"?

"Certainly do but before we go any further how much is this going to cost"?

"Well" replied Geoff "let me tell you how our business operates. Newspapers pay agencies an agreed percentage of the overall cost of the advert so if you were to allow me to place your advertising I would be prepared to initially do the artwork free and just charge you when we have to make changes to the repayment table. As I do not employ anybody full time I pass the work to one of several studios that I can rely on to give a quick turnaround. Their charges are modest so I would be quite happy to do that."

"No, I will continue to place the order, but I do like what you've done so I'll get you to do the adverts and send them to the newspapers we use. " YVONNE " he called out to his secretary "just bring in the newspaper file."

Geoff could not believe it – they were using thirty two local papers in Lancashire, Cheshire, Merseyside and North Wales. Had John allowed him to place them Geoff would have made more money on this one account than his salary of £8500 a year that he'd earned at the Stockport Express. Geoff was both staggered and disappointed. However he did see it as a small acorn and knew that if he was sensible and didn't appear too anxious that he could make capital on this at some time in the future.

Some few weeks later Geoff had a phone call from JOHN ARROWSMITH saying that he had some work that he would like him to do for his building business. This was news to Geoff as he didn't know that he was a builder. There wasn't a lot of work but it was for a housing estate he was building locally. Geoff got all the relevant information he could about the project and produced handout material for prospective buyers. He also prepared advertisements for the Northwich Chronicle and the Northwich Guardian so that was quite a useful and profitable exercise.

However ARROW LOANS was the account Geoff really wanted and he knew that if he played his cards right he would stand a good chance of getting the business.

Time went by and Geoff picked up some useful business both for the advertising as well as the coffee and this included the Lyceum Theatre in Crewe which had over the years had somewhat mixed fortunes. It had recently reopened so Geoff made contact with the new trustee who tried the coffee and was happy for Geoff to supply the restaurant with the Kenya blend. They made an agreement that Geoff would let the theatre have a free box of coffee each week providing that they would allow him a rent free office. They jumped at the offer. Geoff moved all his stock in as well as a desk and chair. This was a marvellous arrangement.

In one of several conversations with JOHN ARROWSMITH Geoff began to sow a few seeds saying that it may be an idea to consider the possibility of using some of the national newspapers instead of so many local papers. In fact he suggested the larger audience could well increase his potential clients by a fairly substantial amount and at the same time reduce the need of the local press.

A few weeks went by without anything further being said on the subject, but Geoff had sown a seed now he was waiting to see what, if anything developed. It came quicker than Geoff expected , for one morning John rang to say that he had been in touch with the Daily Star in Manchester and that if Geoff could match the rate he would be happy for him to place the business.

Wow! Great news thought Geoff. "I'll happily do that said Geoff but tell me what rate they quoted."

"I'll not do that" came the reply "Just see what you can do before I make my mind up". It did not prove to be a monumental task. Their phone number in Manchester was in his copy of BRAD, a publication containing relevant information about all British Newspapers for advertising agencies. He got through immediately explained who he was and that he would like to speak to the person that had spoken to MR JOHN ARROWSMITH recently about the possibility of using the Star for advertising. "Yes of course. I'll put you through to Clare she deals with all the Loans adverts"

Geoff explained to Clare that he ran an agency in Crewe and she had spoken to ARROW LOANS. He ascertained that if he were to place the advertising that he would get the agency commission OK.

"Tell me Clare, what rate did you quote"

"He wanted a eight weeks trial in the Northern edition so I quoted him £10 a single column centimetre"

"Thanks Clare, I hope to be in touch shortly"

Next call was to John. "John I've got the quote you wanted for the Star: for a eight week trial period they will do it for £9.50 a centimetre: how does that compare with what they quoted you?"

"They quoted me exactly the same so you go ahead and book it for the next eight Mondays" John was not one to be bettered!

The Star was never a very exciting paper but it produced some good results and the run was extended, so Geoff increased the rate to £10 a cm.

Encouraged by this Geoff made contact with the Daily Mirror and got a favourable rate from them, but the Mirrors greater circulation was a massive attraction.

John was now totally convinced that his future prosperity lay with the national press. Before long they were in The Sun, News of the World, the Sunday Times, the Sunday Telegraph, Daily Mail, Mail on Sunday. Some little while later the Belfast Telegraph and the Daily Record in Scotland were added to the impressive list.

When Geoff took on the advertising account for ARROW LOANS they had been spending a little over £60,000 a year on advertising. Over the years that Geoff dealt with the company the annual spend was a little short of one million pounds.

But he had an awful shock when he arrived at the Lyceum one morning to find it was locked up and he could not get access. There had been no warning but apparently the council had evicted the trustee who had gone into liquidation. Geoff was not too surprised as he could see that the place was being run in a most haphazard manner. In fact it turned out to be quite a wakeup call to Geoff as he had become reliant on finding suitable accommodation for the business. He decided that he would look around for a desirable terraced house to purchase and adapt it so that he could have his office and coffee stock under one roof. It was in a good location close to the town centre and within walking distance of a printer with whom he was doing quite a substantial amount of work. Geoff was getting along well with the ROWLINSON GROUP and felt that he would like to reciprocate in some way. The opportunity arose and he decided to sponsor a Sportsmen's Evening at the Alexandra Social Club so he contacted the comedian George ROPER who had made his name on the original ITV programme 'THE COMEDIANS'. Through his association with the Lyceum Geoff had become pally with George and he was quite delighted to attend. The show went down really well especially when Geoff won the raffle prize of a mini cruise to Gothenburg.

When the government announced that they were going to put VAT on to all advertising Geoff did not think that it would affect his business too much. However companies that were involved in finance were not allowed to register for VAT. This meant that on all his invoices to Arrow Loans the 15% VAT had to be added, but as Arrow could not reclaim the VAT, so in practical terms a £600 invoice became £690, so this extra money was coming off Arrows profits. In view of this many of their competitors opened off shore offices, or found accommodation addresses to where they could have their invoices sent. These were mainly in the Channel Isles. John was reluctant to follow suit as he felt it was too good to be true. However he discovered it was quite legitimate. In consequence any dealings with Arrow Loans were sent to Geoff Pritchard Advertising Services, Guernsey.   In view of this they found offices on that island and shared the expenses.

All the media were informed and it didn't cause any major problem except the operating costs were quite high.

NOW FOR THE DOWN SIDE !!

The work that Geoff did for Arrow got to be known and admired by similar companies. Although he was delighted to attract this attention he was aware that it was very difficult and unethical to take on business which was a competitor of a valued client.

However Geoff spoke to John on the matter who took the attitude that if other companies were going to advertise in any case then it might as well be Geoff who did the work. Geoff, though, respecting Johns thinking was apprehensive.

Geoff had rented out a room to Nick the son of a pal who was intent on running a mortgage business with his friend Michael. Nick was a former employee of Prosperous Shop and asked Geoff if he would handle their advertising which primarily went into the PEOPLE newspaper each Sunday. This was spotted by the people at Prosperous Shop who rang Geoff to say that they liked what he had done for Nick and would Geoff be prepared to handle their advertising which would also appear primarily in the PEOPLE ?

Although he did agree to do so he felt more than a little uncomfortable with it so treated the situation warily as they did not seem at all organised and had the habit of placing rather expensive advertising into national newspapers without informing Geoff but making sure that the invoices were sent to him. Geoff had to chase them for a cheque to clear their account. They said they would pay him via American Express, but for Geoff not having that facility it was a non-starter.

However he did enquire from American Express about their service and terms of business. A representative from AMEX called and told Geoff that it would take several weeks for it to become operational and that he would have to pay a percentage for each transaction. He spoke to Prosperous Shop who said they would cover that charge. That did not alter the fact that Geoff needed the money NOW. He then hit on the idea that a local Men's Outfitters run by David whom he knew rather well did have this facility for their business. Geoff explained what the situation was and David readily agreed to accept the Prosperous Shop AMEX card. A few days later Geoff received a cheque for the full amount, rushed it to the bank and settled the accounts of the newspapers. Jobs a Good'un thought Geoff as he congratulated himself on having instigated this. A few days later there was a hammering on Geoff's front door. It was ashen looking David who stood quivering with a demand from AMEX for their money back so they had debited his account for the full amount of £12,000. To say he was not happy would be the understatement of the year; he was livid and demanding his money back!

"David" said Geoff, "It's not as simple as that as I have cleared outstanding invoices with it so quite frankly I can't possibly return it to you right now, but let me sort it out. I promise you it will be done today and I will keep you informed as to what is going on"

Geoff phoned AMEX explaining what had happened and they asked for it all to be put in writing. This led to more phone calls and correspondence for most of the week. In the end everything was settled amicably. Or at least it was for David and Geoff who had a phone call from a very helpful young lady at the UK head office in Brighton who said that this had been a most unfortunate incident but there was no need for either David or Geoff to have any concern everything had been resolved. Furthermore she said that Prosperous Shop have had their American Express facility withdrawn. So things turned out better than Geoff had anticipated.

Most businesses that sell goods can, of course, reclaim such goods if the purchaser fails to pay for them. In advertising there is nothing to reclaim. It would be pointless for an agency to say to a debtor that if he doesn't pay he'll take your advert out of the paper. So some caution has to be taken. Several of the double glazing companies were notorious for being, at best, slow to pay.

However Geoff had one such company that paid him regularly at the month end. They were a long standing family concern and it was a pleasure and delight to deal with such nice people. It had been started a few years earlier by a gentleman who was anxious to build up the business which could be taken over in the future by his son and daughter both of whom already worked there. Geoff went along as usual on Monday morning to take the finished artwork for the client to check over before taking it into the Chronicle office. Everything was fine – there were no amendments to make.

First thing Tuesday morning someone from the Chronicle phoned Geoff to ask if it was true that this particular double glazing company had gone into liquidation. "Certainly not" said Geoff who thought it best to give the company a call.

"Yes unfortunately it is so" they said.

This left Geoff 'holding the baby' He had no option but to pay for the space as it was a few hours after the deadline. He was stunned that the company did not have the decency to advise him of what was happening. He had no option but to pay for it knowing there was no way that he could recover the cost.

Was he down hearted? Yes he was. Did he get over it? Of course he did. Would it happen again? Almost certainly - and it did, - almost straightaway !

He had been dealing with what may well be called a family run furniture store in Hanley. Geoff had placed quite substantial adverts in a free delivery newspaper which was one of a great number of what were initially called free sheets that had suddenly sprung up in every town throughout the country. Some succeeded – some were doomed to fail. One morning the proprietor of the furniture store rang Geoff to say that he was terribly sorry but he had been forced to put the company into liquidation. Forms were received to complete, but Geoff knew that it was a complete waste of time filling them in as advertising would be very low down on the administrators priority list. However by a stroke of what turned out to be a bit of good luck in the circumstances as the newspaper they had been using was taken over by one of its rivals. Part of the deal was that they would take on all of the outstanding creditors. Some bright spark in the accounts department had the wonderful idea of amalgamating those outstanding invoices which were renumbered to fall in line with their own accounting system and to make it easier they had put three or four of these invoices and made them into one invoice. This resulted in Geoff receiving a statement showing the new invoice numbers which bore no resemblance whatsoever to the old system or the amount due on each one. Geoff really tried quite hard to establish what they had done and phoned them to say that he needed to know the old invoice numbers so that he could match them up. He told them that there was no way he could pay the debt collection company until they gave him the information he requested. In a matter of only a couple of days they phoned to apologise for the inconvenience they had caused Geoff and said there was no way they could match them up so were writing the debt off!

Geoff felt rather guilty but consoled himself with the fact he had tried very hard.

But if they couldn't do it how could they expect him to ?

Oh well fortune favours the brave -- at least some times.

IT NEVER RAINS BUT IT POURS !

Geoff's business was doing nicely. He had exceeded expectations. He was making a comfortable living. Yes! There had been setbacks, but he learnt how to overcome them and more importantly how to live with them.   Even his old friend at Arrows had to have a go at him. Arrow Loans at this particular time in history had advertised every Monday without fail in the MIRROR for the previous three years and every Monday without fail had been charged £800 per insertion.

Geoff always left the next weeks booking for Arrows until as late as he possibly could. There were dangers with this but generally it worked well for Geoff and his client, but Geoff was always fearful that for whatever reason the paper might close its bookings before Geoff had booked the space. That would have been a disaster, so it was something of a knife edge situation when Helen from the Mirror phoned on a Friday morning. "Geoff have you got John's bookings for Monday yet"

"Not yet" was the standard reply "but I'll let you know in good time".

One particular Friday nobody at Arrow knew where John was. Apparently he'd left the office at 9'oclock and hadn't been seen or heard of since. Time dragged on and it was after 12noon when Helen rang. "Geoff I must have your booking now for Monday or you'll miss out"

"Helen I've tried all morning, the man has disappeared. Can we leave it until quarter past?"

"No we can't ! if I don't get a booking NOW you won't be in"

"Helen I want him in of course I do but he's the one and only person who can sanction it." "Geoff he's paid £800 every Monday for three years. It's obvious he'll want to be in next Monday."

"Maybe you are right but it's too risky"

"Geoff one last offer say yes now and I'll put it in for £500, OK?"

It was too good an offer to miss "Yes OK we'll do it. Have a good weekend, bye".

It was almost 4pm when John rang. "Geoff I'm so sorry not to have spoken to you I've been out until five minutes ago, but no matter as I've decided NOT to go in Mondays Mirror"

"You've done what? You never miss the Mirror"

"I know, but I will not be in on Monday"

"John I've done a great deal for you I managed to get it as a one off for only £500"

"Great price Geoff, but you bought it, you pay for it, because I'm not"

"But."

"No buts you bought it you pay for it".

Did Geoff phone Helen? NO he did not. He thought he'd done a good deal which he had. Not the Mirrors fault. Not Helens fault. Mine and mine alone. Never mind Geoff you may get some of it back tonight when you play Brag !! No chance.

Some few weeks went by and the same thing happened. Friday came . but no John.

Helen phoned for Monday's booking.

"Helen" said Geoff " I did this a few weeks ago and he's refusing to pay me , ONCE is bad enough, so sorry the answer is no"

"Geoff you should have told me"

"You were doing your job, I took my eye off the ball I'm the one to pay for my mistake NOT you"

"Geoff I will make it up to you by knocking £100 off your next five invoices is that OK for you"

"Helen it's more than I deserve but if you are absolutely sure it won't land you in trouble then yes of course I happily accept the offer – thank you"

Geoff had made quite a nice comfortable lifestyle, but he did like a challenge and although by this time he had reached his 70's he enjoyed the thrill that he got by finding fresh business. One such business was the Potteries Motor Transport (PMT) Bus Company in Stoke on Trent. For a while he did a substantial number of promotions with them when they were expanding their services on to fresh routes. He also met Eric Davies a theatrical producer who put on shows at theatres all over the country and wanted large quantities of A5 flyers which were sent to the venues on his behalf.

By and large John was great to do business with. They did have a few minor run ins but they got on extremely well. They do say that business and pleasure don't mix, but that is something Geoff entirely disagreed with for John, Mavis, Dorothy and Geoff frequently enjoyed accompanying one another with a day at a race meeting. They would enjoy lunch at a local hostelry then on to the races at Chester, Haydock Park or Geoff's favourite meeting at Bangor on Dee. They all enjoyed a very modest flutter and if they came away winning a fiver they would be over the moon.

Geoff also enjoyed meeting up with the salesmen from the different newspapers that he dealt with, normally having lunch and a good old natter. However on one such get together they did talk about buying a racehorse between them, and although this never materialised Geoff and John from the MAIL did buy a greyhound together. The dog who was called Beechwood Story was trained by Mickey Cliffe from Wrenbury and had most of his races at Belle Vue. His pet name was Benny and Dorothy and Geoff took great pleasure in taking him for 'walkies' on Sunday afternoons. He was quite a successful dog and won a good number of his races.

Nothing though lasts forever and John rang one day to tell Geoff that he'd had an offer from an advertising agency in Guernsey to say that they would be happy to give John all the agency discount from all of his press advertising and they would handle his business for a weekly fee of £100.

Geoff knew they really didn't understand the business - but he also realised this was a very tempting offer and John would be silly not to at least see how it worked out.

He was right it didn't work out. Geoff thought enough's enough so decided first and foremost to sell the property he had bought as an office.   A local estate agent told him that it could fetch around £35,000 for it.   Geoff decided to rent it out instead and asked the estate agent to find a suitable tenant. They contacted Geoff to say they had found a lady who lived in Crewe but was looking for a place for her son who was living down south and wanted to return to the Crewe area. Geoff was most impressed by the lady who was accompanied by her daughter to view the premises.

They liked what they had seen and Geoff thought that if the son was anything; like his mother he would be OK. Terms were agreed and he moved in.

It turned out that in this case 'like mother, like son' could not have been further from the reality.   His name was Kevin, he was workshy, alcoholic and filthy: a complete contrast to his mother and his sister. He was on benefits but would sooner get paralytic with drink than pay his rent. He was obnoxious. So much so that his mother was in tears over him when she went to see Geoff and begged him to kick her wretched offspring out of the house. Geoff felt really sorry for such a lovely lady and promised he would set the wheels in motion. It took the best part of twelve months to get him out. Geoff decided being a landlord was not really his scenario after that experience so he would sell the house. Geoff was not terribly surprised to get a phone call from JON at the DAILY MAIL He said that John Arrowsmith was deeply regretting parting company with Geoff and would he sound him out to see if he would be prepared to start up again.

Geoff said that he would gladly do so but needed to contact the newspapers to see if his name was still good and that he would get the agency commission once more? They all said yes to this as our accounts had always been kept up to date and in a most satisfactory manner.

Unfortunately the credit crunch and the near collapse of the banking and financial system came into being and so it did not materialise. However it was nice to feel wanted. Shortly after this a lot of companies were offering on-line services which were easy and cheap to set up so all the newspapers lost a considerable amount of revenue.

Geoff had seen the best of it - had enjoyed it – and made a comfortable living through it.

Writing these memories and incidents have not been easy to recollect in the chronological order. Geoff's one regret is that he never had a diary, or to be more correct he'd had diaries as Christmas presents in his younger days, got bored with them about 8th January. However he did buy one in 2004 and has completed the entry for each day every night before going to bed.   He has been known to get up at 2am because he suddenly realised he had not done the previous days entry so wanted to rectify that.   In recent years he has found it to be most valuable in looking when various events had taken place. Each year he buys a diary for each of his grand children, who assure him they are using them correctly.

Geoff is a great believer that you can learn a lot by listening to people of all ages, their rank or status in life is relatively unimportant but a chance remark can change your life by making you think sometimes from a different prospective. Such was the case when Geoff decided to take his granddaughter Megan on a tour around the area of Crewe Green. He pointed out to her the cottage where his grandparents had lived, where his mates had been brought up, the cottage where he had lived, the school he had attended as an infant and where the teacher had lived. The tour was finished off by the front gate of St. Michael's Church where he told her that this was the church he used to attend. Straight away she asked the simple question, "Used to attend, Grandad. Why not now?   This was one of those rare occasions when he was completely stuck for the answer, and said "Do you know what I really can't answer that question. Why not indeed".

When he told Dorothy she was quite amused and said "It takes a six year old to stump you, well done her".

It was shortly after this that Geoff took his car trailer to the home of Ron a friend who was anxious to dispose of the pile of debris from the trees and shrubbery he had been cutting back and wanted to dispose of them at the tip. When Geoff arrived he said to Ron that he would have to sit on the garden wall for a minute as he was not feeling too good and had a pain just below the breast bone. Ron asked his wife Irene to get Geoff a warm drink. When she saw him she said "Geoff you need an ambulance I'll ring for one straight away". The ambulance took Geoff to Leighton Hospital and he had a stent fitted. He was in hospital five days and arrived home five minutes before the Aston Villa versus Arsenal match was being shown live.

A couple of weeks later on a Sunday morning Geoff said to Dorothy that he was going to church and did she want to go with him. "No" was the reply "and I can't see you doing so for long".

However a few weeks later she announced that she would like to go along with him.

That was about twenty-five years ago and neither of them have barely missed a Sunday morning service since. Geoff was asked to go on to the Parochial Church Council (PCC) which he did, and was happy to take on the role of Treasurer which he did for ten years. Both Geoff and Dorothy were asked to be Sides Persons at the church which they were both happy to undertake.   At times when the Church held various events Dorothy enjoyed making scones and cakes to be sold to raise funds.

When the Diocese wanted the accounts done on line it was time for somebody to take over from Geoff.   After that he was asked if he would be the Verger which generally meant attending all the weddings and funerals and making sure that those attending were shown to the right place for them to sit as well as clearing everything up after the service was finished. It was only due to the pandemic that his services were not called upon. Sometimes Geoff takes a stroll around the churchyard where so many of his relatives are buried together with many friends and associates that are now at rest.

CREWE BOWLING CLUB and COLOURFUL CHARACTERS

Although the club has been mentioned previously Geoff felt that it has played such an important part of his life and the lives of many of his contemporaries that he could take this opportunity to give a little of the background.

The club was founded in 1898 by members of the local Freemasons lodge who were anxious to extend their activities and form their own independent group. Originally in Gresty Road, roughly where the first entrance to the Crewe Alexandra F C ground is situated the club moved to its new location after only a few years. The land on which it was built belonged to the Duchy of Lancaster. The only access was along a narrow footpath that led from Crewe Road along what is now the back of the houses on the left of Ludlow Avenue. At that time the estate which is now formed by Ludlow Avenue, Stanhope Avenue and the houses and bungalows on Crewe Road were not even in the town planners minds.

The club house was destroyed by fire in 1938, but was rebuilt fairly immediately.

The bowling green itself is one of the largest in South Cheshire. The club house had no floor coverings but it did have two snooker/billiard tables. In the recreation area were some extremely good solid tables which had a built in ashtray area in the four corners of each table as well as a shelf beneath the table surface which was just the right height to hold a pint glass. This meant that cards or dominoes could be played in comfort without the possibility of spilling a drink. The bar was in the centre of the longest wall facing the entrance. The club had a rack which had the capacity to hold a couple of dozen cues. The snooker tables had a light meter which was fed by old pennies. When decimal coinage was introduces the club kept a healthy stock of those coins which were still being used up to quite recent years. However they were kept behind the bar and members could 'rent them for a new 10pence piece. There was no cloakroom but there were hooks on one of the end walls where coats could be hung.

One evening Geoff and Dorothy had arranged to visit the Odeon Cinema in Crewe to see THE SOUND OF MUSIC with a couple of neighbours. As they had a little time to spare Geoff took his neighbour, called Fred, to get a pint before going to the cinema. As it was raining heavy they wore raincoats. On entering they went straight to the bar and ordered a pint each which they stood at the bar to drink.

They had barely lifted their glasses to take a drink, when the Club Secretary, Wilf, who lived two doors away from Geoff came across saying "This is a gentlemen's club and gentlemen do not do not stand at the bar drinking in their raincoats. Kindly remove them and place them on the hooks provided for that purpose"

"Mr Evans" said Geoff "we are only here for just a few minutes"

"In that case" said Wilf "you can retrieve them in just a few minutes. Now kindly remove them"

"Yes, of course we will, Mr. Evans" Wilf did all he could to keep the highest standard.

Membership to the club was strictly by being proposed and seconded by members of the club who themselves had been members for at least one year. When the application for membership had been displayed on the notice board for a month it was taken down for discussion at the next Council meeting. A set of white and black balls were then passed to each council member who had to place one of those balls in the bag that was passed around. If the potential member passed scrutiny then a white ball was placed in the bag. If two thirds of the balls are white then that person will be duly declared elected.

The newly elected member had to pay a joining fee plus the annual subscription . Geoff's pal Alan Beasley was nominated by his dad Harold , Bills friend. They met up on Tuesday and Thursday evenings most weeks. These were the days that when the entrance door was opened after 8 o'clock in the evening you were met by a cloud of smoke and the bar itself was almost obliterated from sight.

Geoff entered the snooker handicap competition and in the first round was drawn to play against a chap called Mike Warwick. Geoff managed to win, but Mike was a fun sort of person but his regular night was Friday. In consequence Geoff dropped Thursday night in favour of Friday. As time went by they became doubles partners in the handicaps for quite a few years. Unfortunately although they reached the final on two or three occasions they never won the handsome trophy. They both entered the singles handicaps but neither of them ever managed to win. However it was the taking part that really mattered, as well as the drink the winner was obliged to buy for the loser.

There were some really colourful characters about. One pair who went in regularly were Arthur B and Charlie P. Arthur was the owner of a machinery workshop situated right outside what were Geoff and Dorothy's back gate when they lived on Nantwich Road. In the summer months Dorothy usually had a window open that overlooked Arthurs premises, and she often heard the raised voices wafting up from the workshop. Arthur walked with a rather bad limp but from time to time had to leave Charlie in charge whilst he went to see a client. Charlie was a pleasant person but could be described as a bit of a thicko. On one occasion Arthur returned and asked Charlie if there were any messages.

"Somebody rang" answered Charlie,

"Who was it ?" asked Arthur

"Don't know" was the reply.

Then voices were raised

"What d'ye mean yer don't know"

"He didn't say"

"Didn't yer bloody ask?" By now the voices were getting even more raised

"No I bloody didn't ask. If he'd wanted me to know he'd have bloody said"

This would go on for some little while longer then ended by Arthur saying

"Better get your sodding coat and buggar off home. You're a waste of bloody space". With that Charlie would disappear . Next day all was back to normal.

Dorothy actually came out rather well for after such a session Arthur would come to the door with a box of chocolates or a bunch of flowers for Dorothy. He was then quite charming as he offered his apologies before returning to work. In fact he was noted for being a toastmaster at some quite well-heeled functions.

Jack Williams was the younger brother of Ray. Both of them had served their apprenticeships in the Crewe Railway works. In the 1920's and 30,s most apprentices on reaching the age of 21 and coming out of their time would be sacked as the bosses did not want to pay the higher wages of a time served man. So Ray was the first to go. He begged an old pram from a lady who said she had no further use for it. He loaded his pram up with soap and soap powder from a local wholesaler and went from door to door selling to the lady of the house. In those days Crewe centre consisted upon row upon row of railway owned terraced houses, so it was no hardship to canvass them in order to get regular sales. When it was Jacks turn to get the chop he joined up with Ray but also looked for his own enterprise. He was a big strapping powerful young man. At that time there was a furniture store in Heath Street, Crewe and Jack would pop in to see if they wanted any deliveries made. On this particular Saturday morning they wanted a bedroom suite delivered to a house in Wistaston. The only mode of transport they had was a handcart. Jack readily accepted the job which involved a distance of over two miles. The shop proprietors suggested Jack should stand at the front of the cart with his arms locked around the leading bar of the trailer and pull it – in a similar manner to a horse. It was heavy and there was a long way to go!   However once he got the momentum going he was alright. That is, he was alright until he reached the bridge where the railway works general offices were! This was heading towards Edleston Road. The staff were just coming out of the General Offices and they could see Jack was struggling up the gradient. Willing hands gave him sufficient power to get up the bridge. In those days there was a policeman on duty at the High Street/Edleston Road junction. As Jack started his descent the momentum meant that he couldn't slow down because basically the cart was now travelling at a faster rate than Jacks legs. He thought his end had come. Luckily there was no traffic about and the policeman managed to dive out of the way. Somehow Jack kept going and by this time he had sufficient momentum to negotiate the Chester bridge which was only a short distance away. Incredibly the bedroom suite was delivered without a solitary scratch. The brothers were destined for better things.

They decided to start their own warehouse business in Oakley Street, Crewe and supplied many shops in the area. They had managed to purchase a decent sized van which Ray liked to drive (after all he was the senior!)

One particular day it was pouring with rain cold and windy. Ray said to Jack "Come on then our kid you can achieve your ambition today and do the rounds in the van. It'll be good experience for you."

Jack didn't like the idea but accepted gracefully. He had made one or two deliveries, collected the money and set off on his next call. However it was a struggle to get the engine running but after a delay got under way. The same thing happened at the next stop. After some frustrating minutes he got the vehicle going but he was behind on his schedule. At the next call he decided to leave the engine running whilst he conducted the business On returning to the van a policeman was examining the vehicle. "Now lad, don't you realise that it's an offence to leave the engine running whilst unattended"

"Well yes I do officer" said Jack "But I've had that much trouble with it starting again I thought I'd leave it running to make up the lost time"

"Sorry lad, but you are going to lose more time while I take your details, you'll be hearing more about this".

Jack got back later than normal, fed up, hungry and wet through. It didn't help any when Ray stood with a smirk on his face "By jove our kid you've had a real stinker of a day"

"Not as bad yours though" retorted Jack " You've been summonsed"

"How could I be summonsed I've not left here all day and I've done nowt wrong"

"Well you've still been summonsed. You see I left the engine running and this copper booked me. Unfortunately for you I'd got your smock on and the only driving licence I had was in your smocks pocket so I gave him that. See you in the morning our Kid. OK"? The business grew and they eventually moved to the industrial estate down Weston Road. Some few years later it was sold to M6 Warehouses.

A day would seldom pass without Jack having a bet on the horses and it was uncanny how he could pick the winners. One of his pals had the theory that Jack got up as soon as his daily paper THE RACING POST was delivered, made a cup of tea go back to bed to study form, then drop off to sleep and dream the winners name.

Geoff went a time or two with Jack to a race meeting. He would tell Geoff what to look for in a horse, but whatever it was Geoff could never see what it was he was trying to tell him.

Jack was also a former Chairman of Crewe Alexandra Football Club. It always saddened him that his team hadn't done better during his chairmanship years.

Ronnie Dyson was among the small advance party that came from Derby to Crewe to open up the Rolls Royce factory in Pyms Lane, Crewe in about 1936. He was a confirmed batchelor, a very shrewd investor, a good snooker player and an accomplished Crown Green bowler. He won every trophy in the club on several occasions. He could be exceedingly charming and courteous and at the same time be most uncouth. He became personnel manager at Rolls Royce and all those that passed through his hands spoke very highly of him. Although he was well paid he would go into the Army and Navy store to buy an ex-RAF overcoat. He found a set of dentures were left in a hotel wash room. So he pocketed them to see if they fitted him. No they didn't but that didn't prevent him from using them, even though they clattered somewhat.

Arthur Dobson a foreman in the Railway works always smoked a corn cob pipe. He had been chief engineer for the White Star Line Company and had visited many countries throughout the world. He got to know when Dorothy's birthday was and for several years rang to sing 'Happy Birthday to You'. She loved it!

Rocco was a greengrocer and an estate agent. Every year shortly after Christmas he would go off to the village in Northern Italy from where his family had originated and meet up with them. Whilst there he learned quite a bit about cooking. When his wife died those skills came in very useful and he invited certain close associates from the Bowling Club round for supper. It became quite a regular occurrence that Geoff and Dorothy looked forward to. Rocco would explain in great detail the ingredients he used and what part of the world the dish originated from.

Geoff Moss and Brian Robson were auctioneers at Wright Manley who specialised in the auctions held at Crewe Cattle market every Monday. Mossy, a bachelor, lived in Congleton and was frequently the first person in the club in the evening and usually the last one to leave. He was great fun to be with and loved playing a variety of card games in the evening. The stakes were generally very modest and if somebody lost 50pence at an evening's session they'd had a bad night – but they'd had a tremendous amount of fun and enjoyment. One of the older members had been watching television in the TV lounge: it was after 11pm when he emerged to go and catch the last bus that went by his home. Mossy said that he would be passing by where he lived in another half hour or so and he would give him a lift. "So" said Mossy "go and watch a bit more telly and I'll let you know when I'm going".

Some little time later Mossy got up and said to Geoff that he would see him on Monday night and with that he duly departed. Geoff put his snooker cue away and was heading for the exit when the door to the TV lounge opened. "Where's Mossy?" queried the older member. "Oh Lord above he's gone, but don't worry I'll run you home. It's only a five minute walk to my house, so I'll go and get the car" ! Oh Mossy the things I do for you thought Geoff.

Another of Geoff's pals was Sid Webb who was in the club every night and always sat at the same place. During the course of the evening he would despatch six pints of beer, smoke about ten cigarettes and take a flagon of Cider home to be consumed the following day.

He was the shop steward at a large local dairy, and, to put it politely he was very much a political left winger. He was not afraid to air his political views. He got on well with Ron Dyson who was as far right as Sid was far left. However Ron 'used' Sid to good effect by asking him what he would do as a trade unionist under a variety of circumstances. Ron who dealt with the unions at Rolls Royce was often surprised at what Sid came up with and used much of what he'd learnt to very good effect when the occasion arose.

Alf Jennings was the Club President for most of the time that Geoff served on the council. Alf was a former licensee who had the interests of the Club uppermost in his mind. Even so Alf and Geoff did not always see eye-to-eye on various aspects of running the club and Alf was often critical of Geoff's association with Sid. On one occasion Geoff did say to Alf "What you see is what you get with Webby, but I'm sorry to say that sometimes, Alf, you don't see his good side. "If it hadn't been for Webby we would never have had the football burster, or the Waterloo Cup and possibly we would never have had any of the social evenings he introduced, and certainly not the New Years Eve celebrations. I'm sorry to say you seem only to hear his left wing rantings. Thankfully I listen to all of it and discard 95% of what he comes up with, but the other 5% is pure gold to the club. That's the bit I'm interested in and am able to develop to good effect." The first New Years Eve which the Club Council did not want to know about paid the fee of a renowned Comedian, George Roper, Anne Webb, Carol Horton and Dorothy did all the catering for free and did a brilliant job. After paying George his fee and reimbursing the costs of the buffet we had in excess of £250 profit, all of which could have gone into club funds BUT the majority of Council members were not prepared to back our judgement so we sent a cheque to Leighton Hospital for their appeal fund. OK so the club got the profit from bar sales, but it could have been more - so I suggest that we could all look and listen to what our members have to say and learn from the mistakes the council have made."

"Now come on Alf, enough of the politics, your glass is empty let's get you a top up"

Another member of the Council was David Horton, another former licensee. He struck up a good relationship with Sid and Geoff. Sometimes they would all go together with their wives for a long weekend, usually on the North Wales Coast.

David had given up the pub trade and became a fruit and vegetable wholesaler. Geoff had not been too happy with Anthony the club council member whose responsibility it was to look after the bowling green and the machinery that went with the upkeep of the green and the surrounds. On going to see how the greens-man was getting on with preparing the green for the first Monday evening league game Geoff was horrified to see that the turf was cutting up very low on one side and barely touching the other side. The greens-man told Geoff that Anthony had 'serviced' the grass cutter himself as he wanted to save the club money.

Geoff immediately rang Anthony and told him to get here quick.

"What in hells name have you done to this mower. Just look! it's more like a bloody ploughed field, get Haslington Mowers down here straight away while I find someone I can depend on to look after our prime facility in a proper manner".

"I was only trying to save the club money"

"Anthony, the very thing I've always stressed is that we are quite well off financially and if club members do things off their own bat then they are ignoring what the powers that be have authorised and this is a prime example of the reasons why we did that" "Suppose you'll want to replace me with your mate Dave Horton will you"?

"Too right I do"

Thankfully David agreed and did quite a brilliant job.

As chairman Geoff tried his hardest not to miss any tricks. Most of the Councils business was dealt with in an acceptable manner. However like most clubs there are usually two factions which are quite divided in their opinions over the way things are done. Crewe Bowling Club was no exception where two factions were more or less equally divided. Geoff had noticed that one of the Council members did not lean towards one faction or the other. He also spotted that when it came to a vote on something that might cause a split vote the members by the name of Raymond would alternate which faction he would vote with. On the day of the meeting Geoff would study the agenda quite carefully and ascertain what if any of the items were likely to be split. So what he did was to phone Raymond in the afternoon of the day of the meeting and get an assessment of which way he would vote on one such resolution. If Raymond said he would be in favour then Geoff knew that Raymond would be against the next contentious vote. So knowing he was going to vote Yes for the first such item he would be voting No for the second one. So Geoff, as Chairman, knew how to get Raymond to vote the way that he wanted him to. And that thought Geoff to himself is TRUE DEMOCRACY.

Now Geoff had hoped that when the day came for him to give up the chairmanship that his staunch ally David would replace him. Sadly circumstances outside of Geoff's control meant this was not to be.

Crewe Bowling Club became a major part of Geoff's life and he was continually looking for ways in which to improve things. Very often some were obvious, like reviewing the club rules. Are they compatible with the way things were when the club was established in 1898? By and large the answer was yes, but there were some that really did need updating. It was decided to form a select committee who came up with a few suggested additions and amendments. When the committee were satisfied with their recommendations a Special General Meeting was called and the new minutes were approved.

Geoff was approached by club member Alan Clarke who asked if we had ever considered introducing Bridge into the club. Geoff replied that a member by the name of Alan Bates had asked the same question a few years ago when it was decided to put a notice up for the introduction of Bridge and offering tuition. Although the notice was up for several weeks nobody appended their name and so we didn't go ahead. Days later Geoff was talking to Arthur Dobson a long standing club member who was reminiscing about the changes that he had witnessed over the years in the running of the club and said "You know Geoff every time somebody joins or leaves this club the club gradually changes".

Yes thought Geoff, you are right Arthur and with that he saw Alan Clarke and said that he felt it may be an idea to have another shot at introducing Bridge. However as Alan Bates was no longer a member who could we get to give basic tuition? Geoff discovered that two members Ron Dyson and Brian Robson had good knowledge of the game and would willingly give tuition if a reasonable number of members were interested. In a matter of a few days sixteen members had put their name down, including Geoff. This resulted in the game being played so regularly that it was decided to have a competition. The winning pair receiving a cup which was presented by David Bullock a local car dealer.

Philip Johnson was one of the members who had joined in with playing Bridge and he discovered that there was a dedicated Bridge Club in Nantwich which he had started to attend. Geoff rather liked the sounds of it so he partnered up with David Bullock to go on a Thursday evening. Sadly David died so Geoff had to find another partner but Geoff now goes to the Bridge Club more frequently than he attends the Bowling Club.

After serving several years on the Council of the Bowling Club Geoff was flabbergasted when he went into the club on the Tuesday afternoon following the AGM which had taken place the previous Sunday when someone said "Here he is, the new Chairman" Geoff looked around wondering what was going on and whom they were referring to. "Who is chairman then" he asked.

"They want you back. Nobody wants to be Chairman so they want you!"

Geoff couldn't believe his ears so rang Alex Churm when he went home. Alex confirmed what had been said nobody wanted to be chairman but suggested Geoff rang the club secretary Reg Lloyd. He confirmed the situation and suggested that he together with John Bell the outgoing Chairman and Alex meet up that afternoon. Geoff said that he was flattered that his name should be considered for office as he was not even on the council. After a brief discussion Geoff said he would take on the role on two provisos: one was that future meetings be held on a Wednesday evening and not Thursday the second was that he would limit himself to twelve months and not a day longer. This was put to the clubs council a few days later and was accepted. So Geoff was back in office without making any effort and deep down he knew that he now lacked the incentive to really do anything so he put it down as something of an ego trip. At the first meeting Geoff stressed he was in office for no more than twelve months he also expressed alarm that out of those elected members to the council not one of them wanted the chairmanship. He said "You really need to sort yourselves out in the next twelve months as every council member really should be wanting the top job".

Geoff's first step was to invite each member of the council to write down what changes or improvements they would like to see introduced into the club without taking into account the possible cost. Rather surprisingly they nearly all came to the same conclusions. When Geoff spoke to them individually it transpired that although they had thought of these improvements in the past not one of them felt sufficiently confident to put their ideas forward. Basically these were to incorporate the lounge into the main club room to give more space for social events or to make the lounge more user friendly. Others wanted the veranda adjacent to the snooker tables knocked down. Double glazing should be replaced. Quotations were asked for and the double glazing and lounge were duly put into place. Geoff spoke to Madeline Delaney the daughter of club member Rocco Delucchi in her capacity as chairman of Crewe and Nantwich U3A . She was impressed with the facilities but pointed out that several members were from the Nantwich area and their current location was handier. However it was agreed that subject to approval of the club council we would be happy for the U3A to have the facility of the bowling green on one afternoon each week. This was eventually agreed to and they were happy to pay £25 per session into the Bowling Club funds. However that was not the end of it because so many of the U3A members enjoyed the facilities of the club that they were quite eager to become members. In fact forty of them joined the Bowling Club in the first year. Most gratifying. As the year drew to an end Reg Loyd tried very hard to push Geoff into staying on as Chairman. But really he had come back into office and had thoroughly enjoyed it, but NO he would happily come along and enjoy the facilities but would forego the politics. Geoff's love of Crewe Bowling Club where he spent so many happy hours has never diminished, but sadly over the past few years he has not been able to visit very much at all. He became a life member twenty years ago and witnessed the annual general meeting at which it was decided that in future membership was to be opened up to ladies. Some of the old 'die hard' members were furious and quit the club of which they had been members for most of their adult lives.

The club retained its strong Masonic influence and it was difficult to define what it was that made the club such a wonderful place.   Geoff was of the opinion that members had one thing in common – the enjoyment of being with like- minded people keen on upholding the old traditions and standards.   Several members were freemasons even in later years who had absolutely no linkage to the original members.   In fact Geoff was a member for several years without being aware that a high percentage of members were masons. He just knew that whatever the past that the club would continue well into the future. The Masonic influence was quite strong for many years.   Inevitably changes did take place and whilst there was a strong feeling amongst many members that the club had survived extremely well since 1898 it was becoming obvious that changes had to be made.   As the 20th century closed the decision to allow ladies to become members was made. There were a surprising number of ladies who wanted to join and they submitted their application and all of them were successful including Dorothy, Geoff's wife. Maybe it was because he knew the club rules better than most, Geoff paid Dorothy's joining fee and annual subscription immediately the meeting was over. RULE 2 states that no candidate elected by the council shall be deemed to be a member of the club until he shall have paid their first subscription.   So Dorothy had that honour by a short head.   Unfortunately Dorothy much preferred sitting by the fireside, clicking away with her needles as she watched Coronation Street or Eastenders.

Together they loved going to the Greyhound Track at Belle Vue to see their first greyhound run his races. His racing name was Beechwood Story and he had the pet name of Benny. As Dorothy said " I couldn't take him 'walkies' and call to him "Come here Beechwood Story, Benny sounds much better" And as usual of course she was right.

Both Dorothy and Geoff loved cruising. That was something they could not have afforded in their younger days, but they had made sacrifices, and were making decent money through their enterprises. Neither of them were extravagant but they usually did what they wanted to do without worrying over the money. When they bought a new car it would be with them for several years. "After all it will get us to the supermarket and back without any trouble" However Geoff's pal David who was a car salesman said "If everyone was like you the motor car industry would soon close down"

"Well Dave" Geoff would say "Thank the good Lord that they are not all like me"

WHEN GEOFF STARTED TO WRITE THESE PAGES HE FELT AS THOUGH IT WOULD GIVE HIM SOMETHING SPECIAL TO WAKE UP TO EACH MORNING.

DOROTHY AS USUAL ENCOURAGED HIM IN EVERY WAY AS SHE HAD DONE ALL HER LIFE. AS DOROTHY WAS HOSPITALISED FOR WHAT THEY INITIALLY THOUGHT WAS GOING TO BE FOR A COUPLE OF WEEKS TURNED OUT TO BE FOR NINE MONTHS. SADLY SHE LOST THE ABILITY TO STAND LET ALONE WALK SO THIS ENDED THEIR DREAM OF A SUPER CRUISE. GEOFF COULD NOT COPE ON HIS OWN AS DOROTHY NEEDED TWO CARERS TO VISIT FOUR TIMES A DAY SEVEN DAYS A WEEK. SHE HAD ABSOLUTELY NO MOBILITY EXCEPT IN A WHEELCHAIR TAXI WHICH SHE DID NOT

ENJOY. SHE COULD NO LONGER KNIT, SHE COULD BARELY TURN THE TV ON WITHOUT AID. SHE HAD TO SLEEP IN A SPECIAL HOSPITAL BED IN WHAT WAS THE DINING ROOM. SHE WAS 'SEEN TO' BY STRANGERS FOR ALL HER PERSONAL NEEDS. GEOFF'S WRITINGS BECAME DIFFICULT FOR HIM, SO BECAME VERY LIMITED IN THE TIME HE COULD SNATCH TO WRITE. HOWEVER IN APRIL 2021 THEY CELERATED THEIR 64TH WEDDING ANNIVERSARY, GEOFF REACHED THE AGE OF 90 AND DOROTHY ON THE 9TH MAY 2021 ACHIEVED THE AGE OF 88.

THEY HAD A GOOD LIFE TOGETHER AND A VERY GOOD ATTENTIVE FAMILY.

SADLY ON 6TH JUNE 2021 DOROTHY DREW HER LAST BREATH AT AROUND 8.30am IN LEIGHTON HOSPITAL, CREWE.

THANKFULLY SHE NOW HAS NO MORE PAIN. SHE IS A TREMENDOUS LOSS TO GEOFF, JACQUELINE, ROBERT, MEGAN AND MATTHEW AND ALL OF THE FAMILY.

GEOFF HAD NO THOUGHTS OF PUBLISHING HIS BOOK BUT SINCE DOROTHY DIED OF BREAST CANCER HE THOUGHT HE SHOULD TRY TO RAISE SOME MONEY THROUGH HIS EFFORTS TO SUPPORT CANCER RESEARCH.

INITIALLY GEOFF HAD A COMPLETELY DIFFERENT TITLE FOR HIS WRITINGS.

But in the circumstances he has entitled it **THE GIRL ON THE NUMBER 64 BUS**. WELL, here you are then on to the final page.

Thank you for reading my story. It was hard work, but compensated by the fun and pleasure it gave me. Many incidents have managed to escape my memory. However if I do recall any then hopefully I will be able to 'drop them in somewhere.

Confession! All the happenings did take place but some of the names have been changed, as they may have been embarrassed by having their name in print.

I must express my deepest gratitude to my dear wife Dorothy, who sadly died prior to completion. However she did encourage me and gave me her support and backing to see it through.

AND a very special mention of Gillian Bolton of Nantwich. I met Gill in her capacity of Group Leader for the Crewe and Nantwich U3A Writing Group.

Gill is an accomplished and published writer and very kindly agreed to edit my offerings. Her advice and comments were of great assistance to me. But for here encouragement I doubt if I would have ever gone to a publisher. So THANK YOU GILL.

It would be very remiss of me not to mention my family who have helped me recall a few items. I did have a awful happening when I put the computer on to find that somehow the pagination had gone from about 250 pages to 460 pages with the type sizes changed and all sorts which almost made me press the delete button. But I didn't - instead I got my knowledgeable pal Ken Townsend to come and sort it out and my daughter in law Julia came later the same day to refine it to its present standard. THANK YOU ALL SO MUCH.

Geoff had a variety of jobs but was in his element when he was involved in the newspaper industry where he gained rapid promotion in the Display Advertising Department of both the Chester Chronicle Series of newspapers and the Stockport Express group. Eventually he opened his own advertising agency which he developed by placing advertising several days a week in most of the popular daily newspapers. He worked until he was 73 by which time a great deal of advertising was done online. This was no use to Geoff so he called it a day.

Some names have been changed
at the author's discretion to avoid any embarrassment.

In the 1950's the number 64 bus ran from Steelhouse Lane,
Birmingham to Erdington and was operated by the
City of Birmingham Corporation.

My grateful thanks to Jean Crocker for producing the book cover.
She is a graphic designer of great skill who helped me enormously
when I ran my own Advertising Agency.